de Gruyter Studies in Organization 3

Meyer/Stevenson/Webster: Limits to Bureaucratic Growth

de Gruyter Studies in Organization

An international series by internationally known authors presenting current fields of research in organization.

Organizing and organizations are substantial pre-requisites for the viability and future developments of society. Their study and comprehension are indispensable to the quality of human life. Therefore, the series aims to:

- offer to the specialist work material in form of the most important and current problems, methods and results;
- give interested readers access to different subject areas;
- provide aids for decisions on contemporary problems and stimulate ideas.

The series will include monographs collections of contributed papers, and handbooks.

Limits to
Bureaucratic Growth

Marshall W. Meyer
in Association with
William Stevenson and Stephen Webster

Walter de Gruyter · Berlin · New York 1985

Marshall W. Meyer
Professor of Sociology and Economics at the University of California, Riverside
William Stevenson
Assistant Professor of Management at the University of California, Irvine
Stephen Webster
Assistant Professor of Sociology at Kent State University

Library of Congress Cataloging in Publication Data

Meyer, Marshall W.
  Limits to bureaucratic growth.

  (De Gruyter studies in organization)
  Bibliography: p.
  Includes index.
  1. Public administration. 2. Administrative agencies.
3. Bureaucracy. I. Stevenson, William, 1948 –
II. Webster, Stephen, 1954 –   .   III. Title.   IV. Series.
JF1501.M44   1985   350   84-23153
ISBN 0-89925-003-3 (U.S.)

CIP-Kurztitelaufnahme der Deutschen Bibliothek

Meyer, Marshall W.:
Limits to bureaucratic growth / Marshall W. Meyer. In assoc. with William
Stevenson and Stephen Webster. – Berlin ; New York : de Gruyter,
1985. –
  (De Gruyter studies in organization ; 3)
  ISBN 3-11-009865-2
NE: GT

3 11 009865 2 Walter de Gruyter · Berlin · New York
0-89925-003-3 Walter de Gruyter, Inc., New York

Preface

Sociology is fraught with paradox. On the one hand, modern sociology seeks to test mathematically elegant models of social process, like its sister discipline of economics. On the other hand, perhaps more so than economics, much of the subject matter of sociology is intractable to formalization. Sociology assumes values, beliefs, and individual preferences, which are inherently nonrational, to vary and to drive much of behavior. Sociology also assumes that, within the scope of their values, beliefs, and preferences, people behave more or less rationally. The discipline of sociology, then, studies the intersection of nonrational and rational elements in human conduct. Sociology is thus capable of suggesting nonobvious (and therefore, to some extent, controversial) explanations for human conduct. It does not always do so, but when it does sociology achieves results that could not be attained within a framework that assumes the preferences or utilities of all people to be similar.

The study of organizations illustrates the paradox of sociological analysis. The paradox is this: Models approaching if not achieving mathematical elegance have described processes of structural differentiation within organizations, organizational mortality, and the movement of individuals between positions in organizations. At the same time, theorizing about organizations has turned increasingly to arenas where formalization may not prove helpful. The role of culture, of organizational sagas, and even of playfulness and apparently nonsensical behavior now occupies many students of organizations. The phenomenon of power also receives attention. As we approach, in other words, solutions to problems that can be handled with mathematical tools, the more attention is focused on problems where formalization can be maintained only at the expense of substance.

This book attacks a core problem in organizational theory, the growth of bureaucracy. Interest in bureaucracy has waned in recent years, partly because bureaucratic theory has proved an incomplete guide to organizational behavior, partly because public-sector bureaucracies have been held in low esteem. But the issue that gave rise to research on bureaucracies in the first place, the problem of why rational administration has become the principal means of collective action in modern societies, has not waned in significance and has not been resolved. If anything, its significance has been enhanced by recent developments. There is much criticism of public agencies that are bureaucratically managed, yet few workable solutions to the bureaucracy "problem," if it is a problem, have been proffered. This book develops an explanation for bureaucratic growth, but it offers no definitive solution. The difficulty is this: Bureaucratic growth is an outcome of modern concepts of administration that have become deeply embedded in Western societies, as much or more so in the U.S. as elsewhere. Rational solutions to problems, or solutions that are believed to be rational, are for the most part organizational solutions. Problems are confronted by constructing organizations; new problems are confronted by adding more organization to existing structures. Our culture views this problem-organization-problem-more organization cycle as for the most part reasonable and rational. It rarely asks whether the organizations that are the outcome of this process are themselves reasonable and rational.

The reader should be alerted to some of the language used in this book, particularly the term "organization". Organization, as used here, has two important properties. First, the term applies to any organized unit within a bureaucratic system, whether an entire agency, one of its subunits, or one of its sub-subunits. Second, since numbers of organized units within a bureaucratic system may vary, the quantity of organization is variable. These properties may strike the reader as unusual. But they are essential to our argument, which is that bureaucracy has grown because new administrative organization, which is regarded as a rational means of addressing problems, is added continually to existing organization. In the past, researchers have thought of organizations of self-contained units bounded by environments. This simple definition, however, renders the notion of growth in administrative organization almost unworkable. If, for example, the set of offices managing a city's finances is regarded as one organization, then increased or decreased organization within a city's financial functions is impossible—there is a single organization. In the past, researchers have also regarded the number and configuration of offices within a single organization as measuring structural differentiation. Here, the number and configuration of offices are regarded as measuring the quantity of formal organization rather than differentiation because the latter would have hampered explanation of bureaucratic growth. It would have forced us, given the overall pattern of empirical results, to have argued that increased differentation causes growth. We think this implausible. Certainly, this is inconsistent with results reported in the literature. We think it more plausible to argue that increased formal organization causes growth. And it would have forced us to find reasons leading administrators deliberately to differentiate organizations – to create out of on existing organization two or more suborganizations – other than in response to coordination problems caused by growth. We can think of few such reasons for differentiating organizations. By contrast, we can find many reasons for creating new organizational units whose activities differ from existing units and whose formation leads subsequently to growth. These reasons are detailed in the historical account of the agencies studied, which is contained in the third chapter. The reader, then, must always keep in mind that we mean by organization any formation represented and understood as an organizational unit. The reader must also keep in mind two immediate implications of this conception, first, that most organizational units are nested within larger organizations and that many of the latter are nested within still larger units, and, second, that most creation and dissolution of organizations takes place within existing organizations.

Just as the conception of organization used here departs from what has been conventional, so do the units actually analyzed in research. The units that are the foci of the quantitative research described below change from chapter to chapter and, in one instance, vary within a chapter. In some instances, the relevant unit is the entire of set municipal agencies with finance functions; in other instances, units consist of all organizational formations – departments divisions, and sections – having finance functions; in other instances, departments, divisions, and sections are analyzed separately. The reasons for choosing the units analyzed are explained in each chapter. In every instance, however, the units used are all of those that were available to test a given model of bureaucratic growth.

This research on bureaucratic growth could not have been conducted without support from the National Science Foundation. NSF grants SOC77-07626 and SES79-07134 are gratefully acknowledged. The contributions of Robert O. Williams, III, and Leannah Bradley to the construction of historical time series describing finance agencies in Chicago, Detroit, and Philadelphia are also acknowledged with gratitude. Three persons who read the manuscript and commented on it extensively also deserve our thanks. They are Lynne Zucker, David Wolf, and Robert Hanneman. Our wives and children – Judith, Joshua, and Gabriel Meyer, Joanne and Andrew Hale Stevenson, and Debra Webster – are thanked for their loving forbearance throughout the project. No acknowledgement of secretarial assistance is made. The senior author was, with the aid of his IBM personal computer[1] and the Volkswriter[2] word processing software, the senior typist of the manuscript.

This book is dedicated to Peter M. Blau, Quetelet Professor of the Social Sciences at Columbia University. Blau was the first in the U.S. to explore quantitatively the question raised by Max Weber: Why have bureaucratic structures largely displaced other forms of collective action? Studies conducted by the Comparative Organizational Research Program under Blau's aegis yielded insights into the administrative organization of hospitals, universities, manufacturing establishments, and government agencies, the last

---

[1] IBM is a registered trademark of the International Business Machines Corporation.
[2] Volkswriter is a registered trademark of Lifetree Software, Inc.

including the same kind of agencies responsible for the administration of local government finances that are the subject of this book. The problem defined by Blau almost twenty years ago, explaining the size and complexity of bureaucracies, remains the problem addressed here. The approach taken here, however, is different from Blau's. Comparisons are made principally over time rather than across organizations at one point in time. Bureaucratic structures are understood as means of ordering and organizing uncertain environments rather than of achieving economies and efficiencies in administration. And the evaluation of bureaucracy differs from the earlier view. Bureaucracies are viewed as both solving and creating problems, the latter because they tend toward complexity and growth. The limits of bureaucratic growth are reached when complexity within organizations exceed the complexity of problems organizations were intended to address in the first place. These differences in approach and evaluation should not, however, obscure the fact that Blau was first to understand bureaucratic size and complexity as phenomena to be explored and explained in research, and that but for Blau's work the present research would have not been possible.

Los Angeles
November, 1984   Marshall W. Meyer

Contents

Introduction

Bureaucracy is a central institution in modern societies. In the public sector, "bureaucracy" describes agencies with administrative functions, such as the municipal finance departments that are the subject of this book. In the private sector, many functions are organized bureaucratically, but the term "bureaucracy" is an epithet, an accusation that is brandished whenever the flow of paperwork slows or when administrative processes seem to defeat their purposes. Bureaucracy is also a central concept in modern social science, even though the term is used in diverse ways. Sociologists, following Max Weber, have used "bureaucracy" to connote rational, efficient organization; political scientists identify "bureaucracy" with administration of the state; economists use "bureaucracy" to describe non-market organizations whose efficiency properties may be substantially inferior to profit-seeking firms.

Why such diverse perspectives on bureaucracy exist may be of less importance than the simple facts that bureaucratic institutions are ubiquitous, have grown more rapidly than other sectors of society, and are now at the center of the current debate concerning the balance between government and the private sector. This debate is heavily ideological. At one pole, government bureaucracy is regarded as self-serving and inimical to the interests of taxpayers. At the other pole, government bureaucracy is regarded as an essential corrective to distortions arising inevitably in markets, distortions that consign some wage earners permanently to low incomes or unemployment because their skills are obsolete and some industries to technological backwardness because they cannot capture their costs of innovating. Very few data have been brought to bear on this argument. No one has shown whether or not there are limits up to which bureaucracy is a sensible solution to problems and beyond which it is not. It is rather an all-or-nothing proposition. Either bureaucracy is evil, in which case the solution to governmental problems lies in reducing government, or it is not, in which case more government is needed to restore "fairness" and economic health to society.

This book is intended as a first step – a small first step – in bringing objectivity and reason to bear on the debate concerning bureaucracy. Its task is to explain why bureaucracy, which was conceived at the beginning of this century to be the solution to problems of public administration, has grown almost continuously since and appears now to function less well than it once did and perhaps less well than it should. The task is not a simple one because no simple explanation for bureaucratic growth and persistence is adequate. As far as can be determined from the data at hand, no quantitative measure of workload accounts consistently for bureaucratic growth. And bureaucratic growth, while occurring over time, is hardly a function of the aging of individual units of organization. Furthermore, while organizational change follows massive political and economic changes occurring externally, long-term growth patterns are barely perturbed.

Ultimately, it is argued, the logic of bureaucracy itself, which is sustained by beliefs legitimating bureaucratic structures as rational means of addressing complex problems, must be understood as a major source of growth. This conclusion is suggested not only by the failure of simpler explanations for bureaucratic growth but also by two empirical regularities revealed by our data. One is that bureaucratic structure sustains organizational units. The more bureaucratic structure – that is, the more levels of organization and the more units at each level – the greater the survival prospects for a unit, other things being equal. No one steeped in classical organizational theory, which advocates organizing as a rational means of approaching problems, will find this result surprising. What is interesting is that this regularity holds over time and across different levels of organization. The second regularity is that growth occurs contemporaneously with or follows structuring. No one steeped in the history of public agencies will be suprised by this result; organizational units are usually created before they are staffed. What is interesting is that these results yield a dynamic of bureaucratic growth rooted in ordinary administrative behavior, that is, in accepted ways of doing business in public agencies.

0.1 Plan of the Book

The book begins with a discussion of the idea of rational administration. The idea of rational administration, rational administration as an imperative, was invented at about the turn of the century, some years after large industrial firms had developed managerial hierarchies. Rational administration was an attempt to render more businesslike the functions of government, which were at the time riddled with mismanagement and fraud of the "spoils" system. Rational administration assumed that there was a science to administration, that that this science applied with equal force to the private and public sectors, and this science could be encapsulated in prescriptive statements about how best to secure coordination and control. The idea of rational administration asserted, in short, organization to be the solution to problems facing government. Yet the idea of rational administration was fraught with contradictions, especially when applied to democratic government. The uncertainty of many governmental tasks could not be easily reconciled with the level of predictability and control demanded by the rational model of administration.

The problem of bureaucratic growth is outlined in the second chapter. Two issues are raised. One, the empirical problem, is addressed with data showing substantial bureaucratic growth to have occurred in the last fifty years in both public- and private-sector organizations. This pattern is evident regardless of what measures are used to indicate bureaucratization. In fact, some measures show bureaucratization to have increased more in firms than in government. The second, the theoretical problem of explaining bureaucratic growth, is somewhat more complicated. It is argued that neoclassical theory, while beginning from the premise that organization overcomes bounded rationality limits, falls prey to the limits of organizations themselves. The paradox of neoclassical theory is that under irreducible uncertainty, organization poses problems requiring even more organization as the solution. It is argued further that while nonrational models have come closer to identifying this problem-organization-problem-more organization cycle because they are more compatible with systems in disequilibrium, both neoclassical and nonrational theories can be understood as converging on this point. Importantly, the equilibrium assumptions of economists have left them without explanations of bureaucratic growth, even though models of large bureaucratic size and inefficiency abound.

The third chapter outlines one of the central problems addressed in this book – what is organization? It approaches this question by exploring the original purposes of the municipal finance agencies studied and how continual redefinition of these purposes resulted in piecemeal construction of organization whereby small offices were transformed into large bureaucracies. Much of the history of municipal accounting is reviewed in order to illuminate how the demand for financial control resulted in modern budgeting, accounting, and centralization of administrative functions. The upshot of the discussion is an understanding of organization that is somewhat different from the way organization has been defined conventionally in research. Organization is understood exactly as it is in the municipal accounting literature, as organizational units, whether departments, divisions of departments, or sections within divisions. All of these units are treated as organizations in the research reported below.

The fourth chapter describes the surface characteristics of the bureaucracies studied and links them in causal patterns consistent with three models of growth. The surface characteristics include growth in size and in formal organization, rates of birth of organizational units exceeding their death rates, and death rates declining with age. In the first model of bureaucratic growth, the task environmental model, measurable task demands are asserted to affect size directly. In the second model, the inertial model of growth, declining death rates with age are asserted to cause formation of new units in order to accommodate change hence long-term bureaucratic growth. The third model of bureaucratic growth asserts preferences for outcomes tending toward growth, that is, for new organizations as the solution to problems of existing organziation, to be the ultimate sources of growth in large bureaucratic systems.

Four subsequent chapters test the models of bureaucratic growth. The task environmental model of growth succeeds only early in the history of the agencies studied. The inertial model of growth does not succeed at all. The linchpin of this model, the notion that age preserves units of bureaucracy, turns out not to be true. The model of growth as due to preferences for organizational forms that give rise to new organizations and subsequently grow does succeed within the limits of our data. One chapter shows complicated organizational structures to have greater persistence than simple ones, even when other attributes of organizations and their environments are controlled. Another chapter shows growth, on balance, to follow elaboration of organizational structures rather than to precede it.

A final chapter discusses alternatives to bureaucratic growth. It argues that limits to bureaucratic growth are posed by organizational complexity exceeding the same bounded rationality limits that hierarchical organization was intended to overcome in the first place. It argues also that the alternatives to bureaucratic growth are not altogether satisfactory. Organizational failures of the sort discussed in the "new industrial organization" literature do not occur in bureaucracies because essential functions must be maintained and because decentralization, paralleling the industrial model, is impossible. And the model of organizations suggested by contemporary theory, one that emphasizes innovation, permits error, and encourages singleness of purpose, is not appropriate for institutions that heretofore have been organized bureaucratically because bureaucratic work demands control and is intolerant of error. The contemporary model of organizing is particularly inappropriate for the agencies studied given that their task is to maintain fiscal control and consistency in financial reporting. Organizational theory can make a modest contribution to solving the problem of bureaucratic growth provided that theory takes account of the fact that no set of organizing principles applied consistently will always yield positive outcomes in a world fraught with inconsistency. The contribution of research is potentially greater. Research can quantify long-term patterns of bureaucratic growth. Research can identify points at which theories of organizing produce organizations that function poorly. And research, if extended sufficiently, can suggest alternative organizing principles and, indeed, alternatives to formal organization as it is now conceived.

If there is a message in this book, it is that patterns leading to bureaucratic growth are deeply embedded in thinking about organizations as well as in organizational action. This is understandable, since bureaucracy offered substantial advantages over the organizational forms it displaced three-quarters of a century ago. Past a point, however, the advantages of bureaucratic structure and process may have become disadvantages. If this is the case, then organizational theory ought to direct attention toward the phenomenon of bureaucratic growth and away from, to some extent, the design of bureaucratic structures that sustain growth. In a similar vein, organizational research ought perhaps to focus more on the extensiveness of bureaucracy and less on indexes of organizational structures. Both shifts in emphasis can be accomplished without labelling bureaucracy as good or evil. The same forces that gave rise to bureaucracy in the first place and account for its contribution to modern societies may also be those that have propelled bureaucracy's growth past reasonable limits. The task of this book is to identify these forces and to suggest a corrective, if, in fact, one is necessary.

0.2 The Theory in Brief

In explaining bureaucratic growth, this book develops a theory of organization that is somewhat at odds with prevailing ideas. The book begins quite conventionally – the basic variables in the research describe organizational environments, size and structure, and the theories from which the research begins are not obscure – yet its conclusions are not conventional. Why this occurred will be understood by the reader as he or she reads on, provided that he or she is open to new ways of exploring familiar territory.

The theory developed here rests on a set of assumptions that distinguish bureaucracies from other types of organizations. It assumes, for example, that bureaucracies are more likely than other types of organizations to have tasks that are not easily accomplished or whose accomplishment is not easily measured. Business firms, for example, are normally contrained by a "bottom line." No comparable yardstick exists for public agencies. What constitutes adequate municipal accounting and financial reporting, the principal responsibilities of the agencies that are the subject of this research, is often ambiguous and is subject to periodic redefinition. The theory assumes further that bureaucracies seek continually to make sense of indeterminacy. To be sure, where there is stability, bureaucratic process and routine may be

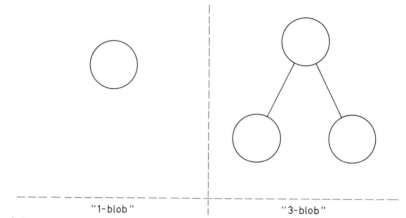

Figure 0.1
"1-Blob" versus "3-Blob" Organization

sufficient to order environments. But under conditions of change, the problem of bounded rationality becomes paramount, and organizational hierarchies are extended in order to map the environment more adequately. The theory assumes lastly that bureaucracies are largely inattentive to the growth of formal organization and of staff. This occurs partly for bounded rationality reasons. The demands made by the environment are such that growth is of little or no salience. Additionally, arguments for maintaining or augmenting organization come from below, from persons closest to unsolved problems, and have more force than arguments for contracting organization. The latter arguments are made, if they are made at all, by persons at higher levels who are less familiar with problems. Inattentiveness to growth also occurs because formal budgeting systems were weak to nonexistent throughout much of the period covered by the research.

The result of uncertain tasks, efforts to map the environment more effectively by augmenting organization, and inattentiveness to growth can be described simply and graphically. Consider Figure 0-1 above. The single circle at the left represents an unorganized aggregation of people. It is called a "1-blob" because there is no differentiation as to level of authority or task. At the right, the three circles connected hierarchically represent a primitive organization. This is called a "3-blob". The theory sketched above argues that "3-blobs" are normally preferred to "1-blobs". Because organization offers substantial advantages over non-organization, "1-blobs" will tend to evolve into "3-blobs" over time. Now consider Figure 0-2. At the left is the familiar "3-blob", but it is represented somewhat differently than before. It is at once a "3-blob" as well as two "1-blobs". The "3-blob" is its totality, while the two "1-blobs" are the subordinate units. At the right of Figure 0-2

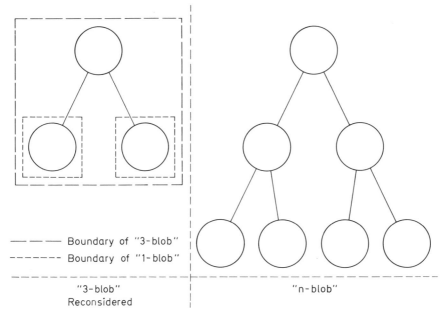

Figure 0.2
"3-Blob" versus "n-Blob" Organization

is the result of the same evolutionary process sketched in Figure 0-1 whereby "1-blobs" become "3-blobs". A new layer of organization has been created. In place of one "1-blob" and two "3-blobs", there are now three "3-blobs". In principle, this process could continue without limit. One could hypothesize that, over time, bureaucratic organizations will evolve toward "n-blobs", where n is unbounded. In fact, however, there must be limits to bureaucratic growth. This book cannot identify precisely what these limits are because they have begun to operate only recently. However, this book can and does argue that these limits do not lie in the kinds of environments conceived conventionally in organizational theory.

The analogy between blobs and bureaucracies can be overdrawn. Units of organization are purposive, while blobs are not. Some minimum criteria of efficiency and effectiveness must be met in organizations; the blob analogy ignores this completely. Nonetheless, thinking about bureaucracies as blobs captures the essence of a paradox to explored throughout this book. On the one hand, formal organization is normally a better means of accomplishing complicated tasks than is non-organization; "1-blobs" will evolve into "3-blobs". On the other hand, should the complexity of tasks be irreducible because tasks are ill-defined or change unpredictably, then organization will evolve toward "n-blobs". This evolution will continue so long as organization is believed to be the best means of addressing complex tasks – which it usually is. Only when the long-term consequences of the organizing process as it now operates are understood will this pattern change.

0.3 Comparison with Other Models of Organizing

As sketched above, the theory of bureaucracy developed in this book appears to depart from more conventional ways of thinking about organizations. It does to some extent, but perhaps less than might be imagined at first. There is perhaps a greater departure from earlier research than from earlier theorizing, but this is understandable since research results usually lag somewhat behind theory.

Two models have dominated both thinking and research on organizations in the last twenty years. One is the rational- or closed-system model, derived from the work of Weber and classical organizational theorists such as Taylor and Fayol. In this model, organizations operate for the most part undisturbed by their environments, objectives are well defined, managers seek optimal ways to attain objectives, and command authority allows managers to control behavior at lower levels of organization. Research focuses on interrelations among organizational elements. The maintained hypothesis is that organizations are configured for purposes of efficiency: Organizational structure increases with size to maintain spans of control within reasonable bounds; administrative overhead increases with complexity to maintain coordination; extensive regulations allow decentralization because the regulations themselves insure consistency in decision-making. The second dominant approach to organizations has been the natural- or open-system model, derived from the work of Katz and Kahn, Thompson, and others. This model assumes that environments, which cannot be controlled, do in fact disturb organizations, but it is otherwise similar to closed-system thinking in that objectives are understood, managers press for attainment of objectives, and control is exercised within organizations if not in the environment. Research focuses on relationships of environmental elements to organizations. The maintained hypothesis is that organizations are configured isomorphic with their environments. In conventional open-systems thinking, isomorphism with environments is achieved through change within organizations. In the framework of population ecology or of organizational evolution, organizations are not free to adapt hence isomorphism occurs through a Darwinian processes whereby units that fit the environment are retained and less fit units dissolved.

The theory developed here does not deny that elements of both the rational and open-system models operate on the bureaucracies studied. The reader will find below that task environments do in fact influence bureaucratic growth, although in different ways at different times and often not at all. The theory argues, however, that the assumptions made by the rational and open-systems models are insufficient to account for long-term patterns of bureaucratic growth and change. Both rational and open-system models, for example, assume objectives to be understood and consistent over time. This assumption is relaxed here. Not only does the environment disturb organizations, but it also disturbs their objectives rendering decision processes sometimes chaotic or, to use the metaphor of March and his colleagues, garbage-can like. Both rational and open-system models assume managers to exercise command authority over organizations. This assumption is also relaxed. Influence or power, whether due to the politics of patronage or the politics of civil service, are ubiquitous and weaken managerial control, consistent with the work of Allison, Pfeffer, and others. Finally, both the rational and open-system models assume formal administrative structures to have instrumental purposes, efficiency in the rational model, isomorphism with the environment and survival in open-system thinking. Here, following the suggestion of John W. Meyer and others, organizational structures are assumed also to have symbolic or representational functions in that they give the appearance of rationality in administration.

The assumptions made here, then, differ from those made in rational and open-system models, but they are hardly without precedent. Quite the opposite, they are accepted elements of contemporary thinking about organizations. The hypothesis derived from these assumptions does, however, depart somewhat from earlier thinking. Previously, organizational size or growth have been considered only in rational and open-system theories. Here it is argued that the intersection of uncertainty and change within organizations, postulated by garbage-can and political models, with the constraint that organizations behave rationally or at least represent themselves as such, postulated by the symbolic model, yields long-term bureaucratic growth. The tasks of public bureaucracies are both complicated and uncertain, internal control is weak, yet rational administration or its appearance must be maintained. The latter is achieved, but at the cost of bureaucratic growth.

The hypothesis is not easily proved. While the dependent variable, bureaucratic growth, can be gauged with some precision, the causal variables – uncertainty, change, and the imperative of rational administration – cannot be. Moreover, since there are competing theories of growth, no one of them can be demonstrated to operate unless the causal variables in the others are controlled, either explicitly by introducing them into statistical models or implicitly by limiting observations to times and places where they can be assumed not to operate. Neither approach to controlling exogenous variation can be adopted fully here. But simply because a hypothesis cannot be proved definitively does not mean that it should not be considered and explored to the extent practicable. The spirit of this book, then, is exploratory. It is driven by the idea that the logic of many modern institutions leads to increased administration and bureaucratization over time, a development that is at first welcomed but later defeats the purposes for which it was intended. Whether or this idea proves persuasive must be decided by the readers of this book, just as they must also decide whether or not we need now to consider means of limiting bureaucratic growth.

Chapter 1
The Concept of Rational Administration

Three-quarters of a century ago, the idea of rational large-scale administration was invented. The idea originated from several sources. One source was the reform movement, which sought an alternative to the corruption of the spoils system that had pervaded U.S. cities in the 19th century. The reformers thought administration separable from politics and sought to infuse businesslike principles in the former. Another source of the idea of rational administration was industry, where a developing managerial class needed justification for exercising authority. It found justification in doctrines of "scientific management" (Taylor, 1911), which attributed to managers expertise beyond the grasp of ordinary working people. A third source, and the one most familiar to social scientists, was the work of Max Weber (1946). Weber celebrated the bureaucratic form as the quintessence of rationality in administration, claiming bureaucracy superior in every respect to the traditional forms that had preceded it.

The idea of rational administration did not originate in a vacuum. Quite the opposite, large centrally controlled organizations have existed throughout history. As Weber pointed out, the Egyptians, Romans, and Chinese had experimented with bureaucratic forms of organization. The Roman Catholic church has been organized hierarchically throughout its existence, and command hierarchy has been universal in military organizations. In the U.S., rational administered organizations appeared first with industrialization. The historian Alfred Chandler has shown that as early as the 1850's, administration and middle management had become important components of business, especially the railroads.

Rational administration and the idea of rational administration are not the same things. The former, rational administration, is a fact, as a means to the end of effective and efficient performance. Chandler, for example, indicates that without scheduling and cost accounting, safe and economical rail transport would have been impossible. The latter, the idea of rational administration, is a belief about how collective activity ought to be organized. The idea of rational administration transforms the fact of rational administration into the imperative that all large-scale activity ought to be organized rationally. It is not a means to an end but rather an end in itself.

This book concerns both the fact and the idea of rational administration. The fact of rational administration of greatest concern here is bureaucratic growth. Bureaucratic growth has been endemic in Western societies in the twentieth century, but it is poorly understood. The idea of rational administration, the imperative that organization follow the rational model, is of concern because it may be responsible for the fact of bureaucratic growth. A key hypothesis we shall explore is that the constraint to maintain rational, formal organization under conditions of uncertainty and change, which often obtain in government, may compel growth.

The argument made here differs from two explanations offered conventionally for bureaucratic growth. One conventional explanation is societal: Literate, complex, and interdependent societies demand more administration than less developed and simpler societies. Another conventional second explanation is individual: Absent market constraints, bureaucrats can more easily augment budgets than their business counterparts. The first explanation ties bureaucratic growth to the larger society, the second to maximization of individual benefits. Neither explanation can be tested rigorously here. And neither has taken account of that possibility the prevailing beliefs about how work ought rationally to be organized have propelled bureaucratic growth beyond reasonable limits.

The central purpose of this book, then, is to trace the connection between the idea of rational administration and the fact of bureaucratic growth. In order to do this, the tautology or near tautology in the argument must be relieved. To hypothesize that the idea of rational administration accounts for bureaucratic growth may be trivial or profound depending upon how intricate a connection is established. Trivially, one could argue that since people normally believe in what they do, there should be a close correlation between the pervasiveness of the idea that one must organize rationally and the extensiveness of rational organization. Less trivially, however, one might show rapid bureaucratic growth began at about the time rational "businesslike" principles were introduced into public administration in the U.S., that bureaucratic growth has followed proliferation of highly rationalized organizational structures, and that highly rationalized organizations have had greater persistence over time than units less rationalized and structured. In other words, complicated bureaucracies that tend toward growth have been retained, while simpler and smaller units lacking the trappings of formal rationality have not been. A preference for the former can be imputed.

Another purpose of this book, assuming that the idea of rational administration can be connected meaningfully to bureaucratic growth, is to suggest alternative organizing principles that might limit growth. The diagnosis of the problem does not suggest an easy cure. Because the prevailing conception of rationality in administration is the problem, rationalistic solutions only compound the problem by adding new administrative process. More subtle thinking acknowledging irreducible indeterminacy in environments that cannot be removed by augmenting bureaucracy is needed. One book cannot complete the task of reworking an entire body of administrative theory that has developed over the last seventy-five years, but the premises of a new theory can be established.

This book has several other purposes. One is to describe as accurately as possible long-term patterns of growth and change among a set of municipal administrative agencies that have been the subject of ongoing research. These agencies are departments of finance, comptrollers' offices, treasurers' offices, and the like, which are responsible for collecting, holding, and disbursing city funds and for maintaining records of transactions. Finance agencies were chosen for study because they are in many ways representative of all bureaucracies and, importantly, because detailed quantitative data describing their internal organization and environments from the 1890's to the present could be found. The question the reader must consider, as we have, is whether the functions performed by these bureaus have expanded by a factor of ten or more during the interval covered by our research, and, if not, then what accounts for growth of this magnitude.

A further purpose of this book is to make use of modern quantitative methods to understand patterns of bureaucratic growth. These methods yield some intuitive results, but also some results substantially at odds with stereotypes of bureaucracy. Not only has substantial growth occurred, which fits stereotypes of bureaucracy, but organizational change has been endemic, which is counter to stereotype. The relationships of environmental change to organizational change and of organizational change to growth are central to the argument in this book but cannot be grasped without the aid of quantitative techniques.

A final purpose of this book is to demonstrate the relevance of sociological concepts to understanding the phenomenon of bureaucratic growth. We shall show that bureaucratic growth is not a simple function of external demand. It is rather a function of organization, or, more specifically, how organizational structures are constructed to maintain rationality or its appearance under uncertainty. The concept of structure, which is central to sociology and distinguishes it from other social science disciplines, is central to this argument. Below, structure will be defined and measured in ways made possible by the unique nature of the data, which are historical time series describing in intricate detail organizational patterns over nearly a century. Structure is shown to be consequential for organizations, a result anticipated in theory but rarely demonstrated in research.

Not all of our purposes can be served in a single chapter. This first chapter, then, will describe the early development of the idea of rational administration and of the finance agencies that are the subject of the research. The growth of both began early in this century, the idea of rational administration in force, and finance agencies in complexity and size.

1.1 Ideas About Organizing

Concepts of rational administration emerged at the beginning of the twentieth century. No specific date for this development can be set. It is clear, however, that prior to the 1890's there was little discussion of administration or management as such, separate from the technical content of business. It is equally clear that by the mid-1910's, some principles of administration that were believed universal had gained wide acceptance. These principles, importantly, have changed little since. The sociologist Charles Perrow explains that no better ideas have been found. Writing of classical organizational theory, he notes that, "all the resources of organizational theory and research today have not managed to substitute better principles" (1979: 58).

Several questions need to be asked of the body of thinking about organizations that developed around the turn of the century. One concerns its content: What practices were recommended and what proscribed? Another concerns its generality: Were the ideas meant to apply to only some types or to all types of organizations? A third question concerns its consequences: Did these ideas in fact contribute positively to organizations, or did they have consequences unforseen by their advocates that detracted from performance, if not in the short run then in the long run? The first and second questions will be addressed in this chapter. The third will occupy the remainder of this book.

Early ideas about organizing – the term organizational theory was not used – were derived largely from experience and intended as practical guides to management. There were several common elements in these ideas, elements that nowadays have become all but universal in organizations. These include command hierarchy, which was borrowed from the military, the positive functions of management, and the imperative of efficiency.

Command Hierarchy

Perhaps the idea most central to early thinking about organizations is command hierarchy. The theme of command hierarchy permeates the work of early management theorists such as Taylor (1911), Fayol (1922), and Weber

(1946). Command hierarchy assumes not only authority, that is, super- and subordination, but also a structure of authority relationships beyond those of individual bosses to their subordinates allowing authority to be exercised across several levels of organization. Control of large numbers of personnel through intermediate managers thus becomes possible. Command hierarchy also assumes pyramidal organizational structures. For any two persons or offices, a superior or office responsible for coordinating their actions is designated. This occurs at all levels of organizations so that at the highest level only one person or unit has ultimate authority. The early theorists believed that absent a structure of authority, control would remain weak and limited to face-to-face contact with direct subordinates. It was also believed that absent pyramidal organizations, ultimate authority would remain diffused and coordination limited. The early theorists' model of command hierarchy was drawn directly from military experience, as indicated by Gulick (1933).

Historically, the idea of command hierarchy appeared after other means of organizing were tried and failed. The immediate predecessor of command hierarchy was contracting within organizations. In manufacturing industry, either individual workers or labor contractors would agree to produce a product by a given date at a given cost but would otherwise retain complete control over work. The contractors acted as agents for labor by negotiating with owners the price of a job, hiring and paying workers for the job, and pocketing the difference between the contract price and actual wage costs. The historian Daniel Nelson describes the position of contractors as follows:

The contractor ... made virtually all the important decisions relating to what, when, how, and by whom the product would be made. In addition, he alone knew – or at least had the opportunity to know – the actual production costs ... Finally, the contractors had nearly complete control over the factory labor force. In many firms the management did not even know how much the contractor's "employees" were paid (1975: 37–38).

In the public sector, contracting took a somewhat different form. Through the end of the 19th century, local taxes were sometimes collected by "farmers" who were permitted to keep a percentage of the take. There was fierce competition for this privilege. Some city treasurers were given a fixed proportion of interest earned on bank deposits to cover office expenses and their own salaries. The percentages allowed tax collectors and treasurers did not appear as expenditures in local budgets. The contracting system was the utmost in simplicity.

No single explanation is offered for the demise of contracting in industry and public management. Some, such as the economist Oliver Williamson (1975), argue that it was inefficient. Others, like Nelson, claim that it threatened ownership prerogatives. In the public sector, contracting for tax collection and the management of municipal treasuries was also corrupt. Much of the impetus for reform arose because basic city functions appeared to have been conducted capriciously or for the benefit of political bosses. Why contracting failed and command hierarchy took its place is not the central concern of this book, however. Of much greater concern are the consequences of command hierarchy.

The early management theorists viewed command hierarchy principally as an instrument of social control, a position shared, ironically, by contemporary critics of management theory (Edwards, 1979). Hierarchy extended social control by allowing authority to span multiple levels of organization, by concentrating ultimate authority in one person or office, and by increasing the likelihood of compliance by offering the possibility of promotion, something not possible when there were only owners and workers. But in addition to extending control, and possibly as a means of augmenting control, hierarchy also contributed to the appearance of rationality in organizations. It did so in several ways. To begin, hierarchy created an unambiguous ranking of offices with corresponding rights and duties. Knowing only the office – not the person – one could also know its prerogatives. Command hierarchy eliminated the redundant, overlapping, and often unpredictable patterns that had characterized earlier organizational forms. Command hierarchy also introduced fixity into organizational structures. Individual persons remained free to enter or leave offices, but relations among offices were formalized in tables of organization, procedure manuals, and the like. In short, command hierarchy introduced an increment of certainty – or at least what was believed to be certainty – into organizations. The idea that organizations could accomplish complicated tasks predictably and therefore rationally was a powerful force, for it allowed permanent solutions. Only recently have scholars begun to suggest that uncertainty and change might be ubiquitous in organizations, but predictability remains an article of faith among practitioners.

The Positive Functions of Management

A somewhat different idea emerging from early thinking about organizations asserted the positive functions of management. Taylor's *The Principles of Scientific Management* (1911), remembered chiefly for its portrait of a hapless Dutchman named Schmidt who is persuaded to load 47 tons of pig iron per day rather than the customary 12½ tons, is in fact a treatise on management responsibility. Taylor exhorted managers to select, train, supervise, and reward their workers rather than relying on old-fashioned "initiative and incentive" systems whereby workers themselves determined how they would go about their tasks. Later, Taylorism became a cult preoccupied with time-and-motion studies, but the greatest impact of *The Prin-*

ciples ... was its assertion of unique management duties and prerogatives.

The idea that management has functions apart from ownership spread rapidly following Taylor. Its development need not be traced here. Its quintessence was Luther Gulick's essay, "Notes on the Theory of Organization" (1937), which is the first chapter in the highly influential volume edited by Gulick and Urwick, *Papers on the Science of Administration.* Aside from stating basic organizing principles – division of labor, span of control, line versus staff, specialization by purpose, process, client, and place – Gulick asked, "What is the work of the chief executive? What does he do?" The answer, according to Gulick who borrowed his ideas from Henri Fayol, is POSDCORB. POSDCORB is, of course, an acronym, standing for planning, organizing, staffing, directing, coordinating, reporting, and budgeting. Each of these functions, Gulick argued, is unique to the office of the chief executive and must be performed in his office, possibly by the executive himself, possibly by separate sections of his office.

As Reinhard Bendix (1956) points out, managerial ideologies had begun to shift even before *Papers on the Science of Administration* was published. From Taylor and Fayol through Gulick, managers were portrayed as expert in administration, the science of organizing. Afterwards, at least until the late 1960's, their expertise shifted to human relations, the science of motivating others to perform. Which expertise most effectively promoted organizational purposes is not at issue here. The crucial point is that expertise was claimed even though it had little scientific basis. Taylor's first book was based on one case, Schmidt, and the *Papers* ... draw their generalizations mainly from the experience of the British general staff during World War I. These shortcomings, however, did not prevent early management theorists from asserting that there was a science of administration and that competent executives were expert in this science. The job of managers was to apply this science, thereby contributing to the appearance if not the fact of rationality into organizations.

The Imperative of Efficiency

A third pillar of early thinking about organizations was its unrelenting press for efficiency. Taylor, for example, justified his prescriptions for managing almost exclusively as means of improving productive efficiency. The efficiencies of scientific management promised both individual and collective benefits. The former would accrue to owners in increased profits and workers as increased wages, the latter to consumers in lower prices hence greater prosperity. Taylor observed, however, that workers' wages could be augmented up to sixty per cent beyond their normal earnings but not more.

A long series of experiments ... demonstrated the fact that when workmen ... are given a carefully measured task, which calls for a big day's work, and that when in return for this extra effort they are paid wages up to 60 per cent. beyond the wages usually paid, that this increase in wages tends to make them not only more thrifty but better men in every way ... When, on the other hand, they received much more than a 60 per cent. increase in wages, many of them will work irregularly and tend to become more or less shiftless, extravagant, and dissipated ... (1911: 74).

It is hardly surprising that early management thinking, indeed almost all management thinking, was ultimately rationalized as a means of promoting efficiency. Efficiency has been and remains a value in most settings, and prescriptions for improving efficiency have always had an audience even if most have remained untested. Modern organizational theory reminds us, however, that efficiency tests can be made only if two conditions are met. First, desired ends or outcomes must be known and agreed to. Second, cause-and-effect must be understood so that the means leading to desired ends and their costs can be identified. What is remarkable about early management thinking is its blithe assumption that these conditions are easily satisfied. Gulick (1937: 191), for example, wrote, "Administration has to do with getting things done; with the accomplishment of defined objectives. The science of administration is thus the system of knowledge whereby men understand relationships, predict results, and influence outcomes ..." It did not occur to Gulick or to his collaborators that objectives might prove elusive, and that even if objectives were understood means leading to them might not be.

Whatever their practical difficulties, the organizing principles of command hierarchy, expert management, and efficiency had substantial academic appeal by the beginning of this century. These principles also had practical appeal as they had worked for the railroads and for manufacturing firms, revolutionizing both transportation and production. It is not surprising, therefore, that the same principles were believed applicable to and appropriate for administration in the public sector.

1.2 Generalizing the Rational Model to Government

Large-scale private enterprise emerged in the U.S. long before there was large government. The interregional railroads were essentially in place by the late 1870's, and most of the major industrial and retailing firms that were to dominate the U.S. economy for the following fifty years had become substantial businesses before the end of the 1890's. Large-scale private enterprise therefore became the model people had in mind when they spoke of rational organization. To be sure, business had borrowed some of its ideas from the military, but it developed other organizing concepts and demonstrated their applicability in nonmilitary settings.

At first, the of idea rational administration diffused slowly. No exact date of its acceptance can be set, but the rational model was well entrenched by the end of the first decade of this century. Chandler (1977: 464–68), for example, notes that the professionalization of management of large industrial firms had extended to almost all functional specialities by 1910. The professional societies for accounting, finance, marketing, and production management were established by this date. And business education had begun by 1910 in the most prestigeous colleges and universities in the U.S. The year 1910 also marked the convening of the First International Congress of Administrative Science in Brussels, which was concerned explicitly with the application of rational concepts to government.

In the United States, the impetus for infusing rational principles into public administration came mainly from the reform movement that first gained momentum in the 1890's. The reformers, particularly the Progressives, had two targets, the trusts that controlled much of U.S. industry, and the political bosses whose machines controlled the cities. The Progressives' antidote for both was big government, which was also neutral, impartial, and objective government. The Progressives' aims were achieved, but, as will be argued below, only at the cost of setting into place forces leading to permanent bureaucratic growth.

Increasing the Size of Government

In an era when government is believed excessive, it is difficult to imagine a time when public opinion favored extension of government in order to balance the power of business. The size of national government and its capacity to regulate business were extended substantially by the reforms of the late 19th and early 20th century. The Interstate Commerce Commission began regulating the railroads in 1887. The Sherman Act, which declared the trusts illegal combinations, became law in 1890, and in 1902 President Theodore Roosevelt launched the government's attack on the Northern Securities Company, which controlled both the Northern Pacific and Great Northern railroads. Previously, government intervention had always been on the side of business. Now, the "public interest" prevailed.

The historian Richard Hofstadter describes vividly how attitudes toward government shifted during the Progressive era:

... reluctantly rather than enthusiastically, the average American tended to rely more and more on government regulation, to seek in governmental action a counterpoise to the power of private business. ... he began to support governmental organization and to accept more readily than he had been willing to do before the idea that the reach of government must be extended . . .

But if the power of the state had to be built up, it would be more important than it had ever been that the state be a neutral state which would realize as fully as possible the preference of the middle-class public for moderation, impartiality, and "law" (1955: 233–34).

The problem, of course, was how to build moderation, impartiality, and "law" into governments that had in the past been the bulwarks of business and city bosses. The reformers' solution was administration divorced from politics.

Removing Politics from Administration

Just as a science of management was sought by industry, a science of public administration was the aim of the early reform movement. The then political scientist Woodrow Wilson was their most articulate voice. In a classic essay on "The Study of Administration," Wilson wrote that public administration "is a field of business. It is removed from the hurry and strife of politics" (1887 [1943]: 493). The object of administrative study was to ground "executive methods . . . deep in stable principle . . . administration lies outside of the proper sphere of *politics*. Administrative questions are not political questions" (p. 494). The aim of administration was efficiency. "To be efficient, [administrative study] must discover the simplest arrangements by which responsibility can be unmistakably fixed upon officials . . ." (p. 497). Wilson advocated centralized authority and unhampered discretion. Montesquieu's notion of checks and balances was untidy and obscured responsibility.

Wilson advocated not only neutral administration, but also administration by experts. "It will be necessary to organize democracy by sending up to the competetive examinations for the civil service men definitely prepared for standing liberal tests as to technical knowledge. A technically schooled civil service will presently have become indispensable". But expertness posed the danger of creating an "offensive official class" (p. 500). This tendency would have to be countered by insisting on civil servants' allegiance to the policies of the government they serve. Indeed, "good behavior" in office would be defined as behavior consistent with the policies of elected officials. Bureaucracy, which to Wilson was an epithet, existed only where the "service of the state is removed from the common political life of the people, its chiefs as well as its rank and file" (p. 501).

Wilson never attempted to resolve the tension between expertness and democratic governance, a problem that has occupied Weber, Michels, and contemporary students of politics (Lipset et al., 1956). Wilson labelled elite administration "un-American." Having done so, he advocated careful study

of European administrative systems to perfect methods of government. "...
all governments have a strong structural likeness; more than that, if they are
to be uniformly useful and efficient, they *must* have a strong structural
likeness ... for all governments alike the legitimate ends of administration
are the same" (p. 502). Wilson believed the French and German models to
be most appropriate for study because they were the most developed administrative bureaucracies, not because their purposes were consistent with
American values. For the U.S., the objective was to construct a federal form
of administration, "systems within systems" (p. 505), to use Wilson's
phrase, that combined vigor in administration with subordination to public
opinion.

Inconsistencies in the Rational Model

In generalizing the rational model to government, the reformers overlooked
some potentially inconsistent elements in their thinking. The basic model
the reformers had in mind was one of citizen control of elected officials who,
in turn, directed the administrative apparatus of the state. This model was
taken from industry, where shareholders exercised control over corporate
managers who, in turn, directed day-to-day business operations. Rational
administration assumed a simple and direct relationship between the desires
of the electorate and the preferences of elected officials. A unity and constancy of purpose rarely present in government, and especially in federal
systems, was taken for granted. If citizens spoke with a single voice, the
rational model might have applied. But since constituencies are diverse and
elected officials normally seek to balance conflicting interests, the rational
model is an incomplete guide to the conduct of public affairs. The rational
model also defined incompletely the relationship of elected officials to their
subordinates. As noted above, U.S. bureaucracy, unlike its European counterparts, was expected to remain responsive to elected officials. But a strong
aversion to the spoils system led the reformers to press for civil service or
merit personnel regulations that substantially insulated career employees
from political pressures. Wilson's solution to this problem, defining good
conduct as compliance with higher authority, was too simplistic. The rational model assumed finally that efficiency measures would guide the
conduct of government as they had guided business. Cost accounting, which
was developed fully by the 1870's, had allowed most businesses to gauge
their efficiency, if crudely, by comparing outputs to expenditures. The same
cost accounting techniques were available to government, but their results
were generally ignored. The simple fact, overlooked by the reformers, was
that the important outputs of government were not easily quantified hence
not easily related to expenditures. Efficiency thus assumed a different
meaning in public administration than in private enterprise. It became un-

derstood as punctuality, honesty, and, above all, conformity to rules and regulations.

Command authority, the functions of management, and efficiency, concepts central to rational administration in business firms, were thus transformed when the rational model was applied to public administration in the U.S. Pluralism and the ethos of democratic governance rendered any simple translation of citizen preferences into administrative action difficult. Managerial prerogatives were constrained by the independence of civil servants and were further constrained by reform innovations such as the initiative and the referendum. And the imperative of efficiency focused attention on procedure rather than outcomes since the latter were so elusive in the public sector. One might question why the rational model remained viable given that some of its key precepts were so severely compromised. The answer is twofold. First, even though the excesses of business were resented by the reformers, its successes were also admired. Second, no alternative model for public administration existed, save for the spoils system for which the rational model was intended as an antidote.

1.3 Max Weber's Synthesis

Max Weber's work, especially his essay on "Bureaucracy" (1946), is understood by most social scientists both as a description of modern bureaucratic structures and as a theory explaining why bureaucracy has displaced earlier forms of organization. The description is straightforward and entirely consistent with the tenets of rational administration outlined above: Bureaucratic organizations operate on the principle of command hierarchy; expert management has responsibility for coordinating work and insuring that directives are, in fact, carried out; the imperative of efficiency precludes other bases for action. The theory explaining the displacement of earlier forms by bureaucratic organizations is somewhat less straightforward. Two arguments are developed. One is necessity. Large, centrally governed states and business enterprises could not be administered absent bureaucratic organization. The second is efficiency. Weber asserted that, "the fully developed bureaucratic mechanism compares with other organizations exactly as does the machine with non-mechanical modes of production" (1946: 214).

Here, it is argued that Weber's theory of bureaucracy, which was written shortly before his death in 1920, can also be understood as an attempt to synthesize earlier management thinking by treating both public and private bureaucracy alike as instances of organization under rational-legal authority. Weber had toured the U.S. in the first decade of the century and was familiar with the politics of reform and with Taylorism. It goes without saying that Weber's participation in German politics also rendered him familiar with European patterns of administration. Weber's larger conceptual framework in which the historical trend toward rationalization of all spheres of conduct drives most social change may have led him to emphasize common elements rather than differences between public- and private-sector organizations as well as between U.S. and European administrative practices. The same conceptual framework may have led Weber to remove – the term resolve is deliberately not used – inconsistencies that surfaced when the rational model of administration was generalized from business to government by the reformers. But having removed some inconsistencies from the reformers' model of public administration, Weber's theory created a new set of contradictions.

Applying the Bureaucratic Model to Public and Private Organizations

Weber argued that the bureaucratic model applies with equal force to governmental and business organizations. The key characteristics of bureaucracy – fixed responsibilities, authority delimited by written rules, selection of officials according to their qualifications – constitute "bureaucratic authority" in government and "management" in business (1946: 196). The principle of separation of personal from official capacities holds in both bureaus and firms. "Public monies and equipment are divorced from the private property of the official ... Nowadays, [this] is found in public as well as in private enterprises; in the latter; the principle extends even to the leading entrepreneur" (p. 197). Thorough and expert training, full-time employment, and expertise based in rules and office procedures are expected in both public and private offices (p. 198). A modicum of social esteem attaches to positions in both private offices or public bureaus; in both settings tangible privileges are attached to the various ranks (p. 199). Generally, the more developed business enterprises resembled most closely public bureaucracies. "The very large, modern capitalist enterprises are themselves unequalled models of strict bureaucratic organization" (p. 215). (Whether firms were models for or modelled after public bureaucracies is not stated.) Weber perceived only one significant difference between public and private bureaucracy. Whereas positions may be held for life in public agencies, no comparable tenure arrangement exists in firms. Weber noted, however, that lengthy employment is "increasingly the case" (p. 202) for private firms organized bureaucratically.

Removing Inconsistencies from the Rational Model

Weber did not attempt to resolve the inconsistent elements that arose when the rational model was transferred from business to public administration but instead defined them out of existence. Weber was unconcerned that the machinery of government should be driven by citizens' preferences. He noted that bureaucracy and mass democracy usually coincided, an observation probably more apt for Western than for Eastern societies, because democracy usually demanded formal equality before the law. But Weber also noted that democratization should not be expected to yield reponsive bureaucracies. Quite the opposite, democracy meant only equal treatment of citizens by the bureaucratic apparatus of the state.

The generally loose term 'democratization' cannot be used here, in so far as it is understood to mean the minimization of the civil servants' ruling power in favor of the greatest possible 'direct' rule of the *demos,* which in practice means the respective party leaders of the *demos.* The most decisive thing here – indeed it is rather exclusively so – is the *leveling of the governed* in opposition to the ruling and bureaucratically articulated group ... (p. 226).

In a similar vein, Weber observed that bureaucracies could not be expected to defer to the preferences of elected officials. "The 'political master' finds himself in the position of the 'dilettante' who stands opposite the 'expert,' facing the trained official who stands within the management of administration" (p. 232). The dilemma that had confronted Woodrow Wilson, the tension between an independent and expert civil service and a civil service responsive to the public and elected officials, was resolved by Weber entirely in favor of the former.

The Problem of Power

Weber's model of bureaucracy is treated by most social scientists as an accurate if not contemporary model of organizations. More so than Wilson or Frederick Taylor, Weber attempted to avoid advocacy, to remove from his observations whatever personal preferences he may have had. To be sure, Weber's writing smacks occasionally of admiration for Prussian methods of administration. But it is far less tendentious that the works of many management theorists who have proffered solutions to problems absent a theory explaining why their solutions should work or evidence indicating that they do in fact.

Precisely because Weber intended his model of bureaucracy, one of his "ideal-typical" constructs, as a description of rather than an encomium for modern organizations, he portrayed rather vividly some of their less desirable features. In particular, Weber noted and was concerned with the effects of bureaucratic systems on power relations. Bureaucracy, first, transformed power by shifting its basis from personal to administrative action. "As an instrument for 'societalizing' relations of power, bureaucracy has been and is a power instrument of the first order – for the one who controls the bureaucratic apparatus" (1946: 228). Bureaucracy, second, weakened the power of leaders, whether elected or hereditary. "The power position of a fully developed bureaucracy is overtowering" (p. 232). The power of bureaus was, in part, a function of their monopoly position and ability to maintain knowledge of their workings as official secrets. Bureaucracy, third, assumed substantially greater permanence and persistence than earlier administrative forms. "The fate of the masses depends upon the steady and correct functioning of the increasingly bureaucratic organizations of private capitalism. The idea of eliminating these organizations becomes more and more utopian" (p. 229).

Weber's attention to power is somewhat inconsistent with his insistence that the value of efficiency predominates in bureaucratic structures. "Modern loyalty is devoted to impersonal and functional purposes," Weber wrote. Bureaucracy is perfected to the extent that it "succeeds in eliminating from official business love, hatred, and all purely personal, irrational, and emotional elements which escape calculation" (p. 216). The dilemma confronting Weber, then, differed somewhat from that which had preoccupied Woodrow Wilson. For Wilson, public administration should be responsive to the public yet businesslike in its conduct of governmental affairs. For Weber, rationalization of administration should eliminate arbitrary power that had characterized earlier forms of administration, but in fact it substitutes power based in knowledge of rules and official secrets for power based in whim. The inconsistency between responsiveness and administration devoid of politics arose in Wilson's thinking because he borrowed the idea of rational administration from the private sector where it had been used to buttress ownership rights and transferred it to government where it was intended to limit the prerogatives of corrupt politicians. The inconsistency between the purely functional explanation of bureaucratic supremacy and the power of bureaucracies described in Weber's theory had a somewhat different source. Having asserted public and private bureaucracy to be essentially similar, Weber could not have minimized the efficiency of the former compared to the latter. Yet his great familiarity with European administrative practices may have persuaded Weber that little could be done to check the power of bureaucratic systems.

The inconsistencies in the Wilsonian and Weberian models of administration are at opposite ends of the same dilemma. Both Wilson and Weber embraced the idea of rational administration, but both were forced to make some unrealistic assumptions in order to purge nonrationalities from their models. For Wilson, good government was administration responsive to the public yet divorced from politics, almost a contradiction in terms. For Weber, efficient administration required that the public have little influence over state bureaucracies, a position inconsistent with any definition of democratic governance save for Weber's own. Wilson was able to open public bureaucracies to their environments by assuming that ideals of good government would prevail over the turbulence of politics. Weber simply closed bureaucracies from their environments. Neither of these positions was tenable, yet without them neither Wilson nor Weber could have transferred the rational model from business to government.

An argument to be pursued in this book is that the idea of rational administration could not be transferred from business to government – or, in some cases, from technical to managerial levels of business organizations – without encountering inconsistencies between predictability and control assumed in the rational model and actual indeterminacy in environments. Given indeterminacy, the rational model yields organizations that are at best temporary solutions to environmental problems. One is left, like Wilson, assuming indeterminacy not to exist, or, like Weber, assuming the environment irrelevant. Another argument is that, in practice, the inconsistencies in the rational model have been resolved by building both predictability and change into organizations, predictability by constructing organizational structures and processes of some permanence, change by continually elaborating these structures and processes. A further argument is that this accommodation of reality to theory has not been costless because it has caused bureaucratic growth. A final argument to be pursued in the last chapter of this book is that bureaucratic growth, an outcome of trying to construct permanent organizations capable of mapping changing environments, is limited ultimately by the senselessness of organizations that result.

1.4 The Rational Model in Early Finance Administration

The movement to render government more businesslike first penetrated local finance administration in the first decade of this century, more than twenty years after Wilson's "The Study of Administration" but at about the same time that doctrines of scientific management and the professionalization of managers had begun to take hold in industry. The effort to reform governmental finances occurred first at the Federal level during Theodore Roosevelt's administration when his Secretary of the Treasury appointed a "committee on business methods" charged with developing office procedures similar to those used in industry. And when the Bureau of Municipal Research, a New York-based reform organization, was founded in 1907, its secretary wrote that, "half of the cities in the United States to-day are either ready now for expert leadership in business methods, or could with little effort be interested in the need for reorganization along business lines" (Allen, 1907: 188). "Business methods," importantly, encompassed comparative financial statements, fund accounting whereby expenditures were restricted to the purposes for which they were appropriated, uniform accounting procedures across city departments, and formal organization adequate for maintaining control of revenues and expenditures.

The Aims of Reform

Reform of local finance administration was intended to remove graft and dishonesty from government and to promote cost-saving techniques. Practices that had functioned acceptably in small and homogeneous communities became less satisfactory with the growth of cities and the rise of machine politics. Throughout the nineteenth century, local fiscal management was highly decentralized. For the most part, department heads were given lump sum appropriations and managed their own accounts. Some departments functioned entirely without appropriations. As noted above, treasurers' offices were often funded from the interest earned on bank balances, and local tax collectors, who kept as remuneration for their services a percentage of the take, often feuded with one another for the privilege of taking citizens' tax payments. Accounts, such as they were, were maintained on a cash basis, and operating and capital funds were commingled. Neither revenues nor expenditures were accrued as earned or obligated, and liabilities were not compared to assets. When obligations were paid, interest-bearing warrants rather than ordinary checks were issued in case the treasury was depleted. And after the fact, expenditures were accounted for in annual financial reports that listed warrants by number and payee, much like a personal check register.

The decentralized system of finance administration, to the extent that administration as such existed, was the utmost in simplicity. Typically, responsibilities were divided among three or four offices, a treasurer who held city funds, a comptroller who supervised collections and disbursements, an auditor whose principal responsibility was preparation of the annual financial report, and an assessor. These offices were often part-time positions, and office staff were sometimes hired on a seasonal basis, when property tax payments were due and at the end of the fiscal year. Organizational practices in government thus lagged substantially behind administration in the private sector at the turn of the century. Firms had few part-time and seasonal positions for office staff, work was full time, and large accounting departments, which the railroads had utilized for three decades, were formed in many of the large industrial firms around 1900 (Chandler, 1977: ch. 13). When the reformers sought changes in the management of city finances, the business model of financial control was available and consistent with their preference for "businesslike" public administration.

The profound influence of the business model on government is perhaps best illustrated by the way that accounting concepts from industry were applied to municipalities. William Lybrand, one of the founding partners of the "big eight" accounting firm of Coopers & Lybrand, acknowledged the hazards of changing municipal accounting and reporting practices so that they conformed more nearly to "ordinary business practice," but he then argued in a 1906 article reviewing Philadelphia's financial report that:

... let us consider what are the principal objects sought to be accomplished in the presentation of a comprehensive annual financial report. The report should present (1) a clear and concise statement of the income and expenses of the corporation during the fiscal period, with like figures of the prior period side by side for comparative purposes, and (2) it should show clearly the financial condition of the corporation as of the date of making the report, with similar comparative data (p. 276).

The reader is reminded that Lybrand is speaking of governmental, not private accounting. The two objectives sought by Lybrand, accurate statements of income and expenditures and of financial condition, he claimed, were ill served by maintaining books on a cash basis. Accrual accounts that balanced expenditures obligated against revenues earned, and capital accounts that separated current from capital funds and balanced indebtedness against governmental assets were needed to describe accurately the financial condition of a municipality, especially if year-to-year comparisons were to be valid.

A third objective in municipal accounting noted by Lybrand but given greater emphasis by others (see particularly Chapman, 1910), was limitation of public expenditures to amounts and for purposes authorized by law. The reformers sought to limit officials' discretion in spending public dollars. The mechanism used to accomplish this was fund accounting in which a separate accounting entity – a fund – was established for each public purpose. Fund accounting, in effect, disaggregated a single municipal budget into several separate budgets, each of which was fixed in an appropriation ordinance. The details of fund accounting cannot be reviewed here. Suffice it to note that the use of multiple funds, as opposed to a consolidated financial statement, has been unique to public accounting but has also been subject to criticism due to the large number of accounts maintained and frequent transfers of funds between accounts.

The three aims of reformed finance administration, accurate statements of income and expenditures, statements of financial condition, and restriction of expenditures to lawful amounts and purposes, gave the appearance of more businesslike management, but they also created some complexities that had not previously been present. Two should be mentioned briefly. First, fund accounting rendered statements of income and expenditures potentially misunderstood because transfers between accounts are treated as both income and expenditure. For example, monies from general tax revenues used to amortize long-term debt are normally entered as expenditures from a general or corporate fund and income to a bond sinking fund. From the 1910's onward, the municipal finance literature has commented on the public's inability to grasp the intricacies of fund accounting. Second, comparative statements of financial condition required that the assets of local government be valued, which municipalities have found even more difficult than industry. While many cities maintain fixed-asset accounts, they do not reflect depreciation of property hence are not of the sort required for a complete statement of financial condition. Thus, just as inconsistencies had occurred when the business model of management was applied to public administration, some difficulties also surfaced when accounting practices from industry were transferred to local government. This did not cause the business model to be abandoned, however. Quite the opposite, the business model was extended and elaborated to fit the circumstances of local government.

Implementing Reformed Financial Administration: The Case of New York

There are few descriptions of how reformed financial administration was first implemented in U.S. cities. Municipal finance functions have rarely excited the public except when massive fraud had occurred, and the accounting profession was unconcerned with organization of these functions at the turn of the century. The innovations undertaken by New York's City's Department of Finance in 1908 did attract attention, however, partly due to New York's position as the major financial center and the largest city in the U.S. and partly due to a public report of the Bureau of Municipal Research recommending reorganization of the Department. The 1908 report as well as the changes implemented are described in a series of four articles (Force, 1909a; 1909b; 1909c; 1909d) published in an early volume of the *Journal of Accountancy.*

The Bureau of Municipal Research recommended and the City's Comptroller concurred that the cash system of accounting should be eliminated and that new standard accounting procedures were needed in New York City. Toward this end, an Expert Accounting Bureau was created. The Expert Accounting Bureau had several tasks. Foremost was an accrual system of accounting in which accounts would be debited when obligations were incurred. "It has been one of the many functions of the Expert Accounting Bureau to dispel from the minds of many of the departmental employees the old idea that book accounts are chargeable only when an invoice and voucher representing an expenditure are ready for actual transmittal to the Department of Finance for payment" (Force: 1909b: 106). A second task was installing and enforcing these procedures in each of the City's operating agencies. The intent was not only uniformity across the nearly 100 City departments supervised by the Comptroller, but also that "the same complete system for departmental accounting will be carried out in this central controlling office." The Comptroller's office was to have, in other words, "a complete file of all papers evidencing, in originals, every transaction occurring in the dependent Departments" (1909c: 182).

Several further recommendations were made by the Bureau of Municipal Research and implemented in the Finance Department. One was establishment of detailed cost accounts apart from appropriation accounts. Just as "cost accounts, in commerce, have become the antithesis to waste" (Force: 1906d: 270), they were expected to promote economy and efficiency in government. Another proposal made and implemented was establishment of a Bureau of Inspection charged with determining the propriety of departmental expenditures and enforcing compliance with uniform accounting standards. This Bureau functioned, in effect, as a postauditing agency. A central purchasing staff was also established in the Finance Department. Finally, the Bureau of Municipal Research also recommended and the Comptroller's office concurred that lump sum departmental appropriations be abolished and replaced by budgets stating the specific object of each category of expenditure. This procedure, which anticipated the form of state and Federal budgets developed almost a decade later, was intended to yield prior cost accounting whereby the objects of expenditures and their costs could be compared before rather than after the fact.

These systems required new staff and organization. But they were also intended to generate far greater savings than costs. To quote Force:

All of the cut-and-dried and old fashioned objections that are first heard in the business world to new systems are put forward. Too much "red tape," "too many clerks," "too much work," and "theoretical ideas" are all thrashed out in turn . . . If cost accounts revolutionize and make the success of large business enterprises they bring returns far outbalancing their outlay. Estimates of annual saving to the city, when thorough and complete reorganization has been once brought about, have been made, which amount from $ 25,000,000 to $ 50,000,000 (1909: 5).

Again, the business model was uppermost in the mind of the reformers.

Two comments about the early innovations in New York's financial management are in order. First, the procedures put in place encompassed most, but not all, of the elements of contemporary finance administration. These elements include a centralized accounting system with balances maintained on an accrual basis, cost accounting, postauditing of disbursements, centralized control of purchases, and line-item budgets. Computerization, program budgeting, and the like, of course, did not appear until much later. Second, the procedures adopted in New York City also caused fundamental realignments in organization. Prior to 1908, primary responsibility for financial management rested with individual department heads. The Department of Finance was little more than a paymaster who disbursed funds upon the request of department heads. From 1908 on, the augmented functions and staff of the Department of Finance enabled it to exercise much greater control over operating departments of government. Organization consistent with the rational model of administration, which in practice meant new organization, was an attempt to cure mismanagement in existing city agencies.

Whether or not the changes occurring in New York's fiscal administration in the first decade of this century were representative of the experience of other cities at that time cannot be determined conclusively. Scattered documentary sources indicate that finance functions in some Eastern and Midwestern cities were similarly reformed, sometimes due to local initiative, sometimes when state supervision of local accounts was imposed. However, the same sources indicate that many cities were slow to adopt modern methods of accounting and financial control. What can be stated conclusively is that realignment of organization – the creation of new offices and responsibilities – did not provide a permanent solution to the problems of financial management of New York City. New York faced fiscal crises in the Depression and again in the mid-1970's. Problems if not crises are endemic in public administration; the theory developed below argues that added administration consistent with the rational model is the normal means of addressing such problems.

1.5 Summary

A brief summary of this chapter may be in order. At the outset, the fact of rational administration was distinguished from the idea of rational administration. At the turn of the century, the most important fact of rational administration was that managerial hierarchies and modern accounting systems had been widely adopted by business and had contributed to the success of many firms. The idea of rational administration, which developed about 1910, attempted to generalize the experience of business to other settings, especially government, in the hope that businesslike methods would replace the inefficient and largely corrupt spoils system. The idea of rational administration did take hold in government, but it contained some inconsistent elements. In particular, the essential uncertainty of many governmental tasks and the insulation of civil servants from managerial influence was not easily reconciled with the level of predictability and control that was demanded by the rational model and had been achieved in business. As a practical matter, it was hypothesized above, external uncertainty was reconciled with the constraints of the rational model by continuous augmentation of formal organization.

Modern administration of local government finances began in the U.S. during the first decade of this century. At that time, business methods of accounting and financial reporting were adopted in New York City, albeit changed somewhat to fit the special circumstances of government. A question that can be raised even at this early point in our inquiry is whether the rational model of administration succeeded in creating order in municipal finances as it had ordered the activities of business. The reader will recall William Lybrand's confident statement of the objectives of local government accounting and financial reporting, which was made in 1906. Seventy-three years later, a leading scholar of governmental finance was much less sanguine that its goals were understood. Writing in *Governmental Finance*, the journal of the Municipal Finance Officers Association of the United States and Canada, Allan Drebin observed that, "The current criticism of governmental accounting may reflect the fact that there has been no general agreement as to what the objectives of governmental accounting and financial reporting are" (1979: 8).

Chapter 2
The Problem of Bureaucratic Growth

This chapter begins the exploration of bureaucratic growth. It operates at two levels. The first level is descriptive, outlining some of the facts of bureaucratization in the U.S. These facts are commonplace and serve only to confirm that measures of bureaucratization have increased substantially over time, that bureaucratization in the private sector has increased parallel to its increase in government, and that bureaucratic growth in industry may have accelerated recently. At the second level, a fundamental question of theory is raised. At issue is not whether propositions in existing organizational theory can be extended to account for bureaucratic growth – certain of them can be, as will be demonstrated two chapters hence. The problem is instead why bureaucratic growth has not been of central concern in theory since it represents organziational change of the most fundamental sort. Neoclassical organizational theory, we argue, suffers the same difficulties as Wilson's and Weber's models of public bureaucracy. On the one hand, there is a strong preference for organization as a means of solving problems. On the other hand, there is acknowledgement that the problems faced by modern organizations increasingly do not admit of definitive solutions. In all likelihood, the preference for organization as a problem-solving device hence for increased organization as a solution to increasingly complicated problems has been so strong that bureaucratic growth has not been understood as a phenomenon requiring explanation. Put somewhat differently, neoclassical theory has been directed toward *how* to organize rather than *whether* new organization is desirable. In contrast to neoclassical theory, sociological thinking has always recognized that there are dysfunctional elements in organizations. But since studies of bureaucratic dysfunctions have been limited to single cases, the possibility that increased complexity and growth are themselves dysfunctions has not been explored. Economic theory has taken a somewhat different stance toward bureaucratic growth. More so than other disciplines, economists have called attention to growth of government, although not to bureaucratization in industry. Economists have, however, been unable to explain this development satisfactorily because their theories suggest that it ought not to have happened: If government is less efficient than private enterprise, it should have shrunk rather than grown.

This chapter focuses first on the facts of bureaucratic growth in the U.S. and then on the question of why growth has not been a central concern of organizational theory. It focuses little on the finance agencies that are the subject of the research described in subsequent chapters. This is a deliberate choice. The reader already has a sense of the origins and intended functions of these organizations. He or she will shortly become apprised of specific developments over the last seventy-five years that may have affected the structure and growth of units charged with administering local finances. But two premises must be established before the details of history and of the research procedures used to test alternative models of bureaucratic growth are presented in detail. One is that the phenomenon of bureaucratic growth is not limited to the agencies studied. Rather, it has occurred both in government and the private sector. The second is that bureaucratic growth has been assumed in organizational theory and therefore not explained by it. The task of this chapter, then, is to document the facts of bureaucratic growth and to make explicit the assumption of growth that heretofore has been implicit in most theorizing.

2.1 Bureaucratic Growth: The Facts

Since the beginning of this century, bureaucratic growth has occurred almost continuously in Western societies. The basic data on bureaucratization were first assembled by Bendix (1956). Bendix constructed three indexes of bureaucratization in industry. One was the proportion of salaried employees. The second was the ratio of administrative – presumably salaried – to production – presumably nonsalaried employees. The third was the proportion of "bureaucrats," persons who were salaried employees throughout their careers, among U.S. business elites. All three indexes increased sharply over time, and increases in the ratio of administrative to production workers in industry occurred consistently across the nations for which comparable data were available. Bendix's data indicate that A/P ratios were about .1 in 1900 and .2 in 1950 (1956: 214).

Bendix's work focused on bureaucratization in industry and was unconcerned with growth in government bureaucracy. Indeed, measures of bureaucratization like those used by Bendix do not apply well to government because most such measures are invariant or inappropriate when applied to the public sector. Almost all government employees are salaried; so much of government is administration that A/P ratios may not be meaningful; save for elected officials, government employees are salaried throughout their careers. The single most meaningful index of government bureaucratization is therefore the size of government.

Growth of Government

There is little dispute about the facts of government growth in the U.S. In 1891, the Federal government had 157,000 civilian employees. This number increased to 239,000 in 1901, 389,000 in 1910, 655,000 in 1920, declined to 601,000 in 1930, but increased further to 1.042 million in 1940 (U.S. Department of Commerce, 1975: Series Y-308). As shown in Table 2.1, Federal civilian employment leapt to slightly over 2 million in 1947 and to just under 3 million at its peak in 1967. Subsequent to 1970, the number of Federal employees has been essentially flat, declining slightly after 1980. By 1983, total Federal employment had dropped to 2.7 million.

State and local government in the U.S. has grown much more rapidly than employment at the Federal level. Total state and local employment cannot be ascertained for years prior to 1929. In 1929, the state and local governmental work force, including education, was 2.532 million, and it was 3.206 million in 1940 (U.S. Department of Commerce, 1975: Series Y-332). As can be seen in Table 2.1, state and local employment reached 4 million in 1949, 5 million in 1955, 6 million in 1959, 7 million in 1963, 8 million in 1965, 9 million in 1968, and 10 million in 1970. State and local government employment continued to increase in the 1970's, reaching 11 million in 1973, 12 million in 1976, 13 million in 1979, and 13.6 million in 1980. Subsequent to 1980, tax limitations and reductions in Federal programs began affecting states and localities so that by 1983 their workforce had declined to 13.3 million.

The rapid growth of state and local compared to Federal employment is due principally to their complementary functions. Save for national defense, few services are rendered directly by the Federal government. Direct service delivery, often funded by Federal dollars, occurs at the local level. For this reason, state and local governmental employment has been more influenced by expansion of governmental programs than Federal employment has been. Federal employment has also been limited somewhat by a policy of contracting for some routine clerical and administrative services formerly performed by civil servants. The respective functions of Federal and local governments render total Federal civilian, state, and local employment the best measure of the size of government, and the ratio of this total to size of the civilian labor force in the U.S. the best measure of the relative size of government. The fifth column of Table 2.1 displays total government civilian employment from 1947 through 1983. Government employment increased almost constantly from the beginning of the series until 1980, decreasing in only two of thirty-three years. Small declines in the governmental labor force, principally in local government, were registered beginning in 1981. This may reflect declining Federal support for localities as well as declining school enrollments. The rightmost column of Table 2.1 displays

Table 2.1
Public Employees by Type of Government and Total Civilian Labor Force, 1947–70 (000's)

Year	Federal Civilian	State	Local	Total Government Employment	Total Civilian Employment	Government/ Nongovernment Ratio
1947	2002	909	2880	5791	57039	.10
1948	2076	963	3002	6041	58344	.10
1949	2047	1037	3119	6203	57649	.10
1950	2117	1057	3228	6402	58920	.10
1951	2515	1070	3218	6803	59962	.11
1952	2583	1060	3461	7104	60254	.11
1953	2385	1082	3580	7047	61181	.11
1954	2373	1149	3710	7232	60010	.12
1955	2378	1199	3855	7432	62171	.11
1956	2410	1268	4007	7685	63802	.12
1957	2439	1300	4307	8046	64071	.12
1958	2405	1408	4484	8297	63036	.13
1959	2399	1454	4634	8487	64630	.13
1960	2421	1527	4860	8808	65778	.13
1961	2484	1625	4992	9101	65746	.13
1962	2539	1680	5169	9388	66702	.14
1963	2548	1775	5413	9736	67762	.14
1964	2528	1873	5663	10064	69305	.14
1965	2588	2028	5973	10589	71088	.14
1966	2861	2211	6316	11388	72895	.15
1967	2993	2335	6539	11867	74372	.15
1968	2984	2459	6864	12307	75920	.16
1969	2969	2614	7102	12685	77902	.16
1970	2881	2755	7392	13028	78627	.16
1971	2696	2747	7437	12880	79367	.16
1972	2684	2859	7790	13333	82153	.16
1973	2663	2923	8146	13732	85064	.16
1974	2724	3039	8407	14170	86794	.16
1975	2748	3179	8758	14685	85846	.17
1976	2733	3273	8865	14871	88752	.16
1977	2727	3303	8989	15019	92017	.16
1978	2753	3414	9039	15206	96048	.15
1979	2748	3607	9755	16110	98824	.16
1980	2869	3688	9976	16533	99303	.16
1981	2769	3731	9968	16468	100379	.16
1982	2725	3744	9728	16197	99526	.16
1983	2731	3723	9598	16052	99103	.16

Sources: U.S. Department of Commerce (1975: Series Y-273, Y-277, Y-280, and D-15);
U.S. Bureau of Labor Statistics (1979; 1983: Tables 10, A-1, B-2).

Table 2.2
A/P Ratios in Manufacturing Industry, 1947–83

	Year							
	1983	1977	1972	1967	1963	1958	1954	1947
All Establishments								
Number	N/A	359928	320710	305680	306617	298182	286814	240807
Employees (000's)	18166	19590	19029	18496	16235	15381	15645	14294
Production workers	12241	13691	13528	13957	12232	11907	12372	11918
A/P ratio	.48	.42	.41	.32	.33	.29	.26	.20
Multiunit Establishments								
Number	N/A	81241	70198	51706	45862	41871	31769	35202
Employees (000's)	N/A	14957	14264	13310	11015	10064	9480	8007
Production workers	N/A	10097	9792	9790	8110	7714	7402	6686
A/P ratio	N/A	.48	.46	.36	.36	.30	.28	.20
Single Units								
Number	N/A	278687	250512	253974	260755	256311	255045	205605
Employees (000's)	N/A	4633	4765	5186	5220	5317	6165	6287
Production workers	N/A	3594	3736	4167	4122	4193	4970	5233
A/P ratio	N/A	.29	.28	.24	.27	.27	.24	.20

Sources: U.S. Department of Commerce (1977: Table 7-1); U.S. Bureau of Labor Statistics (1983).

total governmental civilian employment as a proportion of the nongovernmental labor force – the government/nongovernment ratio. As can be seen in the table, this ratio increased steadily, again almost monotonically, from 1947 through 1970. In 1947, there was approximately one government worker for every ten civilian workers. By 1970, this ratio had increased to approximately one to six, and it remained essentially flat thereafter.

Bureaucratization in the Private Sector

Bureaucratization in the private sector has increased and in all likelihood accelerated since Bendix's initial work on the subject. Data on administrative intensity in U.S. industry comparable to but in somewhat greater detail than those cited by Bendix are reported in the quinquennial Census of Manufacturers. Some of these data are displayed in Table 2.2. In Table 2.2, numbers of production and administrative employees as well as A/P ratios are displayed first for all manufacturing industry and then separately for single unit and multiunit establishments. Single-unit establishments are firms operating at only one site. Multiunits, by contrast, are not independent firms but rather are units within firms operating at two or more locations. For single units, no administrative hierarchy exists beyond individual establishments, whereas each multiunit establishment is tied to at least one other by a common administrative hierarchy.

Several questions can be asked of Table 2.2. The first concerns overall growth in administrative overhead in manufacturing. A/P ratios for all U.S. manufacturing establishments increased dramatically from 1947 to 1983, more than doubling in this interval. The Census of Manufacturers data indicate that this ratio was approximately .20 in 1947 and .42 in 1977, rising steadily throughout this interval. And Bureau of Labor Statistics data show the A/P ratio in manufacturing industry to have reached .48 in 1983. A second question concerns concomitants of this growth in administrative overhead. The Census data indicate this growth to have occurred dispro-portionately in multiunit manufacturing establishments. Numbers of multi-units increased much more rapidly than single-unit manufacturers from 1947 to 1977. Whereas the total number of manufacturing establishments in the U.S. was about 240,000 in 1947 and 360,000 in 1977, an increase of 50 percent, numbers of multiunits grew more rapidly than single-unit establish-ments. The number of multiunits increased 131 per cent, from thirty-five to eighty-one thousand from 1947 to 1977, whereas single units increased only forty per cent, from 206,000 to 286,000. Total employment in single-unit establishments actually decreased in this interval, from 6.3 to 4.6 million workers, while employment increased from eight to fifteen million in mul-tiunits. The Census data indicate further that almost all of the increase in administrative ratios occurred in multiunit establishments. It is of some interest that in 1947, A/P ratios were nearly identical for single-unit and multiunit manufacturers, about .20. By 1977, however, administrative ratios were much higher for multiunits. In 1977, the ratio of administrative to production workers was about .29 for single-unit and .48 for multiunit es-tablishments. The existence of organizational hierarchy coordinating two or more manufacturing units is associated with rapid growth in administration within these units.

Bureaucratization in private employment other than manufacturing indus-try has occurred at almost the same rate as in manufacturing in the U.S. Bureau of Labor Statistics data, which are available in annual series but do not distinguish single unit from multiunit establishments, show A/P ratios to have increased over time for all nonmanufacturing industries. Table 2.3 displays portions of the BLS series for the construction, mining, finance, service, trade, and transportation industries. Total employment is displayed for each industry as are numbers of production workers in construction and mining and numbers of nonsupervisory workers in finance, services, trade, and transportation. A/P ratios are computed by dividing either numbers of nonproduction by production workers or supervisory by nonsupervisory workers. From 1947 ot 1983, the ratio of nonproduction to production work-ers increased from .12 to .35 in the construction industry and from .10 to .42 in mining. Increases in administrative intensity in other industries were

Table 2.3
A/P Ratios in Nonmanufactoring Industry, 1947–83

| | Year | | | | | | | | |
	1983	1980	1975	1970	1965	1960	1955	1950	1947
Construction									
Employees (000's)	3453	4150	3525	3588	3232	2908	2839	2364	2009
Production workers	2566	3213	2808	2990	2749	2479	2477	2101	1786
A/P ratio	.35	.29	.26	.20	.18	.17	.15	.13	.12
Mining									
Employees (000's)	996	996	752	623	632	712	792	901	955
Production workers	699	740	571	473	494	570	680	816	871
A/P ratio	.42	.35	.32	.32	.28	.25	.16	.10	.10
Finance, Insurance, Real Estate									
Employees (000's)	5359	5085	4165	3645	2977	2629	2298	1888	1728
Nonsupervisors	3980	3844	3173	2879	2388	2145	1889	1565	1436
A/P ratio	.35	.32	.31	.27	.25	.23	.22	.21	.20
Services									
Employees (000's)	19297	17478	13892	11548	9036	7378	6240	5357	5025
Nonsupervisors	17065	15549	12479	10481	8295	N/A	N/A	N/A	N/A
A/P ratio	.13	.12	.11	.10	.09				
Trade									
Employees (000's)	19955	20226	17060	15040	12716	11391	10535	9386	8955
Nonsupervisors	17397	17737	15023	13375	11358	10315	9675	8742	8241
A/P ratio	.15	.14	.14	.12	.12	.10	.09	.07	.09
Transport and Utilities									
Employees (000's)	4913	5143	4542	4515	4036	4004	4141	4034	4166
Nonsupervisors	4041	4296	3894	3914	3561	N/A	N/A	N/A	N/A
A/P ratio	.22	.20	.17	.15	.13				

Sources: U.S. Bureau of Labor Statistics (1979; 1980; 1983).

slower, perhaps due to the fact that administration is defined as supervisory rather than nonproduction tasks, perhaps because these industries were not so susceptible to mechanization of work, perhaps because overall growth in nonproduction industries was much greater than in manufacturing, construction, and mining. From 1947 to 1983, A/P ratios increased from .20 to .35 in finance, insurance, and real estate, and from .09 to .15 in wholesale and retail trade. And from 1965 to 1983, A/P ratios increased from .09 to .13 and from .13 to .22 in services in transportation and utilities respectively.

These data suggest no definitive explanation for growth in administration in U.S. industry. Myriad causes could be imagined, from changes in technology that decrease demand for labor to increases in governmental regulation that demand greater documentation of compliance. Whatever the causes of administrative growth, however, it is evident that bureaucratization in industry has paralleled growth in government bureaucracy for at least thirty-five years and has perhaps exceeded growth in government. Increased governmental employment, then, has not been an isolated phenomenon. That bureaucratization has occurred throughout U.S. society suggests the need for a theory of bureaucratic growth rather than one of only governmental growth or of increased administration in private industry.

2.2 Bureaucratic Growth in Organizational Theory

Organizational theory has been largely inattentive to bureaucratic growth, whether in government or in industry. To be sure, models of organizational growth, as distinguished from models of growth in administration have been constructed. Starbuck (1965) classifies such models into four types: "cell-division" descriptions of growth processes, "metamorphosis" models postulating stages of organizational growth, "will-o'-the-wisp" accounts of growth as opportunistic behavior on the part of organizations, and "decision-process" models of growth as the outcome of identifiable decision rules. Two characteristics of these models should be emphasized. First, the causal mechanisms promoting organizational growth are often opaque. The biotic analogy in the "cell-division" model, for example, may be an accurate description of growth processes, but it does not identify conditions causing or limiting growth. Second, few of the growth models focus specifically on administrative or bureaucratic growth. The models describe best the growth of whole organizations, especially business organizations. Their applicability to growth in nonbusiness organizations is unclear.

Several research studies have addressed explicitly administrative growth within organizations. Generally these studies have yielded results consistent with long-term growth in administration. Inkson et al. (1970) discerned continual increases in the extensiveness of organizational structure, hence, by implication, in administration. Holdaway and Blowers (1971) found that while larger school systems had smaller administrative ratios, administrative ratios did not decrease with growth. Hendershot and James found the greatest increase in administration-production ratios to occur in school districts with the slowest rates of growth. Freeman and Hannan (1975; 1978) confirmed a "ratchet" or "bumperjack" effect in administration whereby increases in teaching staff are accompanied by increases in administrative overhead but decreases in staff do not yield decreases in administration. And Daft and Bradshaw (1980) found growth in university administration to be mainly a function of internally as opposed to externally generated demands. Unlike the formal models of organizational growth, these research studies have focused specifically on increases in administration. But like the formal models, and perhaps more so than these models, empirical research on administrative growth has been unable to identify the causal mechanisms promoting growth.

Neither formal models of growth nor research results suggesting a tendency toward bureaucratic growth have been incorporated into organizational theory. This may have occurred because external causes of growth are not captured in either the models or the research studies. But another possibility should be considered, namely that bureaucratic growth is assumed in most organizational theory and therefore does not require explanation. Two branches of contemporary organizational theory are distinguished below, neoclassical models derived from psychology and economics, and nonrational models whose origin is in sociological studies of organizations. The former, neoclassical models, views organizations as purposive and constrained to reasonable or rational behavior in pursuing their objectives. This premise, which originated in scientific management and classical theory, is then extended to propositions describing how organizations are constructed to fit their tasks and contingencies arising in their environments. The assumptions underlying the nonrational models are less explicit. For the most part, these models have been driven by Robert Merton's (1936) observation that purposive action is fraught with unintended consequences. Propositions linking organizational actions to specific kinds of unintended consequences have been developed in various case studies but have not received the same sustained attention that has been given the propositions derived from neoclassical models. Neoclassical theory, it is argued below, attempted to resolve the inconsistencies in classical theory by elaborating formal organization as a means of reducing complexity – in other words, by mechanisms leading to bureaucratic growth. Nonrational models have grasped how the inconsistencies in the classical model yield rigidity in individual behavior and in decision processes that is further exacerbated by, bureaucratization but the only alternative proposed to date is anarchic organizations or "garbage-can" decision making.

The Neoclassical Model

Given its long history and development, no complete outline of the neoclassical model of administration is possible within the confines of a single chapter. It is possible, however, to explore some of the key concepts in the model and to indicate some of its extensions as well as its limits.

Basic concepts. The fundamental concepts of the neoclassical model of organizations were developed by Herbert Simon in his seminal work, *Administrative Behavior* (1947) and elaborated in a later book with James March, *Organizations* (1958). *Administrative Behavior* was written somewhat in reaction to organizing principles prescribed in classical management theory, formalisms such as unity of command, span of control, line versus staff, and division of work by purpose, process, client, and place, and the like. The book was also an effort – a brilliantly successful effort – to understand the relationship of organizational structure to human psychology, something that had not been attempted previously. The critique of classical management theory was straightforward: Some of its principles (e.g., specialization, unity of command) were inconsistent hence useless as guides to organizing. The attempt to understand the psychological basis of organizational behavior was more complicated and should be reviewed in some detail.

Simon began his book by inquiring into the nature of rationality. He established quickly that fully rational behavior is rarely attained because knowledge of alternatives, consequences of alternatives, and preferences among consequences is always incomplete. Indeed, there is a "needle in the haystack" problem whereby the costs of obtaining complete information required for fully rational decisions usually exceeds its benefits. Decisions are therefore not optimal but satisfactory; decision-makers do not optimize but "satisfice." But even satisficing can exceed the bounded rationality limits of individual persons. Formal organization is a means of overcoming these limits. Formal organization helps overcome bounded rationality limits by dividing complicated decisions successively into subdecisions, sub-subdecisions, and so forth to the point where the smallest components can be managed by individuals within their bounded rationality limits. An analogy between organizational process and cognitive process is suggested: Just as individual persons address complicated problems by finding means appropriate to the ends they seek, administrative organizations address complicated problems by dividing them into ends-means chains. Unlike individual persons, however, ends-means chains in organizations can be quite lengthy and are formalized in administrative hierarchy. Each level of hierarchy takes as given the ends established for it at higher levels and determines means appropriate to these ends. These means become, in turn, ends for lower levels. To use Simon's language, each level of organization establishes decision premises that are the basis for action at the next lower level. This process continues until, at the lowest level of hierarchy, operational programs of behavior are in place. Thus, while "it is impossible for the behavior of any single, isolated individual to achieve a high degree of rationality" (Simon, 1947: 79), individuals in organized settings can attain rationality:

The rational individual is, and must be, an organized and institutionalized individual. If the severe limits imposed by human psychology upon deliberation are to be relaxed, the individual must in his decisions be subject to the influence of the organized group in which he participates. His decisions must not only be the product of his own mental processes, but also reflect the broader considerations to which it is the function of the organized group to give effect (1947: 102).

The cognitive basis of neoclassical organizational theory cannot be understated. Participation in organizations is a function of an inducement-contribution balance whereby the rewards offered to individuals meet or exceed rewards from alternative opportunities that have been foregone. Authority operates to the extent that a subordinate "holds in abeyance his own critical faculties for choosing between alternatives and uses the formal criterion of the receipt of a command or signal as the basis for this choice" (1947: 126). Subordinates agree in advance – in return for inducements – to allow superiors' choices to guide their actions within an understood "area of acceptance." The environment of work consists of elements stimulating behavior, which include facts, specific decision premises, and widely shared values. Formal organization orders such stimuli so that each person has the information needed to make the decisions for which he is responsible and so that decisions are made on a consistent basis. Organizational structure, in other words, creates environments – psychological environments – in which behavior more nearly approaches rationality than it would absent organization. The external environment is considered only slightly by Simon, and mainly as imposing constraints of minimum efficiency and effectiveness.

Extensions of the theory. In the mid-1960's, the neoclassical branch of theory began directing attention to the impact of external environments on organizations. Although rarely stated as such, this shift signalled dissatisfaction with Simon's assumption that organizational structure could be derived from organizational goals alone. The theorists in the "open-systems" school of theorizing argued that myriad environmental elements other than efficiency and effectiveness constraints shaped organizations. These included the rate of change in the environment (Emery and Trist, 1965), heterogeneity in environmental elements (Thompson, 1967), interconnectedness among these elements (Terreberry, 1968), dependence on the environment (Pfeffer and Salancik, 1978), and, most importantly, environmental uncertainty.

A number of specific propositions about effects of external environments were developed by open-systems theorists. For example, the greater the number of environmental elements and the greater their heterogeneity, the more "boundary-spanning" required in organizations (Thompson, 1967). The more rapid the rate of environmental change, the greater the amount of coordination or integration required in organizations (Lawrence and Lorsch, 1967). The greater the dependence on a single environmental element, the greater effort to find alternatives to it, to acquire power over it, or to incorporate it into organization (Hickson et al., 1971). These propositions are consistent with Simon's original formulation of the neoclassical model in that they anticipate the complexity of organization to match the complexity of tasks. The cognitive basis of organizational theory was preserved in open-systems thinking, albeit implicitly.

The treatment of environmental uncertainty was much less satisfactory in open-systems theorizing. Two large problems arose. One was conceptual.

There was little agreement as to whether uncertainty was ultimately external to organizations or an internal cognitive state. The second was empirical. In an attempt to bridge external and cognitive interpretations of uncertainty, a number of research studies explored the correlation of "objective" with "subjective" uncertainty measures, the latter called perceived environmental uncertainty or PEU. The results showed virtually no correspondence between the two (see particularly Tosi et al., 1973). Subsequent research explored why external and cognitive measures of uncertainty diverged, and found formal organization to intervene between variability occurring externally and its perception. *Perceived* variability, unpredictability, and unanalyzability of problems were found to be associated with *perceived* uncertainty (Duncan, 1972; Pennings, 1975; Leblebici and Salancik, 1981), but variability, unpredictability, and unanalyzability were also found more likely to arise from changes in work routines than from changes in products or markets. Other studies found structuring of organizations to decrease perceived uncertainty (Huber et al., 1975; Leifer and Huber, 1977). The explanation for this outcome was also found in research: The amount of information used in making decisions increases with the extensiveness of organizational structure (Daft and Macintosh, 1981), thereby increasing satisfaction and decreasing the level of uncertainty that is experienced (O'Reilly, 1980). Research has shown, in short, the extensiveness of formal organization to affect perceived uncertainty, thus correspondences between uncertainty in the external environment and perceived environmental uncertainty to be minimal. Perhaps because of their cognitive orientation, open-systems theorists did not take the next logical step of exploring how new organizations and more complex organizational forms evolve from uncertainty. This work was left to economists seeking to explain large industrial firms as other than means of attaining economies of scale in production.

Neoclassical theory and industrial organization. Several economists, most notably Oliver Williamson (1964; 1975) and Kenneth Arrow (1974), have made use of neoclassical organizational theory to explain the structure of industrial firms. Williamson's work is the most developed, and it will serve as the basis of the present discussion.

Williamson begins with a statement of evenhandedness. While his account of industrial organization emphasizes how market failures give rise to progressively more complicated organizational forms, Williamson argues, at least in the abstract, that market exchange can displace transactions taking place within firms. Indeed, his theoretical framework, an extension of neoclassical organizational theory, is called the organizational failures rather than market failures, framework. The key elements of the framework are uncertainty and small-numbers exchange conditions in the environment and bounded rationality and opportunism in humans. Since the human elements, bounded rationality and opportunism, are ubiquitous, transaction costs, hence failures of markets or of firms, are mainly a function of the two environmental conditions, uncertainty and small numbers. Uncertainty adds to transaction costs by making contracts expensive to write and interpret. Small numbers conditions yield inherently inefficient transactions because normal market forces compelling least-cost behavior are absent.

If one begins, as Williamson does, by assuming that "in the beginning, there were markets" (1975: 20), one finds that simple quid pro quo transactions in the market place, so-called spot transactions, quickly give rise to more complicated arrangements. Large numbers exchange conditions are reduced to small numbers as buyers and sellers become locked into one another. Opportunistic inclinations must therefore be curbed by long-term contracts between parties transacting business. Uncertainty renders fixed-price contracts infeasible, and flexible or contingent contracts are executed instead. But contingent claims contracts are also fraught with uncertainty that arises after the fact when contracts prove ambiguous or inadequate to cover actual events. Contracting parties thus join in a single organization. But the same transactional difficulties that occurred among individual persons are subsequently reproduced in transactions between organizations. Efficiency considerations then impel organizations to join one another, just as individuals had joined in organizations. The classic vertically integrated firm results.

Vertically integrated firms suffer transactional difficulties somewhat different from those affecting individuals and small organizations. Uncertainty and small numbers conditions within firms yield information impactedness whereby the true conditions surrounding a transaction cannot be discerned costlessly. Biases toward organizational persistence, expansion, and internal procurement arise in complex hierarchies because knowledge of the true state of the organization is heavily impacted; communication distortion, and bureaucratic insularity become commonplace since such behavior is easily concealed. Williamson suggests that divisionalized multiunit firms overcome much of the information impactedness characteristic of less developed organizational forms because operating units are held directly responsible for profit. Additionally, strategic planning in the central office guards against information impactedness by assigning firm resources to their highest yield uses. The conglomerate firm, according to Williamson, extends the multiunit form into unrelated businesses but offers the same transactional advantages.

Williamson's work is important for neoclassical organizational theory, but for reasons having little to do with his argument that transaction costs determine organizational forms. To be sure, the transactional perspective enabled Williamson to derive from first principles organizational forms now prevalent among industrial firms. But there is little evidence to substantiate the claim that, for example, multiunit firms are more efficient than their nondivisionalized counterparts. The few extant studies show essentially no effects of organizational form on performance (Weston and Mansinghka, 1971; Armour and Teece, 1978). Williamson's main contribution lies rather in observing, first, that the organizational mechanisms intended to overcome both human and environmental bounds to rationality are themselves subject to failures, and, second, that failures have usually caused simpler organizational forms to be displaced by more complicated ones. The simple facts of organizational structure – Williamson's sociology, if you will – overshadow his explanation for these facts – Williamson's economics. In fairness to Williamson, the claim that he could just as easily have described a devolution from complicated to simple firms and from firms to markets in transactional terms should be noted. But Williamson did not describe such a devolution, for the facts of history have been, at least until this time, of progressively more complicated rather than of simpler organizational forms.

The paradox of neoclassical theory. A paradox that yields bureaucratic growth is embedded in the work of Simon, Williamson, and others and ought now to be made explicit. Organizations overcome bounded rationality limits by reducing large problems into small ones that can be managed within the cognitive capacities of individual persons. But organization itself eventually poses difficulties because it exceeds bounded rationality limits; this is especially the case under uncertainty where the range of problems that can be addressed hence the extensiveness of organization is potentially limitless. Neoclassical theory, then, offers organization as a solution to problems posed by environments but offers few solutions to the difficulties posed by organization save for more organization. Williamson's suggestion that multiunits and conglomerates overcome the limitations of simpler organizational forms is not of general applicability, and the effectiveness of multiunits compared to other types of businesses has not been demonstrated. This paradox – organization poses problems requiring more organization – has not heretofore been explored because attention has been directed to how to organize in face of uncertainty rather than how much organization results. The historical trend toward bureaucratic growth described above suggests, however, that the question of how much organization very much demands attention.

The Nonrational Model

An approach wholly different from neoclassical theory has been taken by models emphasizing unanticipated and largely nonrational outcomes of intendedly rational behavior in organizations. Rather than solving problems in an orderly manner, organizations are depicted as creating problems, as joining solutions to problems in a haphazard way, and as conflictual rather than cooperative. Taken to its extreme, the nonrational model draws analogies between decision processes and the mix of detritus that is found in garbage cans, and between behavior in organizations and anarchy.

Nonrational theorizing is rich but varied. Its diversity precludes any simple account of its development. There are no first principles, like bounded rationality, from which causal propositions have been derived. One of several strands of nonrational theorizing is concerned specifically with dysfunctions of bureaucratic organizations. Its origin is in Robert K. Merton's essay "Bureaucratic Structure and Personality" (1940), which addresses the problem of mindless adherence to rules on the part of bureaucrats. The argument is straightforward: In order to insure reliability of response, bureaucrats are overtrained in rules and procedures. "Displacement of goals" occurs whereby organizational means – rules and procedures – become ends in themselves. Goal displacement persists because, among other factors, bureaucratic virtuosity is the special technical competence of officials and the basis of their esprit de corps.

Several of Merton's students, including Selznick (1949), Gouldner (1954), and Blau (1955) have explored bureaucratic dysfunctions and the more general problem, also posed by Merton (1936), of the unanticipated consequences of purposive action. Not until Michel Crozier's (1964) *The Bureaucratic Phenomenon,* however, was Weber's positive evaluation of bureaucracy shed and emphasis shifted from bureaucracy as efficient organization that in specific instances tends toward inefficiency to bureaucracy as inefficient, wholly dysfunctional organization. Like other sociologists interested in bureaucratic dysfunctions, Crozier based his theoretical inferences on case studies. But unlike other sociologists, Crozier saw bureaucratic patterns of behavior as self-reinforcing and antithetical to organizational goals. The basic elements of bureaucratic behavior in Crozier's model are impersonal rules, centralization of decisions, isolation of hierarchical strata from one another, and parallel, i.e., non-hierarchical, power relationships. These are tied to one another in a positive feedback system or "vicious circle" triggered by unpredictable events not subject to bureaucratic control. Uncertainty, or control over uncertainty, gives rise to parallel power, power to new rules attempting to routinize events, rules to further centralization and weakening of the chain of command. The very weakness of authority, in turn, allows unofficial power to be again exercised when new uncertainties arise, yielding further rules, centralization, and strata isolation.

Crozier's case studies do not preclude generalizing his observations to problems of bureaucratic complexity and growth, even though no direct information about these is provided in his work. Fundamentally, Crozier's model views organizations as arenas where continuous struggles for power occur. Power is a function of control over uncertainty. In business firms where products or markets are volatile, management decisions are the crucial decisions insofar as workers are concerned. In the bureaucracies studied by Crozier, product and market uncertainties were removed due to the monopoly position of state agencies and the rule-bound character of work. Other sources of uncertainty remained, but these were not decided by management and were sources of unofficial power. (Machine stoppages posed the principal source of uncertainty in the industrial monopoly studied by Crozier.) In an effort to neutralize unofficial or parallel power, new rules and greater centralization of decisions were imposed, hence the "vicious circle" of bureaucratic dysfunctions. All that is needed to transform the "vicious circle" into a model of bureaucratic complexity and growth are two commonsense postulates. One is that management seeks control of any source of uncertainty; the second is that new rules and additional centralization demand new staff to insure that management control is in fact effective. These postulates yield a positive feedback model of bureaucratic complexity and growth in which the extensiveness of organization and size are regulated poorly by the environment.

Nonrational theorizing has shifted dramatically in the last decade. Rather than focusing on the unintended consequences of formal bureaucratic rationality, it now describes other responses to uncertainty. One response is "loose coupling" or "decoupling" of day-to-day behavior from organizational structures and rules (Weick, 1976; Meyer and Rowan, 1977). Another is "garbage-can" decision processes containing a much larger element of randomness than was previously acknowledged in theory (March and Olsen, 1976). As March and Olsen note, "individuals find themselves in a more complex, less stable, and less understood world than that described by standard theories of organization; they are placed in a world over which they often have only modest control" (1976: 21). The proliferation of studies in the nonrational tradition is so large that few can be cited much less discussed here. Their importance lies partly in their fit to experience: All observers agree that much of what actually occurs in organizations does not resemble scientific management or anything faintly like it. But studies in the nonrational tradition are also important as indicators of the limits of rational models. Crozier's "vicious circle" of dysfunctions describes the Weberian model of bureaucracy taken to its logical extreme. Contemporary nonrational thinking portrays outcomes when the neoclassical model has been taken to its logical limit, when organization has been extended past the point where it can be understood by participants. What nonrational theory does not offer is a set of principles that could substitute for neoclassical prescriptions as guides to organizing. And the descriptive accuracy of nonrational models may erode as demands for control and accountability in large organizations generally increase, as they have already in educational organizations. While greater bureaucratization is resisted, so are "garbage can" decision processes.

It is of interest that the paradox of neoclassical thinking carrying the assumption of bureaucratic growth – the problems of organization demand more organization – is reproduced partly in nonrational models. The preference for organization in neoclassical theory appears in Crozier's work as constantly increasing bureaucratization. Needless to say, neoclassical and nonrational models evaluate this outcome differently. What neoclassical theory labels as rationality, Crozier calls a "vicious circle" of dysfunctions. It is also of interest that the paradox in neoclassical theory helps explain the breakdown of rational decision making described in nonrational models and therefore why what was previously the antithesis of human rationality is now understood somewhat differently. Much of organizational theory, then, accounts for structure, growth, yet change and unpredictability within organizations, even though it offers no consistent evaluation of these outcomes. No consistent evaluation is possible because while theory searches for optimal organizational forms, the premises of the theory yield a problem-problem-organization-problem-more organization cycle that never settles in equilibrium.

Uncertainty and Organizational Mortality

The above discussion treats bureaucratic growth as an outcome of efforts to maintain formal rationality in uncertain environments. Another approach to theorizing, one differing fundamentally in this implications from the neoclassical and nonrational models, argues that uncertainty is a principally cause of organizational mortality. This theory is known as the population ecology (Hannan and Freeman, 1977) or evolutionary model of organizations (Aldrich, 1979). Its basic premises are these: Organizations are fundamentally incapable of change. They are quickly "locked in" to patterns established at or shortly after the time they are formed. Unpredictable change in environments thus renders organizations progressively less fit over time. Eventually, established organizations are displaced by new ones not carrying so great a burden of anachronism, but new organizations, after overcoming initial resistance, are themselves subject to the same selection pressures that their predecessors were.

Population ecology theory makes specific predictions about organizational survival and mortality beyond these general ideas about forces shifting the composition of organizational populations over time. Placid environments – those changing slowly – favor specialist organizations over generalists that carry considerable excess capacity or organizational slack. More turbulent environments will usually favor generalists that at any particular point in time do not fit perfectly external constraints but do have sufficient change capacity to absorb external shocks. Uncertain environments that change slowly and that impose substantial costs of maintaining generalist capacity, however, may favor specialists.

The critical difference between the theory sketched above and evolutionary or population ecology thinking is in the set of organizations to which they apply. Evolutionary and population ecology theory applies best to small competetive organizations not subject to constraints of rational administration. Aldrich and Riess's (1976) study of succession in small urban businesses exemplifies best the kinds of organizations subject to evolutionary or ecological forces. The theory of bureaucratic growth developed here applies with greatest force where the constraints of administrative rationality are strongest, such as in the finance agencies that are the subject of the research reported below. The imperative of rational administration is the antithesis of competetive enterprise in that it demands solutions to problems within existing organizations, whereas competition permits new organizations to displace existing ones. Importantly, administrative rationality constraints are strongest in precisely those arenas where competition would undermine the objectives sought by organized action rather than enhance these outcomes. Two competing finance bureaucracies, for example, would in all likelihood produce different financial reports for a city, confusing rather than clarifying a city's financial position because there is no way to determine which is most accurate. Two competing police agencies could easily spend as much time fighting one another for "turf" as fighting crime because there is no reasonable way to determine which is most effective.

Bureaucratic growth in industry, which is evident in increased administrative and supervisory ratios, can be understood as an outcome of having competition or quasi-competition alongside rational administration within firms. To use Thompson's (1967) language, in the "technical core" of firms where there is cause-and-effect knowledge, least-cost solutions to problems can in principle be identified and implemented, accompanied sometimes by wholesale changes in organization. At managerial levels, however, the constraint of cost minimization works imperfectly because there is uncertainty as to whether or not problems are ever resolved. Rational administration is maintained at managerial levels, but at the cost of growth. Cost minimization in the "technical core" together with growth at managerial levels of firms yields increased administrative and supervisory ratios over time. Importantly, diminished organizational efficiency may result from this process. Contrary to theories asserting the superior efficiency properties of complex organizational forms, administrative growth may reflect the greater uncertainty of managerial as compared to technical activities in organizations hence incapacity to make cost-minimizing decisions with respect to the former.

In a world of perfect information and competition, administrative growth creating inefficiencies would quickly cause organizations to fail. A causal chain from uncertainty in the environment to administrative growth, inefficiency, and organizational mortality would be predicted, consistent with evolutionary theory. The world is not one of perfect information and competition, however, and for this reason it is possible for both firms and nonprofit organizations to have experienced increased administration and to have declined in efficiency without failing – yet. Ultimately, however, the prediction made by evolutionary theory must hold if only because it approaches trusim. Less fit organizational forms will fail. At issue here is not whether but only when these failures will occur.

2.3 Bureaucratic Growth in Economic Theory

A brief review of economists' attempts to deal with bureaucratic growth is in order. Basically, economic theory has dealt poorly with the problem. For the most part, economists prefer market to bureaucratic coordination of activity on grounds of efficiency. (Williamson's work is in this respect quite heterodox.) There is some empirical support for the preference for private over public ownership, as will be shown presently. At the same time, economists have not been able to explain satisfactorily why markets and firms operating for profit have not displaced bureaucratized organizations that are, presumably, less efficient. No model of bureaucratic growth has been proffered. At best, economic models explain why bureaus may be somewhat larger than counterpart firms, but even these models have been the subject of dispute.

Models of Bureaucratic Behavior

The economists' approach to bureaucracy differs substantially from the approach taken in organizational theory in that it assumes the primacy of acquisitive in contrast to more complex social and political forces shaping organizations. Following the lead of Ludwig von Mises (1944), most economists distinguish "profit" from "bureaucratic" organizations. The former, "profit" organizations, which are typically business firms, engage in voluntary quid pro quo transactions in the marketplace, and their behavior is governed by market forces. The latter, "bureaucratic" organizations, operate in the absence of markets and are governed by detailed rules and regulations. Market forces allow calculation of results for "profit" organizations, whereas little or no calculability of outcomes is possible under "bureaucratic" management. Most economists argue that the ability to calculate results renders "profit" organizations more efficient than bureaucracies, assuming that the two types can be compared fairly. It is not clear, however, that fair comparisons are possible. Often, "bureaucratic" displaces "profit" management when externalities, costs or benefits to persons not parties to a transaction, are attached to activities (Downs, 1967). For example, nonmarket regulation of toxic waste disposal is necessary because simple transactions between producers of waste and those who contract to dispose of it do not safeguard public health. The extreme form of externality is the public good (or evil) where one person's benefit is to the benefit or detriment of all, regardless of who pays. As Olsen (1965) has pointed out, because people are tempted to take advantage of public goods as "free riders" without paying, some form of coercion is usually needed to insure that all pay their fair share. Sometimes coercion takes the form of taxation; sometimes it takes the form of union shop arrangements whereby payment of trade union dues is mandatory; sometimes it takes the form of violence.

Economists have scrutinized closely the growth of government and have concluded on the basis of fairly flimsy evidence that this cannot be explained reasonably. For example, increases in population and wealth do not account for governmental growth (Borcherding, 1977). Economists have therefore turned to formal models of bureaucratic behavior to explain large governmental size. Fundamentally, two types of models have been developed. One treats bureaucrats as budget maximizers. The other assumes bureaucrats (and managers generally) to maximize their discretionary expenditures or "rents" of office. The budget-maximizing model, developed by Niskanen (1971), observes that the transactions in which bureaus engage differ from ordinary business transactions. Whereas firms exchange incremental quantities of goods for incremental or marginal prices, bureaus exchange budgets for promised outputs. A bureau's revenue, thus, is the result of a single transaction with a "sponsor" rather than multiple transactions with customers. This condition, Niskanen demonstrates algebraically, leads budget-maximizing bureaucrats to overproduce in the sense that the marginal cost of outputs always exceeds their marginal value to the sponsor. This result holds regardless of whether or not total output is constrained by available funds. The rent-maximizing model derives from economic analysis of managerial behavior (Marris, 1964). It argues that revenues can be apportioned between producing outputs and other utility-producing expenditures or "rents" of office, and that only the latter, not total budgets, are maximized by rational bureaucrats. Migue and Belinger (1974) have shown algebraically that rent maximization will yield bureaucratic behavior little different from the behavior of price-discriminating monopolists in the private sector. How much bureaucrats overproduce and their efficiency, that is, the ratio of outputs to costs, will therefore depend on the ability of bureaucratic systems to limit discretionary expenditures.

The Efficiency of Bureaucratic Systems

Whether bureaucrats maximize budgets, in which case they overproduce, or maximize rents of office, in which case they overspend, cannot be resolved without substantial empirical evidence of the sort that may never be available. What evidence is available does suggest, keeping in mind the hazards of public-private comparisons, that public organizations are less efficient than their private-sector counterparts. The classic comparison of nearly identical public and private organizations is Davies' (1971) study of Australia's two trunk airlines, Trans Australian Airways (TAA), a government firm, and Ansett Australian National Airways (Ansett ANA), a private firm. The two airlines had similar routes and equipment, and charged equal fares. Per employee, Ansett ANA carried more than twice as much freight and mail, 21 per cent more passengers, and 13 per cent greater revenues than TAA from 1958 through 1968. Had the two airlines not been constrained by law to identical fares and routes, Davies noted, the efficiency advantage of the private carrier, Ansett ANA, might have been even greater. Comparison of privately with publicly owned service enterprises generally yields the same results as Davies'. Municipal utilities tend to have costlier plants and higher operating costs than privately owned utilities, although much of this difference is the result of the small scale of many municipal power plants (Spann, 1977). Private provision of fire protection in Scottsdale, Arizona, is substantially less expensive than in other Arizona cities when relevant community characteristics are controlled (Ahlbrandt, 1973). Private scavengers operate at substantially lower costs than public refuse collections (Savas, 1977), although these differences diminish in suburban communities compared to central cities (Hirsch, 1965).

Evidence suggesting the performance of bureaucratically managed enterprises to be inferior to that of private firms gives at least partial support to models showing bureaucrats either to overproduce or to produce inefficiently. But neither this evidence nor the models to which they lend some credence can account for growth of government bureaucracy or of increased bureaucratization in the private sector, which have occurred parallel to one another. Indeed, if efficiency considerations were paramount, a shrinkage of government and perhaps of private-sector bureaucracy would have been expected given these results. The growth of government, at least until recently, and of private bureaucracy could, of course, be attributed to exogenous demand, but this claim encounters two difficulties. First, within the framework of economic analysis, demand is rarely measured directly but is instead imputed from supply. To attribute bureaucratic growth, i.e., supply of public services, to demand thus approaches tautology. Second, what evidence is available suggests bureaucratic growth to have exceeded growth in measurable demand. This holds not only for government generally, but also specifically for the finance agencies that are the subject of this research as will be shown three chapters hence. The paradox of economic analysis is then this: Whereas economists' preference for market as opposed to bureaucratic coordination of activity is confirmed in theory and research demonstrating the inferior efficiency properties of the latter, bureaucracy persists and, in fact, increases.

2.4 Summary

This chapter began by presenting some basic data on bureaucratization in the U.S. These data showed indexes of bureaucratization to have increased almost continuously for as long as series have been available. Growth of government and of administration in the private sector have been endemic. Why the facts of bureaucratization have not been incorporated into organizational theory was considered next. It was argued that theory has not addressed bureaucratic growth in part because the organizing patterns described in theory presume growth. Neoclassical theory, in particular, has treated organization as a means of overcoming bounded rationality limits and more organization as the solution to problems posed by organization itself. This paradox renders growth almost limitless. The paradox in the neoclassical model that leads to growth is reproduced in certain respects in nonrational theories of organizations. Accounts of bureaucratic dysfunctions have noted "vicious circles" or self-reinforcing patterns of behavior whereby organizational process elaborates over time and performance deteriorates. "Garbage-can" accounts of decision making in large organizations suggest that behavior approaches unpredictability, possibly a result of complexity and growth in administration. In contrast to organizational theory, economic theory speaks directly to questions pertaining to bureaucratic growth. Economists' models of bureaucratic behavior suggest that large size and inefficiency may be characteristic of nonmarket organizations, but the models account neither for long-term growth (except, implicitly, as a function of increased demand) nor for growth in administration in business firms.

Organizational theory, then, contains the essential elements of a theory of bureaucratic growth, although these elements have not previously been recognized as such. Economic theory, although attentive to the efficiency properties of "bureaucratic" compared to "profit" organizations, is less able to account for long-term bureaucratic growth. In subsequent chapters, alternative causal models of growth derived from organizational theory will be developed and tested.

Chapter 3
The Concept of Organization

This chapter begins the discussion of how research can test the ideas about bureaucratic growth developed above. The central hypothesis to be explored in this book, as will be recalled from the first chapter, is that the imperative to organize rationally, which was first articulated in concepts of administration that gained widespread acceptance about seventy-five years ago, accounts in large measure for the fact of bureaucratic growth. The second chapter extended this argument by showing growth to be implicit in most contemporary ideas about organizing. Both neoclassical theory, which treats organization as a means of overcoming limited cognitive capacities of individual persons, and nonrational theorizing, which focuses on unintended consequences in organizations, suggest a tendency toward increased organization in response to unforseen and uncontrollable disturbances. At this point, we must begin transforming this central hypothesis into a set of propositions that can be tested in research. This is not an easy task. Not only must assumptions defining and delimiting organizations and their environments be made, but intermediate causal relations connecting ideas about organizing with their tangible consequences for organizations must also be specified. The first will be the subject of this chapter, while the second will be addressed in the next chapter.

This chapter is concerned with perhaps the most fundamental question that can be raised in research: What concepts of organization and of organizational or bureaucratic growth will guide the present research? Questions of this sort are raised rarely. In the last twenty years, we have proceded on the assumption that organizations were well defined units with identifiable and more or less permanent boundaries. We have assumed that since we knew what organizations were, entities called organizations were the appropriate units for research. This assumption permitted inquiries to focus on interrelations among organizational properties as well as on effects of environments upon organizational properties. Organizations were dissected, as it were, into their relevant properties or dimensions, each of which was treated, in turn, as dependent on other organizational properties and the environment. Foremost among the properties or dimensions of organizations studied are size, organizational structure or differentiation, formalization, standardization, centralization, automation, and the lifespan of organizations themselves. Importantly, the understanding of organizations as well defined entities has pervaded research, whether research has addressed closed-system, open-system, or evolutionary theorizing.

This chapter questions whether this conventional conception of organization remain useful in research. It does so in two ways. It argues, first, that commonsense ideas about organizations and organizing do not require that we think of organizations as fixed, well defined units. In the past, it has been easiest to use a rigid definition of organization in research, but the cost of convenience has been the inability to test a number of important ideas, particularly the notion that the *amount* of formal organization is variable. This chapter argues, second, that the history of the agencies studied does not allow any fixed definition of organizations. The history of these agencies is one of continuous construction of formal organization, of units that are by any reasonable definition organizations themselves. To restrict research to a fixed set of units would be to overlook bureaucratic growth arising from the construction of new units. The first argument can be made succinctly because it is theoretical. The second argument, however, requires considerable historical detail and is therefore of greater length. After these two arguments have been developed, their implications for the choice of units to be studied will be outlined.

3.1 A Revised Concept of Organization

The concept of organization, like the idea of rational administration, is deeply embedded in modern societies. Organization is not only a social science construct. It also carries meaning in everyday life, indicating that people have joined efforts, or organized, in order to accomplish tasks that no individual could complete alone. No precise definition of organization, no attempt to distinguish in all cases that which is organization from that which is not, will correspond exactly to what all people have in mind when they speak of organization. Nonetheless, some general ideas about organization can be developed here. The core elements constituting organization will be outlined first. Static or descriptive concepts of organization will then be compared to ideas about organizing, which call attention to the process of forming and reorganizing organizational units. Finally, the notion that organizations may exist within organizations is introduced. This notion is familiar and assumed virtually everywhere save in quantitative research studies where fixed definitions of organization have been maintained. It must now be incorporated into research so that the extensiveness of formal organization can be treated as variable.

Elements of Organization

There are several elements that appear in almost any definition of formal or large-scale organization. One is identity. Organizations, like many other kinds of human groups, are normally recognized as such by their members and by others. Just as families have surnames and communities and nation-states geographic names, organizations also have names. Sometimes organizational names identify their products and outputs; sometimes, in private industry, names identify the principal owners of firms. A second element in any definition of organization is purpose. Organizations are distinguished from informal groups in that they have reasonably well defined tasks and are, in one way or another, held accountable for the performance of their tasks. Organizations are distinguished from larger groups such as communities and nation-states in that the purposes of the latter are amorphous rather than specific, and in that mechanisms of accountability in the latter tend to be political rather than administrative. A third element of organizations is structure. Generally, organizations are distinguished from other types of groups in that relationships between members and subunits are formally structured, as in organization charts, and are governed by rather specific rules and regulations prescribing duties and responsibilities. Formal structure is not an element of informal groups, and the structure of communities and nation-states, while evident in behavior patterns, is not prescribed formally. Moreover, the same level of detail in administrative regulations that governs conduct in organizations is rarely present in the civil and criminal law of communities and nation-states. A fourth element of organizations is membership and organizational boundaries. Informal groups have no formal mechanisms regulating membership although they are often exclusive, and membership in communities and nation-states, like in families, ethnic, and territorial groups, is a usually matter of birth rather than admission. Organizations, in contrast to other types of groups, certify who is a member and who is not. Persons – and other organizations – not holding membership in a particular organization are outside of its boundaries and thus elements in the environment. A fifth element of organizations is the nature of their interchange with environments. Organizations take inputs from environments and convert them to outputs in exchange for resources. The conversion of inputs into outputs does not so clearly characterize other kinds of group formations.

These five elements of organizations – identity, purpose, structure, boundaries, and interchange with environments – are incorporated, in one way or another, into popular conceptions of organizations, although rarely in such explicit form. To be sure, not all actual organizations contain these elements to the same degree. Radical political organizations, for example, often keep no membership lists; jail inmates, while admitted to custody, are rarely considered to be members of correctional organizations. Nonetheless, most of the five elements are present in one way or another in most of the kinds of social formations that are commonly regarded as organizations.

Organizations versus Organizing

The elements listed above provide a static view, a snapshot, of organizations at any point in time. They do not consider how new organizations are formed, nor do they take into account the possibility that existing organizations may be reorganized or dissolved. The active or gerund form of organization, organizing, conveys the idea that formation, reorganization, and destruction of organizations occur continually. The theoretical literature describes organizing much less well than it describes organization. One concept of organizing, drawn largely from the social psychological and cognitive literatures, argues that organizing processes *implement* rules or procedures in order to reduce equivocality or uncertainty in environments (Weick, 1969: ch. 6). The existence of formal organization is assumed, and organizing consists of its activation. Another view of organizing processes, derived from the literature on symbolic interaction, argues that they *create* the appearance of rational management of problems that, absent formal organization, are believed intractable. John W. Meyer and Brain Rowan observe:

First, formal organizational structure reflects and incorporates prevailing environmental theories and categories ... Organizational actors are constantly in the business of managing categories abstracted directly from environmental theories.

Second, organizational structure has two faces: It conforms to environmental categories and categorical logics, and it classifies and controls activity ...

Third, to accommodate both appearance and reality, organizational structure must always be partially decoupled from actual activity ... Linking the organization as a formal structure with the organization as a network of activities is a major task ... (1978: 108–9).

Meyer and Rowan point out in an earlier (1977) article that organizing is a response to the rise to rational or "institutional" rules of conduct requiring implementation. These rules tend to become more elaborate over time, and for this reason organizing is a continuous process. In contrast to Weick's claim that organizing reduces equivocality or uncertainty, Meyer and Rowan suggest in the third paragraph quoted above that organizing increases the complexity of work because of the tension between task and symbolic demands.

The view of organizing processes taken here differs in some details but not fundamentally from the ideas of Weick and of Meyer and Rowan. Organizing is a response to uncertainty. Sometimes organizing involves only activation of existing structure and procedures, consistent with Weick's argument. Often, organizing involves construction of new formal organization, consistent with Meyer and Rowan. The latter occurs when existing formal organization is believed inadequate to order and make sense of the environment. Importantly, while organizing in the sense of activation of existing structures and procedures can be observed first-hand in contemporary organizations, it is rarely evident in the quantitative historical accounts of the sort available for this research. Thus, for purposes of this research, organizing will be understood as the process of constructing new organization or, in some instances, the process of reordering existing organizational structures.

Organizations within Organizations

Most organizing takes place within existing organizations. Organizing in the sense of implementing structure and processes can take place only in existing units. Organizing in the sense of constructing, reorganizing, and even dissolving organizational units occurs, in all likelihood, with much greater frequency within existing organizations than without. Much organizing activity, then, constructs, reorganizes, or dissolves organizations that are parts of larger organizations, or, in some instances, organizations of which other organizations are parts. The outcome of such organizing activity is organizations within organizations.

The idea of organizations within organizations is not inconsistent with most people's experience. Faculty members, for example, may be simultaneously members of an academic department, a college, a campus, and a larger university system. Academic departments, needless to say, are organizations nested in larger college organizations, which are in turn nested in still larger campus and university organizations. Which of these units consists of the "real" organization to which faculty belong cannot easily be determined. Indeed, it is fruitless to ask because all are at one time or another depending on the problem at hand. For matters of academic merit, departmental units are usually most germane, but matters of retirement are usually determined at the level of university systems, especially for universities that have their own retirement programs. Nor is the idea of organizations within organizations inconsistent with the definition of organizations outlined above. Identity, purpose, structure, membership and boundaries, and interchanges with environments are present for the most inclusive organizations, such as university systems, as well as for the smallest organizations within them, such as academic departments.

The idea that organizations may be created and exist within organizations does, however, shift the approach taken to the problem of bureaucratic growth. A conception of organizations that understands their division into smaller units as structural differentiation and gauges differentiation in terms of levels of authority, numbers of units at each level, and so forth can explain the size and complexity of modern bureaucratic structures only as a function of the scale and complexity of their tasks.[1] A conception that allows organizations to be created and to exist within other organizations introduces variation into the extensiveness of formal organization and therefore allows one to test the two hypotheses that are central to this book: First, that there is a preference for constructing formal organization as a solution to problems, and second, that increased formal organization yields bureaucratic growth. The problem-organization-problem-more organization cycle outlined in the previous chapter cannot be explored so long as a fixed conception of organization is maintained. It can be explored once organizations within organizations hence variation in the extensiveness of formal organization are permitted.

Some technical difficulties are created by the idea of organizations within organizations, and they cannot be brushed aside. The main problem is this: If one treats as organizations both larger units and the smaller units that together comprise the larger units, then the set of units labelled as organizations are not wholly independent entities. In particular, error variance or noise affecting the smaller units also affect the larger units and vice versa, resulting in some bias in statistical estimates. How much bias depends upon the magnitude of common error variance, which is unknown. The best one can do is to control explicitly for sources of error. We would add very quickly, however, that to the extent institutional elements like those emphasized by Meyer and Rowan determine organizations, legally independent organizations are not statistically independent of one another. Similarly, to the extent that firms compete in markets, the behavior of each is not independent of the others. Nonindependence is ubiquitous in social analysis. The idea of organizations within organizations merely renders nonindependence somewhat more obvious in this case than in others.

The concept of organization used here, then, retains the elements of organization appearing in conventional definitions but adds to these elements ideas of organizing and of organizations within organizations. In doing so, it allows the extensiveness of formal organization to vary hence the causes and consequences of the extensiveness of formal organization, among the consequences bureaucratic growth, to be explored.

---

[1] This reasoning is best developed in Blau and Schoenherr (1971).

3.2 The Construction of Municipal Finance Organization

The inadequacy of static definitions of organization is illustrated by some aspects of the history of municipal finance administration in the U.S. Neither the entire history of local finance administration nor the histories of the three cities studied – Chicago, Detroit, and Philadelphia – can be covered in great detail here. There are too many facts and too little space. What can be explored using historical materials is a set of propositions that rather leap from documentary sources at anyone versed in organizational theory. The propositions are as follows: First, the environment presses constantly for control of city finances – for the alternative to control is corruption or insolvency, both of which are abhorrent. Second, control mechanisms designed to improve municipal accounting and financial reporting hence to prevent corruption and insolvency are put into place continually, but they are continually revised as unforseen conditions requiring new controls arise. Third, efforts to achieve control almost always involve the construction of new organization – new units of organization – that does not displace existing organizations but rather is added to it. Organizing is a continuous process, resulting in more complicated and in many respects less manageable or "businesslike" forms of organization than the earlier forms that were displaced.

The Demand for Control

The administration of local government finances provides no direct benefits to citizens. Its benefits are entirely indirect. The functions of finance administration are collection, maintenance, and disbursement of government funds. These functions are performed well, or are believed to have been performed well, when the requirements of law and prevailing accounting standards have been met. But there can be no single or definitive test of finance administration for the simple reason that contingencies unforseen in law and accounting standards arise continually.

The demand for control of local finances arose first from the reform impulse to eliminate corruption that was rampant through the nineteenth century. A. E. Buck's text on municipal finance, titled appropriately *Municipal Finance* (1930), was a early attempt to synthesize experience in financial organization and administration of large cities. The book was a product of research done by the New York Bureau of Municipal Research, and its copyright was held by the same Institute of Public Administration that later published *Papers in the Science of Administration*. Indeed, a chapter on debt administration was contributed by Luther Gulick. A short introductory chapter in the book outlined the "Significance of Municipal Finance." Buck claimed that "scientific financial methods" had prevented the abuses of the

Gilded Age from recurring. As reminders of the latter, the experiences of New York and Philadelphia were cited:

... following the Civil War the treasuries of several of our largest cities were plundered by political rings. One of the most notable of these was the Tweed ring in New York City. Tweed and his supporters drew out of the city treasury more than $ 8,000,000 to build a county courthouse which was estimated to cost $ 250,000. They trebled the bonded debt of the city in two and one-half years ...

Another notable example was the Philadelphia gas ring which looted the city treasury for many years after the Civil War ... It added enormously to the city's bonded indebtedness and pushed the tax rate up until in 1881 the taxes consumed between one-fourth and one-third of of total income accruing to the owners of the taxable property (1926: 4).

An abhorrence of dishonesty is reflected throughout the literature on municipal finance as it has been in almost all prescriptive writings on government since the turn of the century.

Control of fraud was only one purpose of financial administration. Another was control of expenditures intended for the legitimate purposes of government. The demand for expenditure control became especially acute under three circumstances: when costs were rising rapidly, when revenues were shrinking, or when cities' access to credit markets was threatened. During the 1910's, expenditures at all levels of government rose rapidly, due mainly to inflation, population increases, and increased public services (White, 1924; MacDonald, 1924; Lancaster, 1924). This triggered concern for, in the phrase of one commentator, "economy and competency in the public business" (King, 1924: vii). In the era of the Great Depression, economy became the principal imperative of local government as rates of property tax delinquency exceeded twenty-five per cent in the largest cities (Bird, 1935). And when interest rates rose to levels not previously experienced, first in the late 1950's (Balderston, 1957; Chatters, 1957) and later in the early 1970's (O'Leary, 1970), demands for reduced governmental expenditures were again voiced. Needless to say, the financial crises that occurred in several large U.S. cities in the mid-1970's compelled reductions in costs.

A further purpose of finance administration was control of ordinary waste and inefficiency not due to dishonesty. Almost all proposals for reform of financial administration are prefaced by statements of the need to reduce overlap and duplication of services and to improve the output of the municipal work force. But unlike the gross forms of corruption perpetrated by political machines, practices that are merely inefficient are not easily identified much less corrected. Writing in 1923, J. O. McKinsey opined that the efficiency of public services should be judged in terms of "the value of service rendered in terms of dollars spent" (1923: 87). But, as McKinsey noted, no simple test of value exists for public services. Decreased expenditures do not necessarily indicate improved efficiency, just as increased expenditures may not impair efficiency. Rather, McKinsey wrote, the public must have full information so that judgments concerning the value of governmental services can be made at all. The demand for efficiency in public administration was thus tied to the idea of control through accountability whereby officials are held responsible for both the amount and propriety of expenditures. Full accountability, McKinsey added, requires comprehensive financial and non-financial reporting and offers a "very interesting and lucrative field for the public accountant" (1923: 94).

Control of fraud, expenditures, and inefficiency are recurrent themes in the municipal finance literature. Such objectives, the comptroller of the Tennessee Valley Authority wrote in 1941, are "universally recognized as leading to desirable governmental financial and accounting practices" (Kohler, 1941: 4). What was not discussed among practitioners of public finance, perhaps because it was not understood, perhaps because no simple resolution of the problem was possible, was that these objectives could be in conflict with one another. Financial control, for example, is normally accomplished by the well known "diamond principle" whereby every transaction is recorded by two persons and subject to reconciliation by a third.[2] Three persons, in other words, are required for a job that could be done by one absent the need for control. Control is thus the antithesis of economy, and, under some circumstances, efficiency. And, as noted by McKinsey above, economy and efficiency in administration are not necessarily the same things. Just as inconsistencies exist generally between concepts of rational administration and the presuppositions of democratic governance, inconsistencies also exist among the specific demands made on local finance administration. Finance administration is charged with promoting economy and efficiency. It is also charged with insuring that expenditures are in conformity with legislated purposes, which imposes substantial burdens on finance agencies themselves and upon operating agencies whose accounts and reports are subject to the review of finance agencies.

Mechanisms of Control

Many different kinds of financial control mechanisms were implemented in U.S. cities during the interval covered by this research, and controls grew more complicated over time. Some were innovations in accounting, and some were organizational innovations. The accounting innovations made all aspects of financial administration more complex than before. The organi-

---

[2] The application of the "diamond principle" to municipal accounting is discussed by Taussig (1963).

zational innovations also contributed to complexity by extending administrative hierarchies. Almost all organizational innovations were in the
direction of centralization, which in practice meant that existing agencies
lost their autonomy and became subject to control by larger, more inclusive
units.

Accounting innovations. Early practitioners of local government finance
believed that more elaborate accounting records would contribute to the
improvement in control they sought. Three key accounting practices, referred to first as "fundamentals of municipal accounting" (Morey, 1933a) and
later as "major concepts in governmental accounting theory" (James, 1950),
dominated discussions of financial management. One was budgeting, or
budgetary accounting. The second was disaggregation of accounts into independent funds, or fund accounting. The third was the accrual as opposed
to the cash basis of accounting. All three were mentioned briefly in the first
chapter, but greater attention to their intended purposes and their consequences is now required.

– Budgeting. Budgets are so commonplace in modern government and industry that it is difficult to imagine a time when budgeting was innovative
and the focus of public attention. Such was the case the years just before
and after World War I. Prior to budgeting, appropriations were made piecemeal in response to departmental requests. This occurred at both national
and local levels of government. The executive – the President, governors,
mayors – had little control over overall expenditures. Indeed, at the Federal
level, the Secretary of the Treasury, not the President, transmitted departmental requests to Congress. The Budget and Accounting Act of 1921
prohibited departmental requests and placed responsibility for all Executive
Branch expenditures with the President. The Budget and Accounting Act
also required that revenue estimates, comparisons of estimated with actual
revenues and expenditures for the previous fiscal year, and a statement of
the financial condition of the Treasury accompany budget requests (Seidemann, 1924: 40–41). The Federal government had lagged somewhat behind
the states and some municipalities in adopting budget legislation. New York
City had a budget system in operation in 1912, and New York State in 1916.
Some forty-four states and many of the larger cities had budget legislation in
place by 1921.

Great results had been promised from budgeting. An article in the 1915
Annals proclaimed that, "The budget provides a means through which citizens may assure themselves that their effort which has been devoted to
common ends is not used for private gain, is not misused, or frittered
away . . ." (Hatton, 1915: xiv). But by the early 1920's, the promised benefits of the budget had not materialized. L. D. Upson, Director of the

Detroit Bureau of Governmental Research complained of a "constant aggravation of expenditures" (1924: 71). Another commentator called budget laws "mere sops thrown to satisfy the enlightened public demand for information and responsibility" (Lawton, 1921: 472). Still another commentator deplored "general and indefinite" budgetary categories and the tendency of budgets to follow expenditures of the previous year (Goddard, 1924: 432). *The solutions proposed for inadequate budgeting were in almost all instances more detailed budgets.* Upson, for example, suggested that appropriations should be attached to specific activities rather than broad functions (1924: 73). Budgeting fell into disarray during the Great Depression as government deficits mounted – A. E. Buck asked in one plaintive article (1941), "Whither the Budget?" – but shortly after the conclusion of World War II, pressure mounted for replacement of line-item budgets listing personnel and material costs with budgets listing costs per unit of output – for example, the dollar cost of replacing a street lamp bulb (as opposed to the wages of street lighting employees and the cost of bulbs), the cost of fingerprinting a prisoner (as opposed to police salaries and the cost of maintaining jails). Buck (1949) called this approach functional budgeting, but others called it activity (Byers, 1948) or performance (Donaho, 1950) budgeting.

The penultimate step in the trend toward more detailed budgets was PPBS, or Planning-Programming-Budgeting Systems. First utilized in the Department of Defense in the early 1960's, PPPS was believed to be a means of both maintaining financial control as well as economizing on expenditures. Like performance budgeting, PPBS focused on outputs. But unlike performance budgeting, it demanded specification of long-term objectives, of immediate outputs, of short- and long-term costs associated with each outputs, and of costs of alternative outputs that would accomplish long-term objectives (Cotton, 1968: 26–27). Additionally, long-term objectives, so-called programs, were usually divided into sub-programs and, sometimes, further into program elements and sub-elements (Luther, 1968). Suffice it to note that like earlier efforts at budgeting, PPBS did not result in noticeable economies or efficiencies in government. The budget director of Richmond, Virginia argued that planning-programming-budgeting concepts were not flawed. Rather, they were misunderstood: "Proponents of PPBS have too often emphasized the system and its elements, without understanding, or if understanding, failing to explain to others, the intent or purpose of PPBS. In other words, the approach may have been wrong, not necessarily the process itself" (Binford, 1975: 22). The successor to PPBS in the mid-1970's was zero-based budgeting, or ZBB, which attempted to achieve economies by building variations in expenditures into budgets. ZBB began with program concepts but added the notion of alternative service levels, both above and below current levels, and of tradeoffs among them. ZBB attempted to scrutinize all expenditures as if they were new ones, resulting in even more complicated budgetary accounts and more elaborate justifications for expenditures than under PPBS.

While almost all governmental units had adopted some form of budgeting by the mid-1920's, the content and quality of budgets was variable and has remained so since. Some performance or activity measures are present nowadays in most municipal budgets, but full program budgeting remains unusual and zero-based budgeting rare. The fact that PPBS and ZBB have not been adopted universally does not mean that they are believed inappropriate or inferior. Almost no support exists for returning to simpler budgeting methods.[3] Rather, the more complicated budgeting systems have not been adopted for lack of resources and, particularly, lack of trained staff. A lengthy description of zero-based budgeting noted one of its "significant disadvantages":

Foremost is the large increase in the time, effort and paperwork required. Increased time devoted to the budget by City personnel, the need for consultants in the initial implementation, and increased printing costs probably resulted in a net increase of 100 per cent in the costs of preparing the budget (Singleton et al., 1979: 29).

A further disadvantage of ZBB (as well as of PPBS) is its inability to pinpoint possible improvements in service at constant or decreased funding levels. The same article observed that:

... it is desirable to undertake separate measures to promote efficiency and productivity in combination with the implementation of ZBB (p. 29).

– Fund accounting. Through the early 1920's, no distinction between business and governmental accounting was recognized. To be sure, some large cities such as New York had begun to segregate monies intended for capital improvements and pensions from operating funds, and some state regulations governing municipal accounting mandated separation of current from capital and sinking funds (Suffern, 1922), the latter used to retire indebtedness. Nonetheless, business principles still prevailed in government. A thesis presented to the American Institute of Accountants in 1918 argued that "a system of accounts for a public corporation does not materially differ from that of a private corporation" since the purpose of both is "to narrate all transactions, reflect all conditions, and fix the blame for dishonesty ..." (Lyon: 1919: 125). The thesis went on to argue that a general account, a capital balance sheet, and a consolidated balance sheet sufficed to represent fairly the condition of a municipality, just as for firms. And J. O. McKinsey,

---

[3] An article by Philadelphia's Assistant Director of Finance (Durham, 1961) emphasized the advantages of line-item budgets as a means of proposing that expenditure plans be presented in *both* program and line-item form.

cited above for his observation that the outputs of municipalities are not easily valued, claimed nonetheless that the business model should be followed by government. "The chief difficulty ... [in government] is the lack of definite and accountable organization ... It is important to see than an organization chart should be the starting point in the designing of an accounting system for a municipality as well as for a business organization" (1923: 83, 85).

Lloyd Morey, then Professor of Accounting at the University of Illinois, later the University's Comptroller and still later President, was first to argue that fundamental, indeed irreconcilable, difference existed between managerial accounting as used in business and governmental accounting. In a 1926 article, Morey stated that,

Fund, or budget, accounts are peculiar to governmental organizations. They are necessary because the finances of such organizations are carried out in accordance with the budget system, which requires accounts which control and analyze the transactions incident thereto ... in governmental accounting, each fund is a complete entity requiring for its correct accounting a complete balanced set of accounts ... (1926: 77).

The key term here is "entity." Prior to Morey's statement, governments were considered similar to businesses in that the object of accounting was the entire unit of government – a city, county, or state – just as the object of managerial accounting was an entire business enterprise. Fund accounting shifted the focus to individual funds, with revenues and expenditures intended in specific amounts and for specific purposes as outlined in budgets. Morey developed this theme further in a 1933 article:

... a fund is a sum of money or other resources designated to defray expenditures for a certain purpose ... Each fund is a financial entity. The use of funds in municipal accounting is necessary to guarantee the autonomy and integrity of money which is restricted as to the purposes for which it may be used.

In meeting this requirement, the accounts of the general ledger must be subdivided in such a manner as to separately set out all accounts relating to any fund or group of funds. As a result, a complete balance sheet may be compiled for every fund, and such an arrangement is essential to a properly prepared municipal finance report (1933a: 31–32).

Morey's ideas did not fit easily with received accounting doctrine. A reviewer of his 1928 text, *Introduction to Governmental Accounting,* noted that "the average accountant will find himself obsessed by the thought that governmental accounting practice seems to be based on the theory that the longest and most tortuous road is the one to travel in preference to the shorter way to reach the goal" (Rusk, 1928: 74). Nor did his ideas fit easily into accounting curricula. As of 1930, only ten of 42 institutions comprising the membership of the American Association of Collegiate Schools of Business offered courses on governmental accounting. Accounting examinations rarely included questions about government (Morey, 1933b). Nonetheless, spurred perhaps by the deterioration in municipal finances resulting from the Depression and perhaps by the obvious inadequacy of most governmental bookkeeping, the National Committee on Municipal Accounting was formed in 1934 to formulate principles of municipal accounting. The idea of fund accounting was endorsed wholeheartedly (Morey, 1934; National Committee on Municipal Accounting, 1936; 1941). A major publication of the Committee, *Municipal Accounting Statements,* though principally a compilation of forms for financial statements and statistical tables, began with the observation. "A municipality's accounting system must make it possible, among other things, to determine whether or not the municipality is administering its financial affairs in accordance with legal provisions" (1941: 2). The term legal meant budgetary as well as statutory. Both the original and revised editions of the book contained lengthy descriptions of ten different types of funds, including the general fund, special revenue funds, working capital funds, special assessment funds, bond funds, sinking funds, trust and agency funds, utility funds, general fixed assets, and general bonded debt funds. And both editions noted that individual funds could be comprised of sub-funds, each of which was a complete accounting entity.

Subsequent publications of the National Committee on Municipal Accounting, which was renamed the National Committee on Governmental Accounting after World War II, indicated a concern that excessive complexity in accounting could yield unintelligible financial reports. In particular, *Government Accounting, Auditing, and Financial Reporting* (GAAFR), released by the NCGA in 1968, reduced to eight the types of funds suggested. Significantly, one of the eight that had not been recommended previously was an "Intragovernmental Service Fund," an entity created specifically for handling services performed by one agency for the benefit of another. GAAFR noted that "Too many funds . . . make for inflexibility and undue complexity . . . and are best avoided in the interests of efficient and economical management" (1968: 8). The constraint that accounts demonstrate the legality of expenditures, in other words, was an impediment to efficiency and economy in government.

The caution against excessive fund complexity expressed in GAAFR turned out to be too timid. In the wake of the fiscal crises of U.S. cities in the early 1970's, fund accounting was widely blamed for obscuring from the public the true financial condition of local governments. Partly because of the deterioration of city finances, the American Accounting Association (AAA), which along with the American Institute of Certified Public Accountants had previously ignored non-business organizations, asked a research committee to formulate not-for-profit accounting standards. The committee's report stated, in part, as follows:

The lack of a single statement of operations for the entity as a whole and the absence of a single proprietary account to show its financial position can be a disadvantage in the evaluation and control of operations of not-for-profit organizations ...

Because the usefulness of accounting statements on a fund-by-fund basis is limited, it is desirable that attention be given to the development of additional supplementary statements crossing fund lines and combining or consolidating fund information ... (American Accounting Association, 1971: 99).

The 1975 AAA Committee on Accounting in the Public Sector also deemed fund accounting inadequate "except for small and fiscally uncomplicated government units" (1975: 24). The opinions of the American Accounting Association notwithstanding, the American Institute of Certified Public Accountants' *AICPA Guide for Audits of State and Local Governmental Units*, issued in 1974, endorsed almost all of the principles outlined in GAAFR, including the fund basis of accounting.

Two further reports, one produced jointly by the Big Eight accounting firm of Coopers & Lybrand and the University of Michigan (1976), another by a group of accountants at the University of Chicago (Davidson et al., 1977) argued that municipal accounts ought to be as simple and understandable as corporate financial statements. Partly in response to these criticisms, the NCGA relaxed slightly its position that individual funds constituted the only appropriate entity for governmental financial reporting. In a 1979 restatement of GAAFR, it was noted that:

... the individual funds and account groups should continue to be the basic entity reported upon in the comprehensive annual financial report but ... the primary reporting entity focus of separately issued general purpose financial statements should be upon fund type and account group financial information (National Committee on Governmental Accounting, 1979: 25).

Whether the restatement of GAAFR clarified or confused matters is unclear. A number of cities did begin issuing consolidated "citizens'" financial reports in the late 1970's, but many bore auditors' letters stating that these reports did not conform to generally accepted accounting principles.

– The accrual basis of accounting. The idea of accrual accounting has existed as long as accounting itself. Accrual accounts reflect current financial conditions rather than present cash balances. The balance of an accrual account consists of cash on hand, less funds obligated but not yet disbursed (in accountants' language, these sums are encumbered), plus funds earned but not yet received. Virtually all the early theoreticians of municipal finance endorsed accrual methods. Morey, for example, called it "essential," and went on to comment that, "The cash receipt and disbursement system so common among municipalities and other governments in which items are accounted for only when they affect cash is utterly incomplete and indefensible" (1933a: 32). Both the 1936 and 1941 editions of *Municipal Accounting Statements* reflected a strong preference for accrual over modified accrual and cash methods, and some maintained as late as the 1950's that only full accrual accounting was consistent with governmental budgets (James, 1951).

Expert opinion carried little weight with finance officers struggling to make ends meet during the Depression. As property tax delinquencies mounted, one after another city was unable to meet its obligations, even though accrual methods based on taxes owed showed budgets to be in balance. Prior to the Depression, municipalities had routinely relied on short-term loans in anticipation of taxes to meet revenue shortfalls. This kind of financing was unavailable after 1929. The remedy in many jurisdictions was a return to cash accounting. The State of Kansas, for example, enacted a 1933 Cash Basis Law prohibiting municipalities from creating any indebtedness in excess of the amount of funds actually on hand (Barnard, 1935). When New Rochelle's collections fell below 70 per cent of the total tax levy in 1933, an Emergency Finance Commission returned the city to cash accounting (Glick, 1937). These developments were recognized by the National Committee on Governmental Accounting, but only after World War II. In a revision of *Municipal Accounting Statements,* a distinction was drawn between a complete and a modified accrual basis of accounting. The latter, modified accrual accounting, was like full accrual accounting save that accounting statements "do not reflect certain items until they are received in cash" (Tenner, 1951: 71) and was recommended only as a means of complying with statutory requirements mandating a cash basis for revenues.

By the time *Government Accounting, Auditing, and Financial Reporting* was published in 1968, modified accrual accounting was recommended as the appropriate accounting basis *for some but not all governmental funds.* For funds dependent on unpredictable revenue sources such as user and license fees and sales and income taxes where liabilities cannot be established in advance, modified accrual accounting was deemed appropriate. The general fund, which supports most basic governmental services, fell into this category. For funds deriving their revenues from more predictable revenue sources, full accrual accounting was recommended. The National Committee on Governmental Accounting did not have the last word on the issue of the full versus modified accrual basis of accounting, however. The 1971 report of the American Accounting Association research committee took explicit cognizance of the GAAFR statement on the subject but concluded to the contrary, that, "The full accrual basis [should] be considered a generally accepted accounting principle of not-for-profit organizations" (American Accounting Association, 1971: 106). Here, as with fund accounting, the recommendation of the AAA research committee was at variance with the

AICPA's *Audit Guide* (1974), which endorsed without reservation the modified accrual system as outlined in GAAFR.

Innovations in organization. Accounting innovations in municipal finance tended toward complexity in two respects. Accounting principles and concepts grew in complexity – fiscal controls multiplied them over time. Accounting principles were also rendered over time less easily understood and, perhaps, less consistent as they shifted in response to changing conditions in cities. Organizational innovations in municipal finance also tended toward complexity – formal organization increased dramatically. But organizational change, unlike shifts in accounting, was not at all haphazard. Rather, it was entirely in the direction of concentrating ultimate control of municipal finances in a single or small number of administrative agencies.

Throughout the nineteenth century, individual operating departments in U.S. cities were responsible for their own financial affairs. As noted in the first chapter, some agencies, particularly collectors' offices, generated their own operating funds and had license to spend as they wished. Most operating departments, however, depended on appropriations and submitted their expenditure plans directly to legislative bodies for review. Individual departments also managed their own accounts. Purchase orders and payroll checks originated in departments. Uniform pay scales and personnel policies were all but nonexistent until the 1890's, and departments did not coordinate their purchases of supplies to take advantage of quantity discounts. To be sure, the city treasurer's office held most city funds, the comptroller's office countersigned most disbursements, and a city auditor would, after the fact, ascertain whether expenditures were consistent with appropriations ordinances. But what control was exercised over departmental expenditures was weak and, for the most part, after the fact.

Somewhat in reaction to decentralized control of financial management, which in many instances meant no control, A. E. Buck's (1930) text on municipal finance outlined is some detail the pattern of centralized finance administration that has remained the model advocated by most experts in the field. All important fiscal functions, save for budgeting, were to be placed in a single finance department headed by a director of finance responsible only to the mayor or city manager. The principal functions, each of which was to be organized into a separate bureau or division, were control and accounts, treasury, assessments, and purchasing. The bureau of accounts, according to Buck, was to bear responsibility for the auditing of expenditures before they were approved, so-called preauditing. Independent auditors were charged with postauditing of expenditures at the end of each fiscal period. The functions of the treasury, assessments, and purchasing bureaus were those normally associated with these activities, save that they were subordinated to a finance director. Buck also suggested that the finance department administer municipal indebtedness and pensions. A separate bureau for debt management might or might not be required depending on the complexity of a city's debt structure.

The model of centralized finance administration outlined by Buck has not yet been achieved in all cities. As often as not, separate comptrollers', treasurers', and assessors' offices as well as purchasing departments remain (see Meyer, 1979: ch. 5). But financial control has in almost all instances been stripped from individual operating departments. Departments no longer maintain final accounts. The division of accounts in a comptrollers' office or finance department does. Departments no longer issue their own pay checks. The payroll division does. Departments can no longer make their own purchases. The purchasing department or purchasing division of a finance department does. The impact of removing ultimate control of finances from departments to separate administrative agencies is illustrated by a description of Baltimore's central payroll bureau, which was created by the city's Efficiency and Economy Commission in 1924. Its director worte that:

A woeful lack of uniformity in procedure existed under former methods, notwithstanding the waste and lack of control involving appropriations placed at the disposal of the respective departments which operated, in a sense, as private enterprises . . .

For employees engaged, the Central Payroll Bureau requires an *Entry Ticket* duly approved by the department head, indicating the name, address, classification, effective date, and rate applying. These tickets, when applied to the classified and labor groups, are executed in triplicate by the department employing and submitted to the City Service Commission for approval, whereas entry tickets involving employees of other groups mentioned are accepted on department head approval only. These tickets, upon receipt, clear the budget positions-positing or educational units division [of the Payroll Bureau] for verification as applied to a budget positions control record, after which they are referrred to the addressograph operations division where a plate is made, indicating all the facts as shown on the ticket . . .

Department heads receive their addressographed payrolls on the morning of the first day of the payroll period and are required to record attendance daily . . . On the morning of the last day of the payroll period, the payroll sheets are returned to the Central Payroll Bureau, duly executed by the party responsible for the attendance record, countersigned by the department head.

. . . the attendance of the employee is carefully analyzed to determine the salary to which he is entitled. Before proceeding further, however, the payrolls are submitted to the City Service Commission for certification purposes as to names and classifications appearing thereon. All items disapproved . . . are reported by a formal notification thereof attached to the payrolls when they are returned to the Bureau (Bernhardt, 1937: 11, 13, 15–16).

This rather tedious description of the work of Baltimore's Payroll Bureau serves to illustrate how centralization shifted the compensation of workers from a simple transaction between the employee and his department to a complicated one involving workers, their department, three units within the Payroll Bureau, and the City Service Commission. Work multiplied similarly with centralization of other functions. Accounting was removed from operating departments to promote uniformity and honesty. Centralization, however, required that two sets of books be kept and reconciled – one in the department, one in the comptroller's office or finance department – where previously there had been one. Purchasing was also removed from operating departments in order to promote uniformity and honesty as well as economy, but the complexity of transactions was increased at the same time. Absent centralized purchasing, a department head could negotiate directly and speedily with suppliers, often to their mutual gain. Centralized purchasing, at least in theory, removed the possibility of collusion by requiring formal requisitons and competetive bidding administered by an independent agency, a procedure almost always found cumbersome.

The trend toward centralization of finance functions has continued unbroken until this time. Not only have operating agencies of city government given up control of their finances, but unified departments of finance, following Buck's model, are gradually displacing independent assessors', comptrollers', treasurers', and purchasing offices. And some cities have attempted to move beyond Buck's ideas by uniting all administrative functions, financial and nonfinancial, in a single agency called a department of administration or of management.[4] One might reasonably ask at this point whether the stated purposes of centralization, uniformity and economy in administration, were in fact its effects. A strong case could be made that centralized administration of finances achieved uniformity, possibly at the expense of economy. One might ask further why uniformity should have taken precedence over economy. A possible explanation is that finance agencies were aligned to maximize the power of their executives. But this is too simplistic and does not take account of the growth of municipal accounting doctrine that occurred simultaneously with centralization. An alternative explanation suggests that both uniformity and extensive accounting rules were consistent with the machine model of organization, the idea of rational administration that sought in government the same predictability and control that had been achieved in industry.

---

[4] The reader is referred to the May, 1960, issue of *Municipal Finance* for examples of this kind of centralization.

Control and the Construction of Organization

Each of the mechanisms of control discussed above involved, in one way or another, the construction of categories of organization that had not existed absent that control mechanism. Some of the new categories were units of organization represented as such in tables of organization and in budgets. Other new categories were rules and work routines. These were not reflected directly in representations of organizational structure, but they affected organizational structures indirectly due to the new tasks they imposed on finance agencies.

The tie between budgeting and the construction of organization is unambiguous. The structure of budgets, at least early in the history of government budgeting, was no more and no less than organizational structure itself. The two were isomorphic. As demands for greater budgetary control mounted and revenue and expenditure plans were presented in greater detail, formal organizational structure, or at least the representation of organizational structure, and budgetary detail increased in tandem. Later on with PPBS and other innovations, the large number and overlap of budget categories was such that they could no longer be represented hierarchically. Formal organization diverged somewhat from budgets, and it is precisely this divergence that caused many municipalities that had experimented with program budgeting to abandon it. Two comments about the connection of budgeting to the construction of organization are required. First, demands for budgetary control generally increased organization at lower levels of administration. Subunits, sub-subunits, and sub-sub-subunits proliferated, but the basic departmental organization of finance functions was not affected by budgeting, save for the development of centralized budgeting units. Second, while the intent of budgeting may have been to limit expenditures by forcing individual units to make explicit their activities and costs and thereby to compete with each other for scarce resources,[5] its impact may have been the opposite. As will be argued below, the more budgetary hence the more organizational categories, the greater the number of justifications for expenditures and the greater the ease of making opportunistic shifts in these justifications.

Fund and accrual accounting also contributed to the construction of organization, the former due to the proliferation of accounting entities, the latter due to duplication of records. It will be remembered that a fund is a self-balancing and self-contained fiscal entity. One fund's transactions with other funds are represented in explicit interfund transfers, both positive and

---

[5] Padgett (1981) presents a strong case that the Federal budgeting process has had this effect in the U.S. His work, however, is an exception to a long tradition of studies showing budget adjustments to be incremental and upward almost without limit.

negative, just as transactions of one business firm with others are represented in revenue and expenditure statements. Fund accounting demanded increased financial organization in two respects. First, the number of accounts and of financial statements required of cities increased exactly with the number of funds maintained. Second, the number of interfund transfers requiring explicit recognition increased more rapidly than the number of funds due to geometric increase in the range of possible transactions between funds. Accrual accounting added somewhat to the complexity of fund accounting because it required that balances be adjusted by revenues earned but not collected and expenditures obligated but not disbursed. Substantially greater complexity was introduced by the concept of modified accrual accounting. The modified accrual method calculated revenues and expenditures on different bases, the former cash, the latter accrual. For this reason, the difference between revenues and expenditures was rendered an ambiguous measure of change in overall financial condition. Moreover, once the modified accrual basis of accounting became the preferred method for some categories of funds but full accrual accounting remained preferred for others, simple comparisons of financial condition across funds also became ambiguous. No direct connection between accounting changes and shifts in administrative organization can be documented from historical accounts, but some connection surely existed because the newer accounting techniques demanded more functions and probably a larger work force than had been needed previously.

Centralization of finance functions clearly demanded organizational forms that had not existed previously. But whereas the budget process resulted in proliferation of units at lower levels of organization, centralization often yielded new units at or just below the departmental level. Centralized purchasing departments, for example, were created in 1901 in Chicago, 1906 in Philadelphia, and 1920 in Detroit. Centralized departments of finance that placed under the control of a single department head the accounting and control, purchasing, treasury, and postauditing functions were formed in 1953 in Philadelphia and in 1975 in Detroit. Centralized budgeting agencies reporting directly to the mayor were founded in 1955 in Chicago, and in 1975 in Detroit. It is to be emphasized that centralization of functions did not always require new departmental units. The shift of ultimate authority for accounting functions from individual operating departments to a central comptrollers' office or finance department, for example, did not cause these agencies to be formed but did augment their responsibilities hence their internal organization.

One generalization and an observation may be in order at this point. The generalization is that the mechanisms used to secure greater control of municipal finances required more organization – more organizational units, greater differentiation of their functions, more levels of organizational hierarchy. In some instances, particularly in the case of budgeting and of centralization of finance functions, the impact of control efforts on organizational structure was direct and immediate. In other instances, the effects of control mechanisms while less obvious were nonetheless substantial. But in almost all cases, fiscal control and the construction of organization were practically synonymous, in part because the intent to secure control was sometimes best signalled by creating new units of organization, in part because new controls could not have been effectuated absent new organization and staff to carry out these functions. The observation is that control was not always achieved by the mechanisms intended to secure it. This is demonstrated rather vividly by the deterioration of fiscal conditions in the three cities studied in the era of the Great Depression and later in the mid-1970's. Chicago was on the brink of bankruptcy by 1930. Chicago's fiscal distress was due not to excessive expenditures but rather to the failure of the State Tax Commission to authorize an assessment roll for Cook County for two consecutive years. Excessive expenditures brought Philadelphia near bankruptcy in the mid-1930's, and Detroit's treasury was empty by April of 1933 because its dwindling revenues could not support a mounting burden of debt. This pattern was nearly repeated in the mid-1970's. Following the death of Mayor Richard Daley in late 1976, the financial accounts of Chicago were found to be in disarray and to have concealed substantial liabilities for which no provision for payment had been made. In order to bring its budget near balance in 1975, Detroit laid off nearly 2,000 workers and did not fill an additional 1,200 vacancies as they occurred. And in early 1976, Philadelphia's Finance Director, Lennox Moak, who had co-authored the definitive text on municipal financial management (Moak and Hillhouse, 1975) and was then president of the Municipal Finance Officers Association of the United States and Canada, resigned his office in disgrace when it was discovered that he had grossly misrepresented the financial condition of the city in connection with a sale of general obligation bonds. One wonders, indeed whether the finances of large cities were better administered in 1975 than in 1910. If one considers the fiscal condition of municipalities in periods of recession or depression to be an index of success in financial control, then the answer is probably negative.

3.3 An Operational Definition of Organization

Above, the concept of organization was extended beyond elements usually present in static definitions. Organizing processes, it was argued, usually take place within organizations, creating organizations within organizations.

A conception of organization that allows for organizing processes and the existence of organizations within organizations, it was argued, is needed to test the key ideas in this research – that there is a preference for constructing organization as a solution to problems and that the construction of organization yields bureaucratic growth. The history of municipal finance administration in the U.S. was then reviewed. As a result of demands for control of municipal finances, innovations in accounting and organization occurred almost continuously from the first decade of this century onward. Most accounting and organizational innovations were associated with the construction of new formal organization. Thus, demands for control of local government finances, which could never be satisfied, appear to have resulted in nearly continuous construction of bureaucratic organization and, as will be shown below, bureaucratic growth.

At this point, the units to be studied – what we shall call organizations – must be identified so that the hypotheses suggested by theory and history can be tested somewhat rigorously. It should be clear from the above discussion that the extensiveness of formal organization is considered to be variable. Any operational definition that restricts or eliminates variation in the extensiveness of organization will be unsatisfactory. Thus, any definition that restricts the set of units called organizations to those existing at one point in the time cannot be used because it eliminates variation over time in the extensiveness of organization. And any definition that restricts the set of units called organizations to those with particular names or designations, such as departments (as opposed to smaller divisions and sections), cannot be used because it eliminates variation in the extensiveness of organization due to construction of new organization within existing units. Indeed, the history of the agencies studied suggests strongly that the term organization is an eclectic term, applying to any unit created for an instrumental purpose regardless of whether or not that unit is part of a larger unit, which is also called an organization. And, the literature on municipal accounting uses the term "organizational unit" – not department, division, and section – to describe the units to which budget and accounting categories apply. Just as smaller budgets comprise subsets of larger budgets, which, in turn, comprise subsets of even larger budgets, and just as smaller financial accounts are contained within larger financial accounts, which are contained within still larger accounts, smaller organizational units are contained within larger organizational units, which are parts of even larger organizational units. Thus, almost all nominal definitions of organization, whether by name or by hierarchical level, exclude some units as organizations and do not capture all that the environment defines as organizations. This may or may not be important in research. If research focuses on properties of individual organizations such as size, formalization, and the like, then it is of little import whether or not all possible organizational units are captured. But if research focuses on the quantity of organization, particularly increases in organization over time, then all that the environment understands as organization must be treated as such. Measuring the quantity of organization is fundamental to testing the idea that the problems of organizations are, under concepts of rational administration, solved by creating more organization.

The definition of organization to be used here, then, is precisely that used in the municipal accounting. Organizations are those entities understood to be organizational units. Organizations are departments, *and* divisions or bureaus within departments, *and* sections within divisions or bureaus. And in some instances, the set of departments responsible for municipal finance functions is treated as a single organization.

The definition of an organization as a unit at any level of hierarchy is unconventional, but it is not inconsistent with past research practice. To be sure, almost all prior research studies – and such studies are too numerous to cite – have relied upon one or another nominal definition of organization. But these definitions have varied substantially. Sometimes, for example, departments within universities are regarded as organizations, while in other instances universities themselves are the relevant units. Sometimes local offices of state agencies are considered organizations, but in other instances the term organization applies to entire state agencies, including their local offices. Sometimes operating units of divisionalized firms are treated as organizations, but sometimes only the larger firms are. In each instance there has been justification for the particular definition of organization used, suggesting that there is justification for almost any definition of organization so long as it is restricted to purposive groups having boundaries and understood as organizations. Furthermore, the definition of organization as a unit at any level of hierarchy is consistent with the units believed most relevant in the psychological and political science literature on organizations. In the analysis of decisions in organizational psychology, the decision premise is taken as the fundamental unit (Simon, 1957: xii). Individual decision premises are, of course, embedded within broader decision premises, within still broader decision premises in large decision-making systems. In the analysis of bureaucratic behavior in political science, individual bureaus and their subunits are assumed to have considerable autonomy from one another, so much so that ultimate policies more often reflect interunit conflict than cooperation (Miller and Moe, 1983). Only the quantitative research literature has insisted on nominal definitions that restrict organizations to units of a given name or type. In the past, this has served research well, principally by incorporating as a substantive assumption the statistical assumption that the units observed are independent of one another. In this research, the same substantive assumption cannot be maintained because, again, a key idea to be explored here is that one solution to the problems occurring in existing organization is the formation of new units of organization.

The units studied in the research reported below are agencies responsible for the administration of the finances of Chicago, Detroit, and Philadelphia from 1890 until 1975. In one respect, three cities, or organizational systems charged with finance functions in three cities, are the subject of this research. Some twenty-seven different departments charged with finance functions existed[6] in Chicago, Philadelphia and Detroit from 1890 through 1975. These departments also comprise the subject of this research. From 1890 through 1975, some 240 divisions or bureaus, subunits of departments, existed in Chicago, Detroit, and Philadelphia, as did 282 sections, subunits of divisions or bureaus. These divisions and sections are also the subject of this research. Altogether, some 559 distinct organizational units had finance responsibilities in Chicago, Detroit, and Philadelphia from 1890 through 1975. These 559 units did not exist continuously from 1890 to 1975. Quite the opposite, many were in existence for short periods. Their number grew substantially over time, however. There were few organizational units – twelve to be exact – when the interval covered by this research begins and almost fifteen times that number eighty-six years later. This research seeks to explain why such multiplication of organization took place.

The choice of the cities and agencies studied, and the procedures used to define the existence or nonexistence of individual units cannot be justified fully. This is but a complicated way of saying that the quantitative data at hand are imprecise. The data are also insufficient to prove that the hypotheses at hand hold for all organizations, even for all bureaucratically organized systems of administration. All that can be shown is that our observations are consistent with the theory developed above. This is best accomplished by showing that alternative explanations do not account for bureaucratic growth as well as does this theory. Thus, the next chapter will develop alternative models of bureaucratic growth. These models will be tested in subsequent chapters.

---

[6] Units existing for less than two years were not considered in this research.

Chapter 4
Models of Bureaucratic Growth

This chapter develops several models of bureaucratic growth. These models are based in theory but are also derived from the study of finance agencies. They represent a first attempt to formulate specific hypotheses suggested by theory and consistent with surface characteristics of the organizations studied. While the aim of this chapter is to formulate hypotheses rather than to test them, some quantitative data will be introduced since long-term patterns of change must be described quantitatively as well as discursively.

Two theoretical problems are at hand. One is developing a model of growth consistent with our hypothesis that growth is an outcome of a problem-organization-problem-more organization cycle. The second problem is delineating alternative models of bureaucratic growth. Not only must the theory outlined above be tested, but its predictions must be compared to predictions made by alternative and in some respects simpler theories of growth. Two alternative theories will be considered. One treats growth as a function of external task demands. The other treats age, or inertia, as preserving existing organizations hence requiring that new units be formed to accommodate change. As will be shown presently, the surface characteristics of the agencies studied appear not to be inconsistent with the task and inertial theories of growth. Tests of the causal models of growth suggested by all three theories will be undertaken in subsequent chapters.

This chapter is organized as follows: To begin, measures of bureaucratic growth are discussed. Patterns of growth and change among the finance agencies studied and in measures of task demand are then described, and three models of bureaucratic growth consistent with overall growth patterns of these agencies are proposed.

4.1 Measures of Growth

Growth is simply quantitative increase. Bureaucratic growth is, therefore, quantitative increase in bureaucracy. In organizational settings where a clear distinction exists between administrative and nonadministrative personnel, one measure of bureaucratization is the ratio of the former to the latter. Data on A/P and supervisory/nonsupervisory ratios in U.S. industry were displayed in Chapter 2. In settings where almost all work is administrative, as is often the case in government, A/P ratios are not meaningful and total numbers of persons employed is the counterpart measure of bureaucratization. The reader will recall that Chapter 2 also displayed statistics on total government employment in the U.S. Since the work of the finance agencies studied is almost entirely administrative, their size is a more appropriate measure of bureaucratization than A/P ratios, if the latter could be determined.

There is another way to measure bureaucratic growth. While bureaucratic growth can be understood as increased staff, it can also be understood as increased organization. Several advantages are offered by understanding bureaucratic growth as increased organization. First, as indicated in the previous chapter, the history of the agencies studied is one of nearly continuous construction of formal organization as a means of managing change and uncertainties arising in the environment. The historical record suggests, in other words, that organizing was a response to external events rather than a consequence of increased staff. If the immediate response to environmental change is organizing and if formation of organization ultimately increases staff size, then increase in the extensiveness of organization is a valid measure of growth. Second, when one understands bureaucratic growth as increased organization, it becomes possible to ask some questions that cannot be raised much less answered when bureaucratization is understood only as absolute or relative staff size. In particular, treating bureaucratic growth as growth in formal organization allows one to locate the causes of bureaucratic growth in the same factors that cause the rate of formation of organizational units to exceed the rate with which they are dissolved.

Quantifying Organization

There are many potential measures of bureaucratization. Other than personnel counts and indexes of the extensiveness of formal organization, they include the extensiveness of rules and regulations, the degree of standardization of work and the amount of detail contained in job descriptions, and the degree of differentiation and complexity in organizational hierarchies. Where existing organizations are the subject of research, any or all of these measures of bureaucratization can be gathered. But where organizational patterns must be reconstructed from historical sources, as is the case in the present research, only limited data are available. Generally, U.S. cities preserve their financial records – budgets and financial reports – as well as annual departmental reports, where the latter exist. Cities also preserve their legal records, which include appropriations ordinances or statutes. Cities do not maintain outdated procedure manuals, civil service regulations, or tables of organization. Nor do they keep any records of actual working relationships among employees.[1] Thus, only the most rudimentary measures of bureaucratization of finance functions (or of other municipal functions) can be constructed from historical records. These measures include, for every extant organizational unit, its size, as indicated by budget and total staff, and the extensiveness of its formal organization, which is indicated by the number and configuration of subunits present. (In the language of more conventional organizational analysis, the latter comprise measures of organizational differentiation.) Certain quantitative measures describing the environments of the finance agencies studied are also available from official records. These include city size, expenditures, indebtedness, Federal and state subventions, and the length and detail of budget documents themselves.

The organizational units of interest here are, as noted in the previous chapter, departments, *and* divisions, *and* sections of municipal agencies with finance functions in Chicago, Detroit, and Philadelphia. Data describing these units are available from 1890 through 1975. During this interval, the language used to describe different levels of municipal administration came into usage just as organizational units proliferated. Departments were the first and largest governmental units. When units within municipal departments appeared, they were called divisions. And units within divisions were labelled sections when they first appeared. Departments, then, may or may not contain divisions and sections at any point, and divisions may or may not have sections. Thus, while finance administration is normally divided among several departments, departments and divisions are sometimes but not always further divided into smaller units. Finance administration, importantly, is in almost all instances distinct from other municipal activities, such as police and fire protection, public health and housing, public works and utilities, and non-financial aspects of governmental administration. Only data-processing activities serve both financial and non-financial functions, and we have attempted in this research to limit consideration to those data-processing units having principally financial functions.

Given the limitations of historical data, the best quantitative measures of the extensiveness of organization are numbers of organizational units. At any point in time, each of the three cities can be described by how many organizational units had responsibility for finance functions. Furthermore, each department and division with finance functions can be described by the number of units it contained, or, alternatively, whether or not it was divided into subunits. Figure 4-1 illustrates how the extensiveness of organization is

---

[1] Business firms tend to maintain even fewer historical records and thus are much less amenable than government bureaus to the kind of research undertaken here.

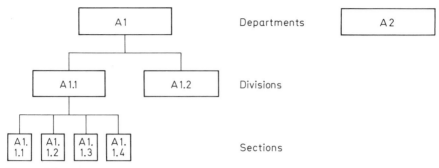

Figure 4.1
Quatifying the Extensiveness of Organization

quantified in this research. A hypothetical "City A" has two departments, "A1" and "A2," with finance functions, one of which has two divisions, one of which has none. One of the two divisions in "A1," further, has four sections, while the other division has no sections. "City A," then, contains eight organizational units serving finance functions. "Department A1" contains six of these units. Importantly, "Department A1" and one of its divisions both have subunits, while the other division and "Department A2" have none. Quantification of finance organization in cities, departments, and divisions is thus achieved by treating as units of organization respectively the departments, divisions, and sections contained within them.

Measuring Births and Deaths

The number of organizational units existing at a given time is, of course, determined by how many existed in the previous period, how many were formed, and how many dissolved. Pinpointing when an organizational unit was formed and dissolved, if it did cease to exist, poses somewhat greater difficulty than defining what are the organizational units of interest. The following definitions of organizational formation, or birth, and of dissolution, or death, were used in this research:

– In general, accounts of organizations given in official records are followed. A birth or formation of an organizational unit occurs at the point it first comes into existence; a death or dissolution is recorded at the point it no longer exists.
– Where dissolution of one unit and formation of a new one to replace it appear to have occurred, a death and a birth are recorded provided that two of three things have occurred: the name has changed, the staff has changed substantially (plus or minus twenty per cent), and functions have changed.
– When two units merge, one death is recorded if the merged unit retains the name of one of the former units. However, should the merged unit have a new name, then two deaths and one birth are recorded.

– When a unit is "demoted" from departmental to divisional status, which among the agencies studied is the most fundamental kind of change that can occur, or from divisional to sectional status, a birth and a death are recorded. "Promotions," which are infrequent, are also recorded as a birth and a death.

These definitions of birth and death of organizational units not only help quantify the extensiveness of organzation, but they also permit one to think of bureaucratic growth as an excess of births over deaths of organizational units. At any point in time, growth in formal organization occurs when more organizational units are formed than dissolved. Forces causing new organizational units to be formed are, therefore, causes of bureaucratic growth. Forces preserving existing units are also causes of growth to the extent that they hold dissolution rates below rates of formation of new units. Also at any point in time, a decline in the amount of formal organization occurs when more units are dissolved than formed. Forces causing existing units to be dissolved are, therefore, causes of bureaucratic decline.

Concepts of Organization and Concepts of Growth

Concepts of organization and concepts of bureaucratic growth are closely linked. If one thinks of organization as a fixed entity with variable properties, then growth in personnel occurs necessarily within organizations. If, however, one thinks of organization as variable, or, better, the extensiveness of organization as variable, then bureaucratic growth can occur through increase in formal organization. Increased organization, to repeat the discussion above, can be understood as an excess of births of organizational units over deaths, and elements causing births to exceed deaths are sought as causes of bureaucratic growth.

Because concepts of organization and of bureaucratic growth are linked, theories of bureaucratic growth also depend upon how organization is understood. If organization is assumed fixed and growth is understood as increased personnel, then growth is usually treated as a simple function of demands for outputs. The environment, in other words, drives growth somewhat mechanistically. But if organization is variable and its quantity increases or decreases, then more subtle models of growth are possible, models in which the causes of growth lie both within organizations themselves and in their environments. For example, by understanding the quantity of organization as variable and bureaucratic growth as an excess of births over deaths of units, one can ask whether growth is due to inertia or increased resistance to change as individual units age. Any preserving effect of age, of course, is not due to the passage of years alone. It is rather an outcome of interdependencies between organizations and their environments that develop over time rather than any simple environmental effect. Similarly, by understanding the quantity of organization as variable and growth as births minus deaths, one can ask whether the problem-organiza-tion-problem-more organization cycle hypothesized above accounts for bureaucratic growth. This model hypothesizes that creating new organiza-tion preserves existing organizations by augmenting their capacity to map their environments. Again, no simple environmental determinism is oper-ating here. Rather, the intersection of external uncertainty with the con-straint of administrative rationality, the latter derived from the larger social environment but also an organizational property, yields this outcome.

Concepts of organization, concepts of growth, and models of growth are thus inextricably tied. Should conventional concepts of organization be maintained, growth is understood as increase in staff and driven principally by environmental demands. Should organization be treated as variable rather than as a fixed entity whose properties are variable, growth is under-stood as increased organization and driven by complicated exchanges between organizations and environments, which reflect external task de-mands only partially. In one of the models of bureaucratic growth devel-oped below, the conventional conception of organization is maintained, and growth is hypothesized to be a simple function of demand. But in the other two models, multiple forces, some within organizations and some without, propel bureaucratic growth.

4.2 Patterns of Growth and Change

At this point, we begin the exploration of growth and change among finance agencies in Chicago, Detroit, and Philadelphia. Changes in key environ-mental elements that can be quantified are first outlined. Growth of staff and of formal organization in the agencies studied is then described, and the frequency of formation and of dissolution of the individual organizational units comprising these agencies is shown over chronological time and by the age of individual units.

Change in the Environment

One of the more troublesome questions facing organizational research is measurement of environments. Whereas properties of organizations such as their size, administrative structure, technology, extent of formalization, and the like are, or are believed to be, readily quantifiable, the same does not hold for environments. The difficulty arises in part because the concept of the environment includes everything outside of organizations. Environ-ments are for this reason not readily delimited. Quantification of environ-ments is also complicated by differences between their "subjective" and "objective" properties. To the extent that organizations focus attention on some problems and divert attention from others, the environment is best measured by the way it is understood by participants. But to the extent that external forces compel organizational responses, the environment is best understood in terms of these forces rather than peoples' perceptions of them. If perceptual and more objective indicators describing environments normally corresponded, no measurement problem would be posed. But numerous research studies, as noted in the second chapter, have suggested that the two kinds of measures are often discrepant.

A further complication, and the one of greatest concern here, is that variation in other than immediate task demands may be difficult to capture. Interdependencies between organizations and their environments emerging over time are often not observable. And changes in prevailing ideas about organizing – e.g., the shift from traditional to rational-legal bases of authority – are also arrayed over time and occur only in the context of fundamental societal change, which is infrequent. Not only is variation in interdependencies sustaining organizations as well as in ideas about organizing sometimes unobservable but quantification of observable environmental elements may be difficult to achieve. For example, the election of a reform mayor is an event that either occurred or did not occur in a given year. It is not a continuous variable. These limitations do not mean that quantitative models of organizational change cannot be tested, but they do mean that models will be partial and will rely on imperfect indicators of the environment. Key developments occurring in Chicago, Detroit, and Philadelphia will be indicated by interventions in time series but not otherwise quantified. The idea of rational bureaucratic administration, which gave rise to the municipal agencies studied and continues to dominate them is not measured at all. It is assumed constant or nearly so over the eighty-six year interval covered by the research. The assumption of near constancy in concepts of rational administration does not imply constancy in organizations, however. A set of ideas for constructing organizations may itself be fixed yet may also be a source of continual organizational change and growth.

Some elements in the task environment for which quantitative indicators are readily available include the size of a city's population, its budgeted expenditures, its indebtedness, and its dependence upon external funding sources, which is measured by the extent of state and Federal subventions supporting municipal programs. Figure 4-2 illustrates changes in these environmental elements over time. The populations of Chicago, Detroit and Philadelphia are displayed in Figure 4-2a. All three cities grew until the late 1950's and then lost population. Philadelphia, the oldest of the three, had more than one million residents in 1890, grew steadily to a peak of slightly over two million in the late 1950's, and declined thereafter. Chicago, which had been

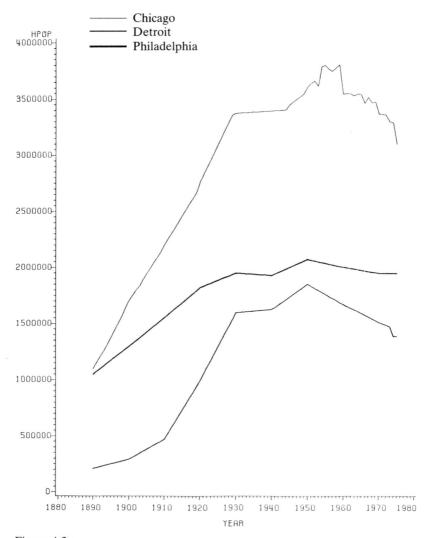

Figure 4.2a
Population of Chicago, Detroit, and Philadelphia by Year

a small community at the end of the Civil War, grew to 1.1 million by 1890, 2.2 million in 1910, and had population of over 3.5 million by the late 1950's. Detroit's population growth occurred somewhat later than either Chicago's or Philadelphia's. Detroit had about 200,000 residents in 1890, 500,000 in 1910, 1.6 million in 1930, and 1.8 million in 1950. Like Philadelphia, both Chicago and Detroit lost residents throughout the 1960's and 1970's.

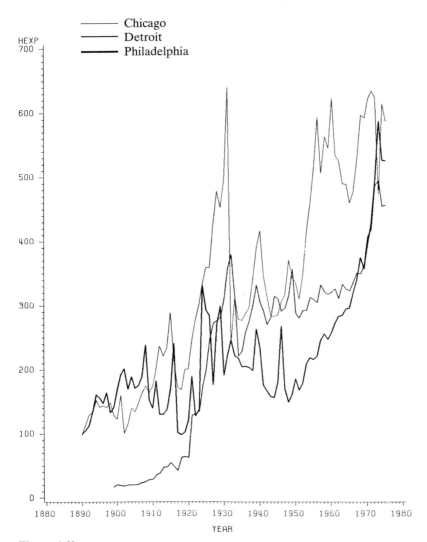

Figure 4.2b
Expenditures (in constant dollars) of Chicago, Detroit, and Philadelphia by Year

The growth of expenditures in the three cities does not follow the same pattern as population growth and decline. Generally, municipal expenditures increased from 1890 to World War I, declined during World War I, increased again until the onset of the Great Depression, declined during the early years of the Depression and then increased, and decreased during World War II and increased again afterwards. Figure 4-2b displays total city expenditures in constant dollars[2] for Chicago, Detroit, and Philadelphia over the 1890–1975 interval. The reader is cautioned that these data reflect budgeted rather than actual expenditures, although they do reflect actual rather than proposed budgets. Additionally, determination of total expenditures is complicated somewhat by the vagaries of fund accounting, which permits some categories of expenditures to be reported twice, once as an interfund transfer and again as a direct expense. A further complication is that municipal functions are not identical in the three cities and these functions shift somewhat over time.

Municipal indebtedness, also in constant dollars, increased over time in Chicago, Detroit, and Philadelphia, paralleling somewhat increases in expenditures. Generally, debt increased from 1890 to World War I, decreased during the years of World War I, increased slowly thereafter until the onset of the Great Depression after which time it increased rapidly, decreased as municipal bankruptcy approached (or, in the case of Detroit, occured) in the middle of the Depression, remained relatively low during World War II, and increased thereafter. Figure 4-2c displays total indebtedness in constant dollars for the three cities over the 1890–1975 study interval. As with the data on budgeted expenditures, the limitations of the data on indebtedness should be understood. They represent, as best as could be determined, the total debt of the three cities, including general obligation and revenue debt as well as short-term tax and bond anticipation notes. For some years, particularly during the 1930's when local finances were in disarray, they also represent estimated rather than actual indebtedness. In years when indebtedness totals were either missing from budgets and financial reports or were patently inaccurate, indebtedness was estimated by interpolation or, in some instances, correction of what could be interpreted generously as typographical errors in official documents.[3]

Federal and to a lesser extent state subventions to municipalities became major elements in local budgets beginning in the mid-1950's. The nature of these aid programs need not be described in detail here. Suffice it to note that the first large Federal housing programs began in 1954 and that revenue sharing funds whose use was less restricted than categorical grants began flowing to cities in 1970. Figure 4-2d displays the growth, again in constant

---

[2] An implicit deflator series in which 1958 = 100 is used to convert actual into constant dollar expenditures.

[3] In several instances (and in more than one city), entire columns of zeroes were omitted from debt accounts; in one instance, short-term debt was understated by a factor of one thousand. The efforts made to correct errors could not, of course, remove systematic misrepresentation of indebtedness such as that now known to have taken place in Chicago in the 1960's and 1970's.

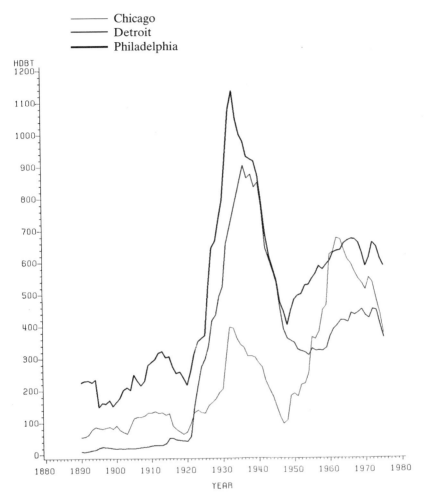

Figure 4.2c
Indebtedness (in constant dollars) of Chicago, Detroit, and Philadelphia by Year

dollars, of Federal and state aid to Chicago, Detroit, and Philadelphia from 1953 through 1975. These funds generally increased from 1953 to their peak in 1973 and declined somewhat in the next two years. It is of interest that Detroit, the smallest of the three cities, received the largest subventions during this period. Although one quarter of these funds are from state subventions, the remaining three quarters reflect the unusual skill of several Detroit mayors, beginning with Cavanaugh in the early 1960's, in obtaining Federal grants.

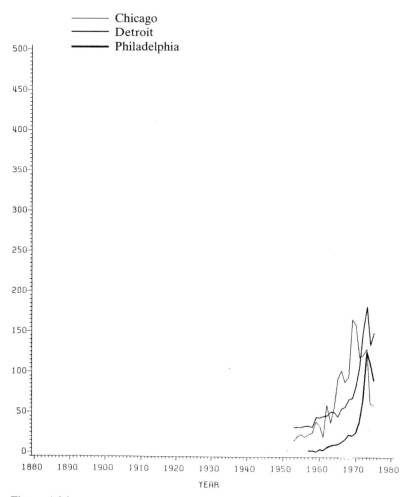

Figure 4.2d
Federal and State Aid (in constant dollars) of Chicago, Detroit, and Philadelphia by
Year

Bureaucratic Growth

The growth of organizations, or bureaucratic growth, is more easily defined
and described than changes in the environment. Conventionally, organizational growth is increase in numbers of personnel attached to an organizational unit, whether an entire administrative bureaucracy or one of its
departments, divisions, or sections. Organizational growth is thus not the
same thing as business growth, which is normally understood as increase in

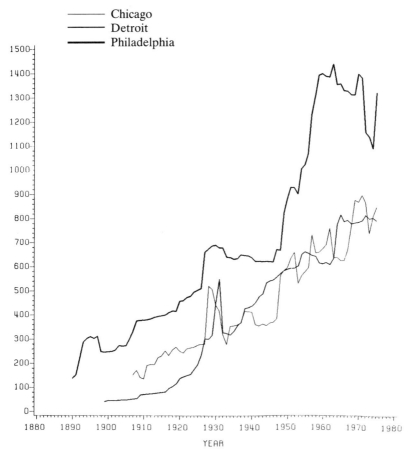

Figure 4.3a
Total Employees in Finance Functions of Chicago, Detroit, and Philadelphia by
Year

sales. Less conventionally but perhaps more literally, organizational or bureaucratic growth can be defined as increase in formal organization or of
formal organizational structure. Both of these definitions of growth are used
here.

Growth of agencies responsible for finance functions in Chicago, Detroit,
and Philadelphia is endemic over the 1890–1975 interval. This holds for both
personnel counts as well as measures of organization. Figure 4-3a displays
total numbers of employees performing finance functions in the three cities
for the years for which complete data are available. Series begin in 1890 for

Philadelphia, in 1899 for Detroit, and in 1907 for Chicago.[4] In 1907, Chicago's finance functions required 152 employees; this number grew to 850 in 1975. Detroit had 41 persons employed in various finance functions in 1899. This number grew to 794 in 1975. And Philadelphia, which had 138 finance personnel in 1890, employed 1325 by 1975. Growth in organization paralleled somewhat growth in personnel in the three cities. Figure 4-3b displays the total number of organizational units – departments, divisions, and sections – existing in each year in each of the three cities. All three cities divided finance functions among four organizational units in 1890. Chicago had a Comptroller, a Treasurer, and Departments of Collections and Special Assessments; Detroit had Departments of Accounting and Assessment as well as a City Comptroller and City Treasurer; Philadelphia had an Assessor (whose department was called Revision of Taxes), a Comptroller, a Treasurer, and a Revenue Department. By 1975, Chicago's finance functions were divided among 63 units (including six departments, thirty divisions, and twenty-seven sections), Detroit had fifty units (four departments, nineteen divisions, and twenty-seven sections), and Philadelphia had 63 units (eight departments, twenty-five divisions, and thirty sections).

Total employment in the finance functions of Chicago, Detroit, and Philadelphia fits an exponential model of growth somewhat better than a linear model. The extensiveness of bureaucratic organization in these cities increases linearly with time, however. The upper panel of Table 4.1 displays regressions in which employees are estimated as a linear function of time (or year) for the three cities, from the first year in which total size is available through 1975. The goodness-of-fit measures, the R^2's range from .873 for Philadelphia to .960 for Detroit. Growth of staff, importantly, is somewhat faster than linear. When second-order terms are added to the regressions as is done in the second panel of Table 4.1, their coefficients are positive and significant for two of the three cities. In the third panel of the table, the logarithm of size to the base ten rather than linear size is estimated as a function of year. Here, the R^2's are slightly higher, ranging from .897 for Detroit to .938 for Philadelphia. The estimates displayed in the fourth panel of Table 4.1 add a second-order term to the previous model; the logarithm of size is estimated as a function of year and the square of year. The coefficients of the second-order terms are negative and significant for Chicago and Detroit but nonsignificant for Philadelphia, suggesting that the rate of exponential growth decreases over time for two of the three cities. Impor-

---

[4] Several departments in Chicago and Detroit had no personnel budgets as late as 1898 in Detroit and 1906 in Chicago. Employees were paid percentages of revenues (in the case of tax collectors) or of interest earned on city funds (in the case of treasures). Who was paid how much was left entirely to the discretion of department heads.

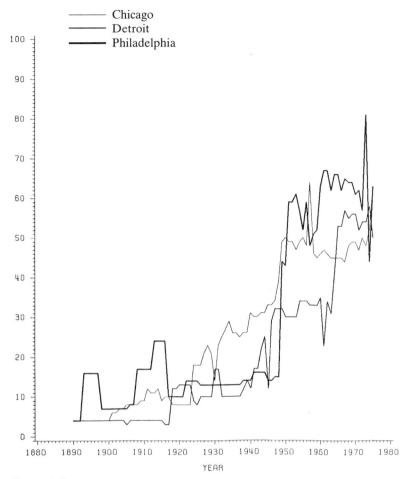

Figure 4.3b
Total Organizational Units in Finance Functions of Chicago, Detroit, and Philadelphia by Year

tantly, the R^2's in this model, which range from .908 for Chicago to .973 for Detroit, are higher than those in the three previous models. Increases in staff in the finance agencies studied, then, occur exponentially, but the rate of exponential growth tends to slow over time.

The extensiveness of formal organization for finance functions increases over time at an increasing rate, but a second-order linear rather than a exponential model fits patterns of growth best for two of the three cities. Table 4.2 displays estimates in which numbers of organizational units are

Table 4.1
Regressions of Size (Y) on Year (x_1) and Year^2 (x_2)

	Model: $Y = x_0 + b_1x_1$	
Chicago (1907–1975)	$Y = 55.44 + 10.14x_1$**	$R^2 = .887$
Detroit (1899–1975)	$Y = -155.4 + 11.81x_1$**	$R^2 = .960$
Philadelphia (1893–1975)	$Y = 57.5 + 14.89x_1$**	$R^2 = .873$
	Model: $Y = x_0 + b_1x_1 + b_2x_2$	
Chicago (1907–1975)	$Y = 104.5 + 2.73x_1 + 0.74x_2$**	$R^2 = .902$
Detroit (1899–1975)	$Y = 137.8 + 10.8x_1$** $+ .010x_2$	$R^2 = .960$
Philadelphia (1893–1975)	$Y = 239.2 + 3.15x_1 + .130x_2$**	$R^2 = .905$
	Model: $\log x_{10} Y = x_0 + b_1x_1$	
Chicago (1907–1975)	$\log_{10} Y = 2.08 + .010x_1$**	$R^2 = .901$
Detroit (1899–1975)	$\log_{10} Y = 1.56 + .019x_1$**	$R^2 = .897$
Philadelphia (1893–1975)	$\log_{10} Y = 2.36 + .010x_1$**	$R^2 = .938$
	Model: $\log_{10} Y = x_0 + b_1x_1 + b_2x_2$	
Chicago (1907–1975)	$\log_{10} Y = 1.97 + .016x_1$** $- .0001x_2$*	$R^2 = .908$
Detroit (1899–1975)	$\log_{10} Y = 1.09 + .044x_1$** $- .0003x_2$**	$R^2 = .973$
Philadelphia (1893–1975)	$\log_{10} Y = 2.36 + .010x_1$** $- .0000x_2$	$R^2 = .938$

* $p < .05$
** $p < .01$

regressed on year. For Detroit and Philadelphia, the best fits are obtained when total numbers of units are estimated as a function of year and the square of year. The R^2's for this model, shown in the second panel of Table 4.2, are .934 and .902 for the two cities respectively. For Chicago, however, the best fit obtains in a model estimating the logarithm of total units to the base ten as a function of year and the square of year. The R^2 for this model, shown in the fourth panel of Table 4.2 is .915. Whether the second-order linear or exponential model best fits growth in bureaucratic organization is perhaps less important than the fact that such growth characterizes the systems under study and accelerates rather than abates over time.

Table 4.2
Regressions of Total Structure (Z) on Year (x_1) and Year^2 (x_2)

	Model: $Z = x_0 + b_1x_1$	
Chicago (1890–1975)	$Z = -3.46 + .689x_1{**}$	$R^2 = .909$
Detroit (1890–1975)	$Z = -7.06 + .624x_1{**}$	$R^2 = .821$
Philadelphia (1890–1975)	$Z = -3.78 + .737x_1{**}$	$R^2 = .676$

	Model: $Z = x_0 + b_1x_1 + b_2x_2$	
Chicago (1890–1975)	$Z = -.539 + .480x_1{**} + .003x_2{*}$	$R^2 = .915$
Detroit (1890–1975)	$Z = 5.34 - .261x_1{**} + .010x_2{**}$	$R^2 = .934$
Philadelphia (1890–1975)	$Z = 13.5 + .500x_1{**} + .015x_2{**}$	$R^2 = .806$

	Model: $\log_{10}Z = x_0 + b_1x_1$	
Chicago (1890–1975)	$\log_{10}Z = .623 + .015x_1{**}$	$R^2 = .918$
Detoit (1890–1975)	$\log_{10}Z = .412 + .016x_1{**}$	$R^2 = .908$
Philadelphia (1890–1975)	$\log_{10}Z = .791 + .012x_1{**}$	$R^2 = .706$

	Model: $\log_{10}Z = x_0 + b_1x_1 + b_2x_2$	
Chicago (1890–1975)	$\log_{10}Z = .478 + .026x_1{**} - .0001x_2{**}$	$R^2 = .947$
Detroit (1890–1975)	$\log_{10}Z = 4.70 + .012x_1{**} + .0001x_2{*}$	$R^2 = .912$
Philadelphia (1890–1975)	$\log_{10}Z = .939 + .001x_1 + 0001x_2{**}$	$R^2 = .744$

* $p < .05$
** $p < .01$

Time-Dependence of Change

Growth in formal organization is the result of an excess of births over deaths of units. Here, annual probabilities of birth – the proportion of units existing in a year that were not in existence the previous year – and of death – the proportion of units in any year that do not continue until the next year – are considered as functions of chronological time.[5] Several questions are raised

---

[5] Annual probabilities of birth and death are similar but not identical to transition rates, which are estimated in some of the chapters below. The reader is referred to the explanation of transition rates at the beginning of Chapter 6.

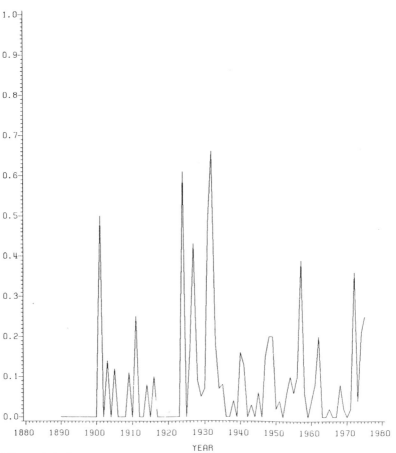

Figure 4.4a.1
Annual Probabilities of Formation of Organizational Units in Chicago

in examining these probabilities. One is whether formation of new organizational units occurs continuously or is characteristic of certain periods but not of others. A second question is whether dissolution of existing units is also a continuous process. A third question is whether rates of formation of new units exceed rates of dissolution of existing organization throughout the series or whether, contrariwise, there are identifiable "spurts" of both growth and decline despite the overall trend toward growth. Although all of these questions cannot be answered fully in this chapter, suggestive answers are possible and important to the explanation of bureaucratic growth. Should births and deaths be concentrated in short intervals, one would look to events occurring in these intervals as the causes of growth. But should

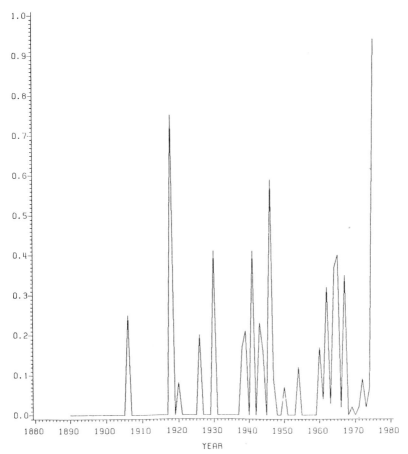

Figure 4.4a.2
Annual Probabilities of Formation of Organizational Units in Detroit

births and deaths be spread over many years if not the entire interval studied, one would seek the causes of bureaucratic growth in other than immediate events.

Annual probabilities of formation and dissolution for organizational units responsible for finance functions in Chicago, Detroit, and Philadelphia are displayed in Figure 4-4. Although there is considerable year-to-year variation in the likelihood of both births and deaths, several patterns are evident. First, both birth and death probabilities are much lower prior to 1910 than after, save for some early births in Philadelphia. Not only, then, was there relatively little formal organization in the last decade of the 19th century, but such organizations as did exist prior to 1910 had much greater stability

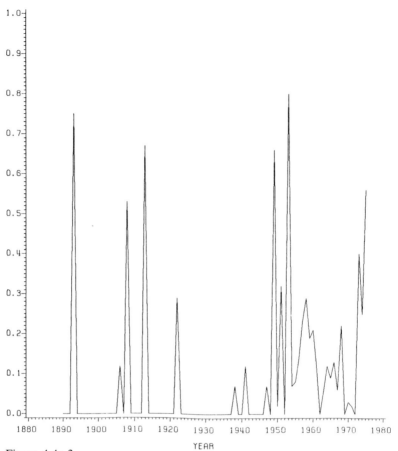

Figure 4.4a.3
Annual Probabilities of Formation of Organizational Units in Philadelphia

than organizations existing after this date.[6] This pattern is of interest because concepts of rational administration were introduced into municipal
finance functions in the first decade of this century. The development of
formal organization beyond rudimentary departmental units occurred at the
same time that ideas of rational administration took hold. Second, comparison of birth and death probabilities in Figures 4-4a and 4-4b shows the

[6] When one regresses annual birth and death probabilities on year over the 1890–1975 interval,
a significant upward trend in both of these probabilities is found in both. This trend, however,
is entirely an artifact of the difference between the pre- and post-1910 intervals. Neither from
1890 to 1909 nor from 1910 to 1975 do birth and death probabilities increase significantly. Birth
and death probabilities are, however, approximately four times higher beginning in 1910 compared to earlier.

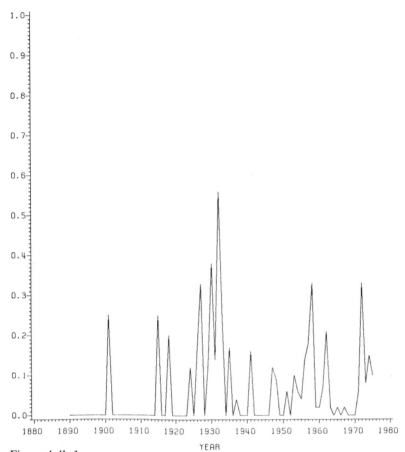

Figure 4.4b.1
Annual Probabilities of Dissolution of Organizational Units in Chicago

likelihood of births to exceed the likelihood of deaths throughout. As one would expect, given nearly continuous growth of personnel and of formal organization, there are no sustained intervals in which probabilities of dissolution exceed probabilities of formation of organizational units. Third, also as would also be expected given continuous increase in formal organization, there are many more peaks or "spikes" in birth than in death rates. For all three cities, there are twelve instances in which half or more of the organizational units with finance functions were formed in a single year. There are only three instances in which half or more of existing units were dissolved. Importantly, the peaks or "spikes" in birth probabilities are not confined to points at which finance functions were reorganized totally. Complete reorganization of departmental units managing city finances oc-

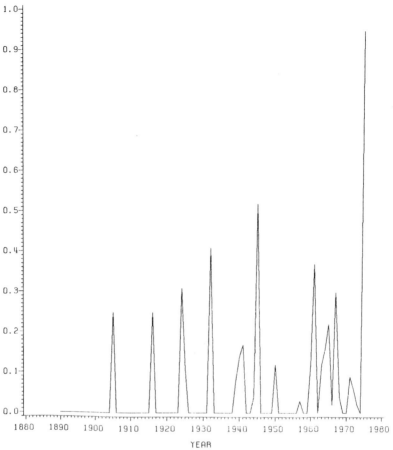

Figure 4.4b.2
Annual Probabilities of Dissolution of Organizational Units in Detroit

curred only twice – in Philadelphia in 1953 and Detroit in 1974 – in the interval covered by our series. High birth probabilities at other times reflect major additions of organization within existing departments or the creation of new departments, such as centralized purchasing departments, that did not alter patterns in existing departmental units.

Consistent with long term growth in formal organization, higher probabilities of birth than of death characterize the units studied. However, both births and deaths are low until 1910 and increase thereafter. There are no sustained intervals when probabilities of dissolution exceed probabilities of formation of individual units. And high birth rates are not confined to points at which total reorganization of finance functions occurred. These patterns

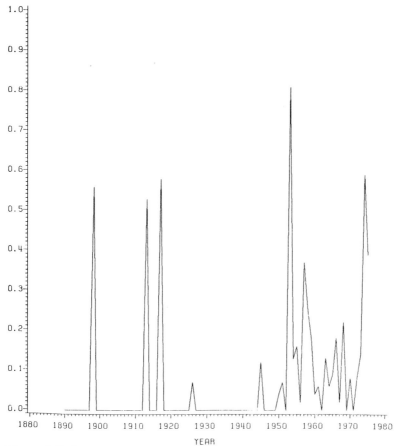

Figure 4.4b.3
Annual Probabilities of Dissolution of Organizational Units in Philadelphia

suggest that ideas about rational administration had some impact on the finance agencies studied, although how much impact is not clear. Certainly, the second decade of this century marks the point at which rapid formation of formal organization first occurred in these agencies. Whether or not the precepts of rational administration account for growth in formal organization and not only change remains to be explored.

Age-Dependence of Change

An excess of births over deaths of organizational units may be due to inertia. Once established for a few years, existing organizations may be difficult to dissolve or replace even though new units are needed to address contingen-

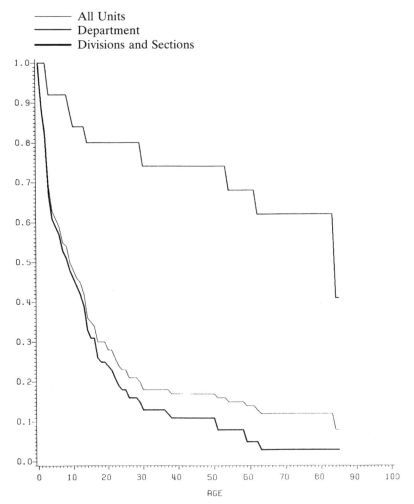

Figure 4.5a
Survival Plot for Organizational Units

cies unforseen initially. Inertia within organizations may be due to any
number of factors, including learning, sunk costs, ties with other organizations, and legitimacy. Stinchcome (1965) describes such a pattern as reflect-
ing "liabilities of newness" whereby mortality among organizations is
greatest in their first few years of existence.

As a first step in exploring descriptively the relationship of age to rates of
dissolution, survival functions for organizational units are plotted in Figure
4-5a. The vertical axis of Figure 4-5a is the percentage, running from zero to

100, of units surviving to a given age. The horizontal axis is age. Three plots are displayed in Figure 4-5a, one for all organizational units responsible for finance functions in Chicago, Detroit, and Philadelphia, one describing only departmental units in the three cities, and one describing divisions and sections. All three plots have the expected concave shape – the percentage surviving is not expected to drop linearly with age since a linear survival plot is mathematically equivalent to increasing probabilities of dissolution with age. Moreover, the survival plot for departments is substantially above that for divisions and sections. For example, 84 per sent of departments covered in the research survived to age ten and 80 per cent to twenty years of age, while 44 per cent of divisions and sections survived ten years and 34 per cent twenty years. It should be noted that there are very few deaths among units over sixty years of age. Dissolution rates above this age, especially for divisions and sections, are in effect zero. Thus while the concave shape of survival plots does not necessarily indicate that death rates decline with age, the fact that deaths are all but nonexistent among older units does suggest age-dependence.

As a second step in describing the relationship of age to organizational dissolution, logarithms of the survival curves in Figure 4-5a are plotted in Figure 4-5b. Since age-independence of death rates is equivalent to a constant probability of dying regardless of age, a linear log survival plot would indicate no effect of age on mortality. In fact, the log survival plots displayed in figure 4-4b are not linear. They are concave, indicating that the highest probabilities of dissolution hold for the youngest units. There appear to be liabilities of newness or advantages of age for the agencies studied. Age or its concomitants, then may account for the excess of births of deaths of organizational units and thus for bureaucratic growth.

Summary of Growth and Change Patterns

From 1890 through 1975, measures describing environments of agencies responsible for finance functions in Chicago, Detroit, and Philadelphia vary in different ways. City populations increase, then decrease. Real dollar expenditures and indebtedness fluctuate with economic conditions caused by war and depression. Federal and state subventions begin flowing to cities in the mid-1950's and increase until just before the series terminate in 1975. Measures of growth and change in these agencies exhibit somewhat more predictability over time. Growth of employment in finance functions is nearly continuous and is exponential; growth of formal organizational structure is also nearly continuous and is faster than linear throughout the interval covered by the research. Organizational formation and dissolution are infrequent prior to 1910, but from 1910 on probabilities of formation are higher than probabilities of dissolution. Dissolution rates for organizational

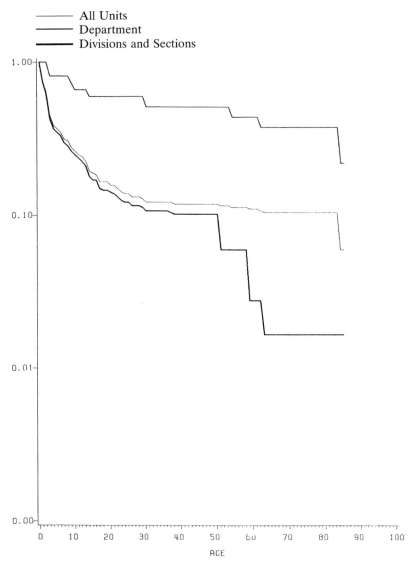

Figure 4.5b
Log Survival Plot for Organizational Units

units do decline, or appear to decline, with age, however. Survival plots indicate that older organizations are less likely to die than older ones. These surface characteristics of finance agencies are consistent with several possible models of bureaucratic growth.

4.3 Models of Growth

Three models of bureaucratic growth are developed here. Each is conceptually simple, although complicated to test, and each is consistent with the patterns of change in organizations and environments observed above. One of the models treats growth as a function of quantifiable task demands arising in the environment. The second model treats growth as a function of inertia in existing organizational units. The third model explains growth as an outcome of preferences for organization as the solution to problems arising externally, of the problem-organization-problem-more organization cycle we have hypothesized to be endemic to organizations. There is a fundamental difference between the first and the other two models. In the first model, environment and organization are isomorphic. Change in organizations follows environmental change. In the second and third models, by contrast, existing organization is retained despite shifts in the environments, and new organization is formed to accommodate change. The second and third models differ, however, with respect to the mechanisms causing retention.

Model I: *Task Determination of Bureaucratic Growth*

The idea of task determination of bureaucratic growth corresponds most closely to accepted ideas in organizational theory. Open-systems theory and to some extent the theory of organizational evolution, although not recent applications of this theory, anticipate that quantitative measures of tasks, demand for outputs, or niches in competitive environments will correspond closely to the size of organizations, and that growth in tasks, demand, or niches will yield corresponding growth in organizations. In open-systems theory, this task environment determines the size of an organization, which, in turn, gives rise to internal differentiation into subunits and sub-subunits. In evolutionary theory, niche width and variability determines both the existence and size of individual organizations. While some short-term mechanisms of persistence within organizations are recognized in evolutionary theory, demands and constraints arising in the immediate environment are ultimately determinative.[7] In both open-systems and evolutionary thinking, causality runs almost entirely from environments to organizations, and in both instances there is no possibility of long-term organizational growth or decline, whether in staff or in formal organization, absent corresponding shifts in environmental constraints or demands.

---

[7] Aldrich's (1979: ch. 8) discussion of persistence underscores the inconsistency of evolutionary theory on this point. If, in fact, evolution governs organizational populations as it is alleged to govern biotic populations, then persistence mechanisms are of little long-run consequence. If persistence mechanisms are of consequence, then evolution is an incomplete theory of organizations.

Figure 4.6a
Task Determination of Bureaucratic Growth

Figure 4-6a displays the causal paths anticipated by task determination of bureaucratic growth. The environment, which in the task model is understood mainly quantitatively, gives rise to size, and size in turn gives rise to the extensiveness of formal organization. Increases in task demands, then, are expected to yield bureaucratic growth directly, while decreases should yield decline in the task model.

Model II: *Bureaucratic Growth as an Function of Inertia*

The idea that inertia preserves existing organizations is also accepted in organizational theory, although it has not received the same sustained attention as the task model. Two differences distinguish the inertial from the task model of bureaucratic growth. One concerns the nature of environments. In the task model, environments consist mainly of quantitative demands and constraints, variation in which should cause variation in size, hence organization. In the inertial model, environments encompass other elements, such as legitimacy, vested interests, networks of association, and the like, which tend to sustain organizations for reasons having little to do with their efficiency in performing tasks. A second difference concerns the nature of organizations. The task model treats all organizations as alike. The inertial model distinguishes new from existing organizations and argues that established organizations are much more likely to survive than new ones. The notion of "liability of newness" describes the differences between new and established organizations, but it does not explain these differences.

Casually, the inertial model of bureaucratic growth argues that environments create organizations, which in turn act upon environments so as to perpetuate their existence. Environments, therefore, maintain existing organizations. But environments also create new organizations when existing units are inadequate to meet demands. Figure 4-6b shows causal paths run-

Figure 4.6b
Bureaucratic Growth as a Function of Inertia

ning from the environment to existing organizations and from existing organizations back to the environment. This causal loop denotes persistence of established units. Figure 4-6b also shows a path from the environment to the formation of new organizations as well as paths from both existing and new organizations to size. Bureaucratic growth, thus, is the outcome of accumulation of organizational units over time, the latter due to inertial processes.

The inertial model of bureaucratic growth parallels in some respects incrementalist theories of budgeting (Wildavsky, 1964), which argue that government growth occurs inevitably as new interests demand accommodation alongside established interest groups. A test of the inertial model of bureaucratic growth is, therefore, a partial test of incrementalist theory.

Model III: *Bureaucratic Growth as a Function of Preferences for Organization*

The idea that preferences for organization drive bureaucratic growth has not heretofore been explored in research but, as noted above, is suggested strongly by theory. The model of growth as a function of preferences maintains the distinction between existing and new organization made in the inertial model. But the preference model views the environment quite differently. Whereas the inertial model asserts environments to protect existing organizations, the preference model asserts environments to contain ideas about organizing as an effective means of solving problems as well as ideas about specific forms of organization appropriate to given purposes. The first and second chapters of this book presented some of the ideas about organizing that yield preferences for increased organization, and the third chapter outlined some of the organizational patterns that emerged for municipal finance functions, given preferences for organizing in response to uncertainty.

Causally, the model of bureaucratic growth as a function of preferences for organization argues that environments gave rise to existing organizations and continue to give rise to new organizations. As indicated in Figure 4-6c, the paths *from* the environment to existing and new organizations are identical in the preference and inertial models. However, the preference and

Figure 4.6c
Bureaucratic Growth as a Function of Preferences for Organization

inertial models differ as to the mechanisms sustaining existing organizations. In the inertial model, existing organizations become more closely tied over time to their environments, which in turn sustain organizations. In the preference model, new organizations sustain existing organizations because the environment views organizing as efficacious and appropriate. The inertial and preference models yield similar long-term outcomes, higher rates of formation than of dissolution of organizations hence bureaucratic growth, but they posit different causal mechanisms leading to this result. In the inertial model, there is near inevitability of growth because legitimacy and vested interests protect existing organizations. In the preference model, growth is less inevitable because its source lies ultimately in ideas about organizing, which have changed in the past and may, like the organizations they have created, change again in the future.

Testing the Models

The three models of bureaucratic growth will be tested to the extent that the data permit in the chapters below. All three are plausible given the patterns of growth and change described in this chapter. The task model holds some promise since quantitative growth in environments parallels growth in organization to some extent. The inertial model holds some promise since mortality of organizational units appears to decline with age. The preference model is also promising because high rates of formation of organizational units appeared around 1910, at the same time as concepts of rational administration gained widespread acceptance, and did not decline substantially thereafter.

Promise and proof are very different matters. The appeal of the task determination as a model of bureaucratic growth is that all of its elements are measurable and quantifiable. The size of a city, its expenditures, and its indebtedness, for example, can be entered directly into quantitative models. Inertial and preference models of growth, by contrast, posit environmental forces that may not be unobservable and certainly are not quantifiable. In order to explore these models, environments must be inferred from behavior of organizations that is observable and quantifiable. The reader's forbearance with this approach is asked. There is no reasonable alternative given that the environmental forces posited in the inertial model – vested interests, legitimacy, and the like – cannot be recovered from historical sources, and given that the environmental forces posited in preference model – organization as a solution to problems – are so pervasive as to be invariant over much of the interval studied. Thus, while the theories addressed in this book describe ultimately interactions between organizations and their environments, much of the quantitative analysis used to test these theories focuses on organizations themselves.

Chapter 5
Task Environments and the Growth of Bureaucracy

This chapter explores the proposition that task demands determine the size of bureaucratic organizations. Organizational theory maintains that, in general, environments rather than internal processes ultimately govern organizations. Various mechanisms through which environments operate are specified in theory. One such mechanism is adaptation, the shifting of personnel and resources and rearrangement of administrative structures to match changes arising externally. Conventional open-systems theories (Thompson, 1967; Katz and Kahn, 1978) treat adaptation as the principal source of change in organizations. Another environmental mechanism is selection, i.e., births and deaths of organizations. Selection theory argues that organizations have less flexibility than is indicated by the adaptation model of change (Hannan and Freeman, 1977). Because organizations cannot change, many units go out of existence and are replaced by others whose fit to the environment is better. A third environmental mechanism is representation or institutionalization, the process whereby organizations are constructed so as to conform with expectations defining how they ought reasonably to appear (Meyer and Rowan, 1977). Adaptation theory assumes organizations to act rationally to accommodate the environment, selection theory makes no assumptions about the rationality of organizational action, while institutional theories of organizations direct attention to maintaining legitimacy, which is fundamentally non-rational.

Whatever the mechanisms promoting change in organizations, and whatever the rationality of organizational action, most theories of environmental determination are consistent with the hypothesis that, other things being equal, bureaucratic size is a function of task demands. The adaptation model, for example, suggests close correspondences between measures of task or workload and size. The selection model suggests several kinds of possible task environment-organization correspondences. One is derived from economic theory: Whether among firms or within complex bureaucratic structures, overstaffed units will be replaced by leaner ones, leading to a balance between task or workload and staff (Penrose, 1959). Another correspondence suggested by the selection model links variability in the environment to slack or excess capacity in organizations: The wider the range of environmental fluctuations, that is, the greater the range of possible task demands, the greater the diversity required within organizations hence the greater the excess capacity at any point in time (Hannan and Freeman, 1977; Aldrich, 1979: 56–61). Even the institutional model predicts task determination of organizations in some respects. Institutional theory views correspondences between environments and organizations as principally symbolic hence the size of bureaucracy more a function of categories of activity deemed obligatory for rational action than of task demands arising externally (Meyer and Rowan, 1977). To the extent that organizational categories can be quantified, they can be treated as indicators of tasks and their relationship to size ascertained.

One might imagine that, given its simplicity and its centrality to the ideas about environmental determination, the relationship of quantitative task demands to quantifiable dimensions of organizations, especially size, would have been explored fully in both theory and research. This is not the case. To be sure, theorizing about firms has recognized the existence of task environments relevant to goal setting and attainment (Dill, 1958) and of expectations concerning task demands that shape behavior (Cyert and March, 1963: 84–99). Taxonomies of environments, however, rarely mention much less take systematic account of environmental variations in demand (see reviews of such taxonomies in Katz and Kahn: 1978: 124–30; Pfeffer and Salancik, 1978: 63–68; Aldrich, 1979: 63–70). And the resource-dependence perspective, which might seem logically to link organizational size to task demands, focuses instead on the consequences of power – control over resources – for the actions of organizations (Pfeffer, 1983).

Research studies, like theory, have focused only slightly on correspondences between task measures and organizational size. In some instances, the two are treated as inseparable, and their relationship is left unexplored. Blau and Schoenherr (1971), for example, found community size and the size of employment security agencies to be so highly correlated that the latter – size – became a surrogate for the extensiveness of tasks. In other instances, research has shown inconsistent effects of task demand on size. Meyer (1979) found substantial correlations between task measures and the size of local finance agencies at two time points, but he also found these correlations to decrease over time such that, longitudinally, task demand was associated with declining size. And in still other instances, no effects of task measures on size have been found. Fennell (1980) found the range of hospital facilities, which was in turn a strong predictor of hospital size, to be mainly a function of physician's and administrators' preferences and not significantly related to patient characteristics. Research focusing on organizational processes but not specifically on environments also suggests no consistent relationship between task demands and size. Economies of scale in administration (Blau, 1970) indicate that organizational growth should occur at decreasing rates as task demands increase. Decreasing administrative overhead with supervisors's experience (Pfeffer et al., 1983) suggests that organizational learning should yield slower growth in size than in tasks over time. But the ratchet pattern of bureaucratic growth whereby administration increases with workload but does not decrease when work is slack (Freeman and Hannan, 1975) suggests a different outcome, namely more rapid increases in size than in tasks.

In short, while most models of environmental determination are consistent with the hypothesis that size follows from task demands, theory has been for the most part inattentive to this relationship. Research studies have also not been centrally concerned with effects of environments on size. Research on organizational processes suggests that economies of scale and learning may yield slower growth in size than in tasks, but that persistent increases in administration may yield faster growth in size than in tasks. In short, little is known about the conditions under which correspondences of task measures with size do and do not hold.

The central question to be explored in the chapter is to what extent bureaucratic growth is, in fact, due to variations in task environments, and, by implication, to what extent size is due to other causes, principally inertia and institutional constraints. It is acknowledged that bureaucratic systems are limited ultimately by available resources: The environment will at some point control growth if only because budgets cannot exhaust societal wealth. But short of this extreme where the proposition that environments determine organizations becomes truism, there remains the question of whether the proximate causes of growth lie in task elements or elsewhere, or, alternatively, when the proximate causes of growth lie in task demands and when they lie elsewhere. Contemporary organizational theory, much in contrast to early case studies that focused almost entirely on behavior within organizations, very much favors environmental explanations, especially those linking tangible organizational outcomes to tangible forces operating externally. It does so, in part, because alternatives to the environmental model are not stated in ways that allow them to be tested easily. Precisely this reason requires that the impact of task environments on size be tested before alternative explanations for growth are pursued.

This chapter is organized as follows: To begin, the description of growth in the finance functions of Chicago, Detroit, and Philadelphia developed in the previous chapter is reviewed. The issues posed by exponential increases in size are then addressed. Separating the effects of task measures from other possible causes of bureaucratic size, especially time itself and antecedent or constant conditions, becomes difficult in that increases in size are nearly constant over time. Models treating the total size of all organizational units with finance responsibilities in the three cities as a function of various quantitative indicators of the task environment are then estimated. While most task indicators bear strong relationships to size during the interval preceding 1933, such relationships decline to nonsignificance later. Models of size as a function of qualitative changes in the environment likewise yield mainly degenerate results with one exception: Bankruptcy halted (but did not reverse) growth of Detroit's finance functions during the Depression years. Possible effects on growth of changes in municipal budgeting and financial reporting, almost all of which occurred in the post-World War II era, are then reviewed but not estimated quantitatively. Alternatives to the task environment explanation of bureaucratic growth are discussed in conclusion.

5.1 The Problem of Exponential Growth

In the previous chapter, growth of the agencies responsible for finance functions in Chicago, Detroit, and Philadelphia was shown to be a function of year. Linear size increased at an increasing rate with time; the logarithm of size increased steadily with time for each of the four cities, although the rate of increased declined somewhat in the later years. Not only could long-term growth be described by a simple model of the logarithm of size as a function of time, but this model fit the data very well. Overall, more than ninety per cent of the variance in size was accounted for by time.

The very high correlation of time with size is consistent with several alternative explanations of growth. Exponential increase in size (or straight-line increase in the logarithm of size) could be caused by other variables also increasing exponentially with time. For example, uninterrupted increase in task demands could account for the high correlation of size with time. Exponential increases in size could, alternatively, be caused by a bureaucratic tendency never to eliminate organizational positions. To the extent that administrative positions ratchet upward because once in place none can be removed, time is a surrogate for the growth process. Alternatively, exponential growth could be a function of history, which may have placed the agencies studied on a growth trajectory, or of forces pressing continuously for increasing size, such as the management objective of growth. Choosing among these explanations creates some difficulties, however. The effects of elements associated with time, such as task demands, and of time itself may be inseparable due to multicollinearity, while the effects of constant properties of organizations, whether they lie in history or in organizations themselves, may be indetectable because they are invariant.

In this chapter, the size of the organizational systems studied will be estimated as a function of task measures. Time appears both explicitly and implicitly in these models, but only as a control. Its effects, where they are explicit, are not interpreted causally. Constant properties of the units studied are only implicit in the models tested below. In subsequent chapters, effects of time and of constant conditions will be estimated, but only after the mechanisms through which they are hypothesized to operate are specified and introduced explicitly as causes of bureaucratic growth.

Time appears in the models below in several ways. First, since the plots of environmental variables and size displayed in the previous chapter suggest growth and increases in environmental measures to correspond in some intervals but to diverge in others, the series are broken into segments that represent different historical eras. The first era runs from 1907 through 1932, corresponding approximately to the Progressive era, World War I, and the post-World War I years. (Because of incomplete series, years before 1907 are excluded from this analysis.) The second era covers the Depression, New Deal, and World War II, and post-World War II era, from 1933 through 1952. The third era begins in 1953 and runs to the end of the series, covering the period in which cities became increasingly dependent on Federal grants for housing and urban renewal and, beginning in 1970, on unrestricted Federal revenue sharing funds. No claim is made that the breaks between 1932 and 1933 and between 1952 and 1953 represent the only points of fundamental change in the series. Rather, these are points of significant change when definitions of tasks hence relations between task environmental measures and bureaucratic growth can be expected also to have changed.

Time is entered into some of the models of bureaucratic growth below as a surrogate for continuous environmental pressures for growth. As will be shown presently, time or year is the only continuous variable predicting growth consistently across the three cities. Effects of elements varying discontinuously, such as the Great Depression, can be estimated only after causes of size operating continuously are controlled. Since variables other than time have either intermittent or nil effects on size, the variable time represents the continuous causes of growth when estimating effects of discontinuous variables.

5.2 Effects of Task Measures on Bureaucratic Size

The effects of task measures on the size of municipal finance functions in Chicago, Detroit, and Philadelphia are now estimated. Models treating size as a function of task measures varying continuously are considered first.

Table 5.1
Simple GLS Regressions of Log_{10} Size on Measures of Demand (Constants Omitted)

	1907–1932	1933–1952	1953–1975
Chicago			
Log_{10} Population	1.845**	8.164**	—1.592**
Expenditures · 10^{-5}	.076**	.076#	.057*
Indebtedness · 10^{-5}	.016	.048	.014
Budget Pages · 10^{-2}	.025	.466**	.045**
Federal/State $ · 10^{-5}	–	–	.076*
Year	.017**	.016**	.008**
Detroit			
Log_{10} Population	1.374**	3.521**	—1.089**
Expenditures · 10^{-5}	.235**	.042	.033#
Indebtedness · 10^{-5}	.126**	2.079	.046*
Budget Pages · 10^{-2}	.553**	.001	.060
Federal/State $ · 10^{-5}	–	–	.035
Year	.037**	.015**	.006**
Philadelphia			
Log_{10} Population	2.251**	4.644**	—5.842**
Expenditures · 10^{-5}	.007	.010	.009
Indebtedness · 10^{-5}	.030**	—.008	.048#
Budget Pages · 10^{-2}	.128[a]	.119**	—.016*
Federal/State $ · 10^{-5}	–	–	—.024
Year	.012**	.008**	.005#
Three Cities			
Log_{10} Population	1.520**	4.160**	—1.285**
Expenditures · 10^{-5}	.065**	.016	.018*
Indebtedness · 10^{-5}	.025**	.004	.010
Budget Pages · 10^{-2}	.336**[a]	.003	—.000
Federal/State $ · 10^{-5}	–	–	.024
Year	.016**	.013**	.007**

# $p < .1$
* $p < .05$
** $p < .01$
[a]   1919–1932 only

Attention then turns to the impact of qualitative shifts in task environments on size.

Effects of Continuous Task Measures

The effects of continuous measures describing the task environments of finance agencies are estimated in three different ways. To begin, size is treated *within each city* as a function of each of the task measures taken one of a time. Series for the three cities are then pooled, and a separate generalized least squares regression is used to estimate the effect of each of the task measures, again singly, on size. Finally, all continuous task measures are included in a single regression model estimating size. In all instances, models are estimated separately for the three historical intervals described above. While several of the continuous task measures had statistically significant effects on size over the entire 1907–1975 interval, these effects proved nonsignificant in most instances once observations preceding 1933 were removed from consideration.

Effects of Task Measures Entered Singly into Models

Table 5.1 displays simple generalized least squares regressions of five task measures and year on the logarithm of size – the number of positions budgeted for municipal finance functions – for the three intervals. One regression is estimated for each of the task measures for each of the three historical intervals. The uppermost three panels of the table display separate regressions for each of the three cities, while the lowest panel displays a single estimate in which observations for the three cities are pooled. Not displayed in Table 5.1 are the constants terms in regression equations. Also not displayed in the lowest panel of the table are coefficients of dummy variables for two of the three cities (Chicago and Detroit) in the pooled regressions. The effects of the task measures should be described seriatim.

– Effects of population. The total size of finance functions increases significantly (at the .05 level or below) with city population in the 1907–1932 and 1933–1952 intervals but decreases with population in the 1953–1975 interval. These effects hold within all three cities and in the pooled regression of population on size.

– Effects of municipal expenditures. In the 1907–1932 interval, size increases significantly with real dollar expenditures[1] for two of the three cities. From 1933 to 1952, there are no significant effects of expenditures on size; in the interval beginning in 1953, real dollar expenditures increase size significantly for Chicago only. In the pooled regression, real dollar expenditures affect size significantly only in the 1907–1932 interval.

– Effects of municipal indebtedness. In the 1907–1932 interval, size increases significantly with real dollar indebtedness for two of the three cities. As with expenditures, there are no significant effects of indebtedness in the 1933–1952 interval. In the interval beginning in 1953, indebtedness increases size significantly in Detroit only. In the pooled regression, real dollar indebtedness affects size significantly only in the 1907–1932 interval.

– Effects of budget pages. Numbers of pages in municipal budgets are considered to be a crude measure – no adjustment, for example, is made for

---

[1] As noted in the previous chapter, municipal expenditures and indebtedness are adjusted by an implicit deflator series in which 1958 = 100, i.e., a 1958 dollar is valued at 100 cents.

type size – of the complexity of task demands facing finance agencies. No consistent pattern of effects of budget pages on size appears in the models estimated separately for each city. Size increases significantly with budget pages for only one city in the 1907–1932 interval but for two cities from 1933 to 1952. From 1953 though 1975, however, budget pages increases size in Chicago, has no effect in Detroit, and decreases size in Philadelphia. In the pooled regressions, a significant effect of budget pages on size appears only in the first historical period, which is confined to the 1919–1932 interval in this instance because Philadelphia had only scattered appropriation ordinances but no single budget document prior to 1919.

– Effects of Federal and state subventions. As noted above, Federal and state funds flowed to municipalities in significant amounts beginning in 1953. For Chicago, Federal and state aid measured in constant dollars is significantly associated with the logarithm of size in the 1953–1975 interval. Federal and state funds have no significant impact, however, on the size of finance functions in Detroit and Philadelphia.

– Effects of Year. Year is a surrogate for variables increasing linearly with time and causing the logarithm of size to increase (or size to increase exponentially). Year, or time, is not considered a causal variable, but it should be recognized that the variables for which Year is a surrogate may not admit of more direct measurement. The estimates in Table 5.1 show size to increase with Year consistently across the three cities and over time. Indeed, Year is the only variable appearing in Table 5.1 that increases size consistently across cities and over time. The effects of Year, or elements increasing linearly with Year, on size decrease somewhat over time in both the regressions for individual cities and the pooled regression. Year remains statistically significant in all instances, however, save for Philadelphia in the 1953–1975 interval when its significance is at the .1 level.

Overall, the simple GLS regressions indicate task measures to increase size in the 1907–1932 interval but not to increase size consistently thereafter. Year, which is a surrogate for variables increasing linearly but not measured directly, increases size throughout. Task elements appear to govern the size of bureaucratic systems only in the earliest historical period for which data are available. Whether this pattern is due to historical shifts that propelled size independently of task demands after 1932, or whether it is an artifact of age whereby bureaucracies are more open to environments at the time of formation than later cannot be determined from these data.

Effects of Multiple Task Measures

Table 5.2 displays the results from three generalized least squares models in which the measures of task demands are introduced simultaneously. The upper panel of the Table contains results of estimating of multiple task

Table 5.2
Multiple GLS Regressions of Log_{10} Size on Measures of Demand (Constants Omitted)

	1907–1932	1933–1952	1953–1975
Chicago			
Log_{10} Population	1.585**	3.844**	—.377
Expenditures $\cdot$ 10^{-5}	.030*	.069*	.045*
Indebtedness $\cdot$ 10^{-5}	—.018	.010	—.013
Budget Pages $\cdot$ 10^{-2}	–	.101	.028#
Federal/State \$ $\cdot$ 10^{-5}	–	–	.034
Detroit			
Log_{10} Population	.655**	.377	—.645
Expenditures $\cdot$ 10^{-5}	.099*	.037*	.045
Indebtedness $\cdot$ 10^{-5}	.037#	—0.32**	.025
Budget Pages $\cdot$ 10^{-5}	–	—.068**	.069#
Federal/State \$ $\cdot$ 10^{-5}	–	–	—.044
Philadelphia			
Log_{10} Population	1.364**	5.270*	—5.686**
Expenditures $\cdot$ 10^{-5}	.003	—.009	.006
Indebtedness $\cdot$ 10^{-5}	.021**	—.019*	.007
Budget Pages $\cdot$ 10^{-2}	–	.073	—.014#
Federal/State \$ $\cdot$ 10^{-5}	–	–	—.115
Three Cities, Omitting Year			
Chicago	—.469**	—1.325**	.002
Detroit	—.103*	.082	—.327**
Log_{10} Population	1.252**	4.444**	—1.053**
Expenditures $\cdot$ 10^{-5}	.020**	.013	.013
Indebtedness $\cdot$ 10^{-5}	.021**	.005*	.008
Budget Pages $\cdot$ 10^{-2}	–[a]	.004	—.002
Federal/State \$ $\cdot$ 10^{-5}	–	–	—.001
Three Cities, Including Year			
Chicago	—20.828**	—9.479*	—19.654**
Detroit	—83.866**	—2.491	—17.114*
Log_{10} Population	—.899**	1.947*	1.074
Expenditures $\cdot$ 10^{-5}	.016*	.015	.007
Indebtedness $\cdot$ 10^{-5}	.020**	.005*	.003
Budget Pages $\cdot$ 10^{-2}	–[a]	.005	—.010#
Federal/State \$ $\cdot$ 10^{-5}	–	–	—.038*
Year	.011**	.007**	.004#
Chicago $\cdot$ Year	.011**	.005#	.010**
Detroit $\cdot$ Year	.043**	.001	.009*

# $p < .1$
* $p < .05$
** $p < .01$
[a] Not estimated for 1907–1932. For 1919–1932 interval, budget pages was not significant in multiple regressions of log_{10} size on measures of demand.

demands *within* each city. The middle and lower panels display pooled regressions indicating the effects of multiple task demands across the three cities. The effects of Year on the growth of size are omitted from the models displayed in the upper and center panels, but Year (and interaction of city with Year) is included in the model displayed in the lower panel of the table.

The upper panel confirms the inconsistent effects of task demands on organizational size within each city found in Table 5.1. For Chicago, expenditures increase size in the first and third time intervals, population is a significant predictor of size in the first two intervals, and budget pages and Federal and state revenues are barely significant predictors of size in the third interval. In Detroit, all task demands, with the exception of population, have significant effects in the first two intervals, but no task demand has a strongly significant effect in the third interval. Population has a significant effect across the three intervals in Philadelphia, although its impact is negative rather than positive in the third interval. Indebtedness also changes from a significant positive to a negative effect from the first to the second interval in Philadelphia.

These results are summarized in the pooled regressions in the middle panel of Table 5.2. Here it can be seen that task demands had significant effects from 1907 to 1932, but little impact thereafter. Population appears to have significant effects across the three time periods, but comparison of these results with the upper panel indicates that the significant effect of population on growth in the third interval is due mainly to its large negative coefficient in Philadelphia.

It might be suspected that the strong effects of population are but artifacts for upward growth in other unspecified variables, at least in the first two intervals when population was increasing uniformly in all three cities. To account for the effects of simple upward growth, Year is included in the pooled regression displayed in the lower panel of Table 5.2. As suspected, using Year as a surrogate for variables causing upward growth produces significant effects for Year across the three time periods. The coefficient of population now reflects the effects of population net of upward growth and is rendered less significant than before as a predictor of organizational growth in the second and third intervals. Additionally, there are significant differences between the three cities in the rate of upward growth net of other variables in the first and third, but not in the second, intervals. We cannot explain differences in rates of upward growth in the first interval. In the third interval, however, fiscal and organizational turmoil in Philadelphia caused substantial variation, both upward and downward, in employment in the city's finance functions in the late 1960's and early 1970's.

In sum, the effects of task demands tended to be more consistently significant in the earliest time period, from 1907 to 1932, than later. Year, as a surrogate for upward growth net of measured task demands, had significant effects in all three intervals. The effects of task measures entered simultaneously into models are similar to effects of the same measures entered singly, as discussed above.

Qualitative Shifts in Task Environments

Possible effects of qualitative or discrete shifts in environments altering the tasks of municipal finance agencies are now examined. Four kinds of changes are explored qualitatively. These include accession of a new mayor, the period of the Great Depression, implementation of civil service or merit personnel systems, and imposition of municipal wage or income taxes. In each case, the maintained hypothesis is that these discrete changes in environments account to some extent for the impact of Year on size hence the trend toward bureaucratic growth. Thus, new mayors might be expected to add staff, the Depression to shrink staffs or hold them at unusually low levels such that growth occurred rapidly with economic recovery, and civil service and income taxes to increase both numbers of as well as the rate of increase of staff. Almost none of these expectations are confirmed by the data at hand.

The generalized least squares regressions displayed in Table 5.3 estimate the logarithm of size as a function of Year, dummy variables representing points at which qualitative shifts occurred or during which environments differed qualitatively from earlier intervals, and the interaction of the dummy variables with Year. The variable "new mayor," for example, was coded one during the first year of each mayor's term of office and zero otherwise. The "Depression" variable is coded one for the years 1930 through 1940 and zero otherwise. Civil service or merit personnel systems existed from 1912 on in Detroit, from 1951 to the present in Philadelphia, and not at all in Chicago; the "civil service" variable is coded one for years when such personnel systems were in place. Municipal income or wage taxes were enacted permanently in 1939 in Philadelphia and in 1962 in Detroit; the "income tax" dummy variable is coded one beginning in these years.

The dummy variables describing qualitative changes in environments and their interactions with Year have little significant impact on patterns of growth. The regressions in the uppermost panel of Table 5.3 show accession of a new mayor not to affect the size of finance functions at all in Chicago and Detroit. In Philadelphia, however, changes in administration increase size by an amount that approaches statistical significance and decrease slightly the yearly growth rate for finance functions. The Depression has no effect on growth patterns for Chicago and Philadelphia. Growth of Detroit's

Table 5.3
Effects of Qualitative Changes on Log_{10} Size

	Chicago	Detroit	Philadelphia
Constant	2.274**	1.869**	2.531**
Year	.010**	.017**	.009**
New Mayor	—.006	.002	.016#
New Mayor · Year	—.001	—.000	—.001*
Constant	2.241**	1.865**	2.532**
Year	.010**	.170**	.009**
Depression	—.121	.498**	.017
Depression · Year	.005	—.014*	—.000
Constant	–	1.760**	2.529**
Year	–	.050*	.009**
Civil Service	–	.175	.130
Civil Service · Year	–	—.034	—.002
Constant	–	1.812**	2.525**
Year	–	.021**	.010**
Income Tax	–	1.120#	.009
Income Tax · Year	–	—.021*	—.001

\# $p < .1$
* $p < .05$
** $p < .01$

finance functions did cease during the Depression years, more likely than not due to the city's bankruptcy in 1937 that forced both financial and administrative consolidation. The interaction of year with the Depression dummy variable has a coefficient of $-.014$, which is significant and which when added to the long-term growth rate of .017 yields virtually flat size for the ten-year interval. Civil service has no effect on the size of finance functions for either Detroit or Philadelphia, nor does Philadelphia's wage tax. The income tax enacted in Detroit in 1962 appears to flatten rather than accelerate growth of finance functions; in all likelihood both the tax and declining rates of growth are responses to fiscal stringencies.

With one exception, then, qualitative environmental shifts either bear no significant relationship to growth of municipal finance functions or yield unexpected changes in growth patterns. The exception, the impact of the Great Depression in Detroit, is of some interest. It suggests, first, that some events do interrupt long-term patterns of growth, but, second, that bureaucratic growth may be interrupted only by events that are truly catastrophic, such as governmental bankruptcy. Absent events of such magnitude, shifts in task environments may have little impact on long-term growth patterns. The pervasive impact of Year or time is not reduced when changes in ad-

Table 5.4
Innovations in Municipal Budgeting

	Chicago	Detroit	Philadelphia
Proposed vs. enacted budget	1957	1974	1953
This year vs. last year	1957	1974	1953
Activity descriptions	1957	1974	1953
Justification for new items	1957	1974	1956
Performance budgeting	1957	1974	1958
Program budgeting	–	–	1968

ministration, civil service regulations, or in revenue sources are introduced into models explaining the size of bureaucratic systems, but its impact is removed temporarily by municipal bankruptcy triggered by the Depression.

Recent Innovations in Budgeting

The information contained in municipal budgets and financial statements increased substantially over the interval covered by this research. Much of this increase is in the number of items or "lines" in budgets and is captured, albeit imperfectly, in the number of pages in budget documents. Some of the increase, however, is in the amount of information provided for each budget item or "line." The simplest budgets, which were common until the 1950's, indicated only the personnel and expenditures allotted to each function or organizational unit. These are called line item budgets. Beginning in the early 1950's, however, additional information was attached to each item of expenditure. Public budgets, for example, began to reflect differences between proposed and enacted expenditures. Comparison of proposed with previous years' actual expenditures were added as were descriptions of the responsibilities of each organizational unit, discursive justifications for new budget items, and costs per unit for each activity undertaken by municipal agencies, the last known as performance budgeting.[2] Some localities followed the Federal model by developing full program budgets in which expenditures are classified at four levels of specificity – program, sub-program, element, and sub-element – as well as on a line item basis.

Table 5.4 displays dates at which some major innovations in municipal budgeting were adopted in Chicago, Detroit, and Philadelphia. These innovations were implemented simultaneously in 1955 in Chicago and in 1974

---

[2] For example, performance budgets state the average cost of fingerprinting a prisoner, the per acre cost of mowing median strips in expressways, and the average cost of replacing a street-lamp fixture.

in Detroit. During these years, budget staffs in Chicago and Detroit also became responsible directly to mayors rather than to department heads. In Philadelphia, budgeting innovation occurred more gradually, culminating in massive (and largely inpenetrable) program budgets of the late 1960's and early 1970's. The innovations listed in Table 5.4 occurred relatively late in the time series when the growth of finance functions slowed somewhat compared to earlier years. For this reason, all would appear to diminish growth rather than to increase it. Since budget innovations contribute substantially to organizational process, one might expect them to accelerate growth, consistent with the discussion in the third chapter.

One possibility that is suggested but cannot be proved from the data at hand is that recent budgeting innovations, like earlier budgeting innovations, were both consequences and causes of growth. Historically, growth occurred in all municipal functions, not only finance, and such growth may have been disproportionate to task demands. Certainly, growth in municipal services was disproportionate to revenues in the post-World War II years. By 1975, both Detroit and Philadelphia suffered extreme fiscal stringencies, and Chicago's finances were found to be in disarray after the death of Mayor Daley. Almost all of the innovations listed in Table 5.4 can be understood as means of limiting expenditures or, at a minimum, of drawing attention to new items of expenditure and significant increases over previous years' budgets. Similarly, centralization of responsibility for preparing city budgets can be understood as an effort on the part of mayors to exercise greater control over increasingly scarce resources. To be sure, the innovations in budgeting adopted in the three cities studies also reflect fad and fashion in organizational design, or what DiMaggio and Powell (1983) call "institutional isomorphism." It is nonetheless possible that their intended if not actual purpose was to slow growth in services and expenditures, and it is clearly the case that they did not cause any immediate acceleration of growth of municipal finance functions.

Summary of Results

Task measures predict the size of bureaucratic systems inconsistently. From 1907 through 1932, continuous measures of task demand such as municipal population, real dollar expenditures, and real dollar indebtedness are associated with size, and the effects of task measures hold when all are entered simultaneously into a single equation predicting size. From 1933 on, however, continuous task measures predict size poorly or not at all. Qualitative or discrete shifts in task environments such as changes in municipal administration, adoption of civil service, and imposition of city income or wage taxes also have little or no effect on size or rates at which size increases over time. For one city, Detroit, one qualitative change, the Great Depression, did halt bureaucratic growth. In all likelihood, this occurred because of municipal bankruptcy.

One variable predicting size consistently across the three cities and over time is Year. Other things controlled, the size of finance functions in Chicago, Detroit, and Philadelphia tends to increase each year. Possible explanations for this outcome need to be explored in some detail. Such explanations will be pursued in the concluding section of this chapter.

5.3 Conclusion: Why does Year cause Growth?

The empirical results developed above admit of no simple interpretation, and it may be that no single interpretation of them can be demonstrated unambiguously to hold. Growth of finance functions in Chicago, Detroit, and Philadelphia is more a function of Year, of time itself, than of indicators of task demand that were captured in this research. But Year, or time, is not a sufficient explanation for growth, for it points to no underlying cause of persistent augmentation of staff. Causes of growth other than the task measures used above that would yield exponential or nearly exponential growth over time must therefore be considered. Three possible causes of exponential growth are reviewed here. One is peoples' preferences for growth, which generate pressure for larger budgets and staffs. Another is age, which can render existing programs and bureaucratic units more difficult to displace with time. A third is a preference for new organizations, which differs from a preference for growth in existing organizations in that new organizations shift tasks not only quantitatively but also qualitatively.

Individual Preferences as an Explanation for Growth

Other things being equal, organizational growth can be assumed to be preferred to constancy or decline. Certainly, this assumption is embedded in economists' accounts of firm behavior (see especially Penrose, 1959), and there is no reason to believe that public bureaucracies differ substantially from firms in this respect (see, in particular, Tullock's [1965] account of bureaucratic empire-building). But because growth is preferred to its alternatives does not mean that growth always ensues, at least among firms. Quite the opposite, what evidence is available shows that the vast majority of business enterprises to be small, to have failed to grow (Aldrich, 1979; Carroll, 1983). And firms that have grown have almost always done so in proportion to demand for their products or services. The data on municipal finance functions do not indicate whether a higher proportion of public agencies than of private firms actually realize their preferences for growth. But they do show finance agencies' growth to have exceeded demands for their outputs, at least those outputs that can be measured reliably over time.

The crucial question, then, is not whether preferences drive bureaucratic growth but why preferences for growth are possibly less constrained by task demands in bureaus than in firms. The answers to this question will occupy much of the remainder of this book. Individual preferences, however, will not be considered as causes of growth but rather as an invariant element in organizations.

Age as an Explanation for Growth

Exponential bureaucratic growth may be a function of organizational age, which, in turn, is a function of time. To the extent that age decreases the likelihood that individual units of bureaucracy can be displaced, overall organizational size can only ratchet upward as new units are formed to accommodate external changes. Whether or not aging contributes to organizational size will be explored in detail in the next chapter. To anticipate some of the discussion below, it should be noted that effects of age are not easily separated from effects of time when both are assumed to operate. And even if an age effect can be established, the specific mechanisms through which age affects organizations must still be determined.

Preferences for New Organizations as an Explanation for Growth

Bureaucratic growth may also be a response to continuous accumulation of new organizations, as opposed to growth in existing units. The distinction between forming new organizations that address new tasks and expanding existing units is imprecise, but it corresponds roughly to the difference between doing more kinds of work and doing more of the same. The measures of task demand utilized above may have tapped the latter better than the former, hence there remains the possibility that finance agencies grew continuously throughout the interval studied because their functions expanded in ways not captured by either quantitative or qualitative task measures.

It is a commonplace observation that the functions of U.S. cities increased over the interval covered by this research (Liebert, 1976). Cities assumed responsibility for health and welfare programs beginning in the 1930's and became conduits for large Federal programs aimed at revitalizing urban centers following World War II. These represented new activities for cities and augmented city work forces substantially. Whether or not these activities were qualitatively new for finance agencies is less clear. A strong argument can be made that the impact of augmented municipal responsibilities on finance administration is reflected fully in real dollar municipal expenditures, debt, Federal and state grants, and the complexity of budget documents. Growth in finance functions beyond increases in such quantitative task measures may require explanation in terms of new activities undertaken *within* finance agencies, not outside of them. One argument to be examined below is that the essential indeterminacy of bureaucratic work yields accumulation of tasks hence new organizations over time as new problems arise. The test of this argument is whether or not bureaus that have added to their own tasks and formal organization, as distinguished from tasks arising from measurable external demands, are advantaged compared to bureaus that have not.

Chapter 6
The "Liability of Newness" in Public Bureaucracies

This chapter begins the inquiry into causes of bureaucratic growth other than immediate task demands. It concerns specifically whether or not inertia in existing units renders then difficult to displace, leading to increased numbers of units over time. The idea that inertia accumulates in organizations, or that there is a "liability of newness" whereby newer organizations are less likely to survive than old ones, was first articulated by Stinchcombe in his classic article on "Social Structure and Organizations" (1965), and it has become a key proposition in organizational theory since. "Liability of newness" asserts, in Stinchcombe's words, that". . . as a general rule, a higher proportion of new organizations fail than old. This is particularly true of new organizational *forms,* so that *if an alternative requires new organization,* it has to be much more beneficial than the old before the flow of benefits compensates for the relative weakness of the newer social structure . . ." (p. 148).

Recently, the idea of "liability of newness" has been incorporated into formal models of organizational change processes. These models, which will be described below, treat rates of dissolution or failure for organizations as functions of chronological age and of other variables. In some recent research studies that have analyzed data on organizational survival, the "liability of newness" has been confirmed: Younger organizations have had higher instantaneous death rates than older ones (Hannan and Freeman, 1981; Carroll and Delacroix, 1982; Freeman et al., 1983; Carroll, 1983). The interpretation of these results has varied. Sometimes these results are treated as confirming a population-ecology model in which organizational forms are subject to selection like biotic populations occupying ecological niches (Hannan and Freeman, 1977). Sometimes they are taken as evidence of "institutionalization" of organizational forms over time (Zucker, 1983). And sometimes no particular interpretation is proffered for the empirical finding that older organizations fail less frequently than younger ones (Carroll and Delacroix, 1982). All of this research, it should be noted, concerns nongovernmental agencies. The one extant study of mortality in government agencies (Kaufman, 1976), suggests no "liability of newness": "Organizational death seemed to claim victims in all age categories without systematic discrimination" (p. 60). Casstevens' (1980) reanalysis of Kaufman's data also indicates no age dependence of death rates, and Carroll's (1983) review of both Kaufman's and Casstevens' work confirms this result.

This chapter addresses both substantive and methodological issues surrounding the "liability of newness." Substantively, it asks whether there is inertia or "liability of newness" among the finance agencies that are the subject of this research and, if there is, whether it is of sufficient magnitude to account for long-term bureaucratic growth. Methodologically, this chapter asks whether the kinds of models normally used to test for "liability of newness" can yield unambiguous results. The substantive and methodological issues are largely inseparable. This chapter argues that in many instances where organizational death rates appear to decline with age, alternative explanations for this result are possible and, indeed, are plausible. It argues further that no fully satisfactory means of testing such alternative explanations may be available given the limitations of the models normally used to estimate age-dependence of death rates. It argues also that "liability of newness" is best understood as a causal hypothesis asserting certain consequences of age to preserve organizations. And it shows that, at least among the agencies studied, little inertia or "liability of newness" remains once variables affecting mortality other than age are controlled.

6.1 The Model

The basic model used to test for variations in organizational mortality is one in which an instantaneous rate of failure or transition is estimated as a function of other variables. The instantaneous transition rate in instances where the state change is from existence to nonexistence can be defined as:

$$r(t) = \lim \triangle t \rightarrow 0 \ [\text{Pr}(\text{death between t and } t + \triangle + \text{ alive at t})]/\triangle t$$

where $\triangle t$ is an infinitesimal interval. A *constant* rate model in which transition rates do not change is usually of the following form:

$$r(t) = \exp[b_0],$$

where b_0 is invariant across the units studied. The exponential form is used to constrain $r(t)$ to nonnegative values. An *age-independent* model in which transition rates do vary but not with age introduces variables $x_1 \ldots x_n$ as causes of $r(t)$ such that

$$r(t) = \exp[b_0 + b_1 x_1 + \ldots],$$

where $b_1 \ldots b_n$ are coefficients of variables $x_1 \ldots x_n$.

Age-dependent models of transition rates are normally of two forms. One form, the Gompertz (1825) model, assumes mortality to increase or decrease from an initial rate $\exp[b_0 + b_1x_1 + \ldots]$ at an exponential rate c per unit of time t. Formally, it is as follows:

$$r(t) = \exp[b_0 + b_1x_1 + \ldots] * \exp[c_0t].$$

Another form, Makeham's Law (1869), adds an age-independent term to the above equation such that

$$r(t) = \exp[a_0] + \exp[b_0 + b_1x_1 + \ldots] * \exp[c_0t].$$

This age-independent term, a_0, is best understood as a long-term asymptotic death rate that is approached as age approaches infinity. It should be noted that a and c parameters in the age-dependent models can be assumed constant, or they can be estimated as functions of variables $x_1 \ldots x_n$, just as the b parameter is in the above equation.

Time- or period-dependent models of transition rates can also be estimated. The simplest time- or period-dependent model adds one term to the constant rate model above such that:

$$r(t) = P_i * \exp[b_0],$$

where P_i's are coefficients of dummy variables, each of which has a value of one for the time period it represents and zero otherwise. For example, if two time periods were specified and P_1 estimated to be double P_2, then transition rates would be twice as high in the first period as in the second. In theory, estimates of time- or period-dependence in age-dependent models can also be made. The least complicated form of such a model, parallel to the Gompertz model above, would be:

$$r(t) = P_i * \exp[b_0 + b_1x_1 + \ldots] * \exp[c_0t],$$

where the P_i's are coefficients of dummies for historical periods and t is chronological age. Needless to say, more elaborate time-dependent models of age-dependence in transition rates can be imagined.

Transition rates can be understood intuitively as the inverse of the length of the period or "spell" at the end of which a unit changes or undergoes a transition to another state. Units occupying a state for nearly infinite intervals have transition rates approaching zero. Units changing states more than once per unit of time have transition rates greater than unity. In principle, then, transition rates have a lower bound of zero and no upper bound. In fact, given that the transitions of interest here, from existence to nonexistence of organizational units, occur only once in the lifetime of a unit, the upper bound of such rates in this research is one. If organizational mortality, that is transitions from existence to nonexistence, were distributed uniformly over time, then rates of organizational mortality would not differ from annual probabilities of dissolution, which were displayed two chapters above. The fact that mortality is not distributed uniformly over time, however, means that mortality rates and annual probabilities of dissolution do differ and have somewhat different substantive meanings.

The method of maximum likelihood is used to estimate transition rates. Ordinary least squares methods would yield results identical to maximum likelihood were none of our observations censored, that is, were all units observed until they went out of existence. This condition cannot be achieved in most nonexperimental research, however. The advantage of maximum likelihood techniques is that they permit probabilities of events, such as organizational mortality, and censoring to be estimated jointly. Relatively unbiased estimates of transition rate models are therefore possible. Tuma's (1980) RATE algorithm was used to estimate transition rates in this research. The reader is referred to Tuma's work as well as to Coleman (1981) for mathematical expositions of transition-rate models.

The idea of "liability of newness," which asserts mortality rates to decline with age, suggests that the c coefficients in the age-dependent models should be negative and differ significantly from zero. In the Gompertz model, then, "liability of newness" hypothesizes death rates to decline from an initial rate $\exp[b_0]$ (or $\exp[b_0 + b_1 x_1 + \ldots]$) to zero at a negative exponential rate c_0 (or $c_0 + c_1 x_1 + \ldots$). In Makeham's law, death rates are hypothesized to decline from an initial rate $(\exp[a_0] + \mathrm{ep}[b_0])$ to an asymptotic rate $\exp[a_0]$ at a negative exponential rate c_0 where variables other than age do not affect mortality. Where variables other than age are expected to influence mortality, the a, b, and c parameters are treated as functions of $x_1 \ldots x_n$.

Conditions Affecting Estimates of Age Dependence

Two conditions can influence estimates of age dependence in the Gompertz model as well as in Makeham's law apart from the true magnitude of the c parameter in the population studied. One is population heterogeneity. Another is censoring of observations.

Population heterogeneity that is undetected or uncontrolled will often exaggerate apparent age-dependence of death rates. It will always do so when heterogeneous populations are in equilibrium, that is, when all failed units are replaced. In his discussion of nonlinearity in long survival plots, which was observed in Chapter 4, Carroll (1983: 8) noted that:

Time-[or age-] dependence in the transition rates is one interpretation for non-linear log survivor plots; another, equally plausible, interpretation is population heterogeneity. That is, if the data contain several subgroups, each characterized by time-[or age-] independent rates of different values, then the log survivor plot might be nonlinear. Unfortunately, there is no definitive method for choosing between these alternative explanations. Instead, the investigator must explore the data for heterogeneity and then finally make a decision on time-dependence in light of substantive considerations.

This can be understood intuitively. Consider two populations, A with a high death (and birth) rate, B with a low death (and birth) rate. Neither death rate is age dependent. A constant fraction of each population dies every year. Both populations are in equilibrium since births equal deaths for each. Their relative proportions will not change over time. The average age of population B, however, will exceed the average age of population A because the members of A die young and are replaced while the members of B live longer. Imagine now that variable X accounts for the difference in mortality between populations A and B; imagine X high in the high mortality population A and low in the low mortality population B. Variable X, which is associated positively with mortality, is therefore associated inversely with age. The problem of heterogeneity can thus be stated quite succinctly: Variables that cause mortality may also be associated inversely with age. The analyst who cannot or does not control all potential causes of mortality in age-dependent models runs the risk of imputing a spurious relationship of age to death rates.

Censoring of observations can have the opposite effect of population heterogeneity by masking age-dependence in death rates. Censoring occurs when observations commence after some or all of the units under study have been founded (left censoring) or before some units have died (right censoring). Carroll's (1983) review of some 52 studies of organizational mortality concluded that *"the performance of the age-dependent models depends solely upon the level and type of censoring in the data"* (1983: 16). Specifically, age-independent models of mortality fitted best those data sets where there was substantial right-censoring and censoring was highly correlated with age such that long-lived units were substantially more likely to be censored than others. Age-dependent models fitted best those data sets where there was little right-censoring or where censoring was uncorrelated with age.

Heterogeneity and Censoring in Organizations

In biotic populations, neither population heterogeneity nor censoring need pose substantial problems in estimating age-dependent models of mortality. Investigators normally limit observations to homogeneous groups and attempt to observe population cohorts until all members have died (Benjamin, 1965: 19–21; Boughey, 1968: 27–30; Pianka, 1983: 102; Pielou, 1969: 49–52; Poole, 1974: 11–16).[1]

In organizational populations, heterogeneity and censoring pose substantial and related problems. To begin, no set of organizations, no matter how similar individual units are as to type or function, can be considered homo-

---

[1] Interestingly, "liability of newness" or high juvenile mortality in biotic populations is limited to many fish, invertebrates, insects, and plants but is not characteristic of humans, most other mammals, and birds (Pianka, 1983: 107).

geneous. Two decades of research studies comparing organizations quantitatively – so numerous are such studies that none need be cited – have shown substantial variation to exist in their properties. To the extent that any organizational property can be reasonably expected to influence mortality, it must be controlled explicitly in time-dependent models of death rates. This holds whether or not such properties are readily measured. Some key concomitants of organizational survival, such as the quality of management, are extremely difficult to gauge quantitatively. Importantly, the use "representative" populations of organizations in research compounds rather than mitigates the heterogeneity problem in this instance. Valid results can be expected only when organizational populations are homogeneous or when sources of heterogeneity are controlled (McKelvey, 1982; McKelvey and Aldrich, 1983).

Heterogeneity potentially affecting organizational mortality rates occurs in environments as well as in organizations. Business cycles and political changes may (or may not) cause failure rates to shift over time net of other things. Certainly, it would not be prudent to assume these kinds of environmental changes to have no effects on mortality. In principle, controlling heterogeneity in environments poses no greater difficulty than controlling heterogeneity in organizations – one either selects a set of organizations whose environments are constant or controls statistically for variable properties of environments. The latter is accomplished most directly by introducing into models variables describing environments explicitly. Often, however, explicit environmental measures are not available, and historical periods or intervals are used as surrogates for them. For example, one might reasonably expect failure rates among municipal agencies responsible for financial functions to increase during the era of the Great Depression. One can test this expectation by estimating models of organizational mortality in which historical era is controlled. This is accomplished most parsimoniously by adding to age-dependent models of transition rates one or more dummy variables for historical era as in the equations above. But if such models cannot be estimated – and we were altogether frustrated in our efforts to estimate age-dependence in period-dependent models that included dummy variables for historical era – then transition rates must be estimated less parsimoniously *within* each historical era or period. Some censoring of observations that span two or more historical intervals occurs, however, when rates are estimated within eras. Because such censoring may be correlated with age, estimated effects of age may be biased downward.

The upshot of the discussion is this: Estimates of the Gompertz model and Makeham's Law are vulnerable to heterogeneity in organizations or in environments, which if not removed or controlled can exaggerate age-dependence in death rates. Not all sources of heterogeneity in organizations and environments can be identified, much less measured and controlled. Moreover, in some instances heterogeneity occurring due to variation over time in environments can be removed or controlled only by censoring series, which may attenuate estimates of age-dependence. The interpretation of Gompertz and Makeham's Law estimates, thus, is rendered ambiguous.

6.2 Age-Dependence in Death Rates

The previous chapter estimated models treating total employment in finance agencies of Chicago, Detroit, and Philadelphia as functions of task demands. Employment in finance agencies and task measures were available, for the most part, for each city for each year from 1907 to 1975. Each observation was, in other words, a city in a given year; three cities times sixty-nine years yielded a total of 207 observations. In this chapter, entirely different kinds of observations or units are used. Models of organizational mortality are applied to the 559 organizational units – departments, divisions and sections – responsible for finance functions in the three cities from 1890 to 1975. Each observation describes the entire period or "spell" of existence of each of these units. Among other characteristics of the units coded are its first and last years of existence, its name and organizational location, and its size. Certain characteristics of the three cities also describe "spells" of existence of each unit. Of some importance in this and the following chapter are changes in municipal administration, which one would expect to increase, and do in fact increase, organizational mortality net of other things. "Spells" of existence are also described by the measures of task demand used in the previous chapter, but none of the task measures had significant effects on mortality.

Two simplifying assumptions are used in the analysis below. First, certain kinds of deaths of organizational units are not considered. For the most part, deaths of departments, divisions, and sections, are recorded when units disappear. The circumstances surrounding dissolution of units may vary, however. Divisions are subunits of larger departments, just as sections are subunits of divisions. In the great majority of instances where individual divisions and sections went out of existence, the departments and divisions of which they were parts continued. In some cases, however, deaths of divisions and sections occurred simultaneously with dissolution of larger departments and divisions. Deaths of the latter sort, so-called dependent deaths, are excluded from this analysis since they are clearly caused by factors leading to dissolution of larger units and may be unrelated to the age of individual divisions and sections. Including dependent deaths in the analysis would degrade any age-dependence of mortality. Second, the Gompertz model rather than Makeham's Law is estimated below. In estimates of Makeham's Law, the long-term asymptotic death rate, a_0, was found to be only marginally significant before and nonsignificant after covariates were added to the initial death rate, b_0. This result is not surprising as the survival plots displayed in Chapter 4 suggested mortality to be virtually zero for units age sixty or older.

Concomitants of Mortality

Table 6.1 displays maximum-likelihood estimates of the Gompertz model for Chicago, Detroit, and Philadelphia units with finance functions over the 1890–1975 interval. In the first panel of the table, the initial death rate, $\exp[b_0]$, is estimated without covariates. In subsequent panels, hypothesized covariates of the initial death rate are added one at a time.

The uppermost panel of Table 6.1 shows that, absent covariates, the initial (age zero) instantaneous death rate for organizational units is estimated to be .087 and to decline at the exponential rate of .034, or 3.4 per cent per year. Both the initial death rate and its rate of decline are highly significant. In the second panel of Table 6.1, a dummy variable coded 1 if a unit is a department, as opposed to a division or section, is added as a covariate of

Table 6.1
Effects of Age and Other Variables on Death Rate (N = 559)

	exp[b]	c
Parameter	.087**	−.034**
Parameter	.087**	−.018**
Department	.182**	
Parameter	.121**	−.016**
Department	.222**	
Log Size	.729**	
Parameter	.100**	−.015**
Department	.230**	
Log Size	.752**	
New Mayor	1.887**	
Parameter	.125**	−.015**
Department	.227**	
Log Size	.735**	
New Mayor	1.654**	
Chicago	.739**	
Detroit	.782#	

  # $p < .1$
** $p < .01$

the initial death rate.[2] The model continues to estimate the initial death rate to be .087, but is also estimates departments to die at a rate of .182 times that for other units, which is significantly smaller than initial death rates for divisions and sections. Importantly, the rate of decline of the initial death rate drops dramatically compared to the first model. Whereas the exponential rate of decline of mortality was estimated to be .034 in the original model, it declines (absolutely) to .018 when the dummy variable for departments is added.

The logarithm of size – number of employees – to the base 10 is added in the third panel of Table 6.1, and in the fourth panel a further variable, a dummy for change in municipal administration, is added as a covariate of the initial death rate. The effects of both are highly significant. Increased size decreases organizational death rates, while new mayors increase death rates substantially. Importantly, both reduce slightly the estimated age-dependence of mortality. With log size added to the model, the exponential rate of decline of death rates is .016; with change in administration also added, it is .015. In the bottommost panel of the table, additional dummy variables for two of the cities, Chicago and Detroit, are also introduced. While Chicago has significantly lower (by a multiple of .739) death rates for organizational units than Philadelphia, Detroit does not. The dummy variables for city have practically no effect on age dependence of mortality. To four digits, the c coefficient is estimated as .0151 without the city dummies and .0148 with them in the model.

The Impact of Historical Change

The impact of historical change – environmental changes arrayed over time – are now considered. The histories of Chicago, Detroit, and Philadelphia from 1890 though 1975 cannot be reviewed in detail here. It suffices to note that three kinds of events had profound impacts on cities, city finances, and the organization of finance functions in this interval. One was municipal reform, which occurred in Detroit in 1918, in Philadelphia in 1953 when a Home Rule charter was granted by the Commonwealth of Pennsylvania, and not at all in Chicago. Both Detroit's and Philadelphia's reforms were accompanied by partial reorganization of finance functions. Detroit, for example, created a centralized purchasing department, removing from department heads authority to buy goods and let contracts. Philadelphia created a centralized finance department responsible for accounting and control functions as well as for budgeting. The second event affecting all three cities was the Great Depression. The Depression bankrupted Detroit

---

[2] Death rates for divisions and sections are identical, hence no dummy for divisions is used.

by 1937 and nearly bankrupted Philadelphia. Chicago deferred tax collections for two years (and continues to this date to collect taxes a year late) by funding city operations from short-term borrowing. In each case, some adjustments in the organization of finance functions occurred. The third event affecting cities was Federal funding of urban programs, which began in the Eisenhower administration in 1953 when the Federal housing and redevelopment grants were initiated.

Three historical eras are suggested. The first spans the 1890–1932 interval, the era of municipal reform in the U.S. if not in all of the cities studied and the World War I years. The second spans the 1933–1952 interval, which includes the Depression, the New Deal, and World War II. The third, 1953–1975, is the post-World War II era. Two questions are raised. One is whether organizational mortality varied across these eras. There is strong reason to believe that it did. The other is whether age-dependence in organizational mortality can be estimated across eras without some censoring of observations. We found that, as a practical matter, it cannot be.

A single period-dependent model of age-dependence in death rates was first attempted. This model added dummies for the three historical eras, the P_i's in the equations above, to the Gompertz model. Convergence of maximum-likelihood estimates, however, could not be attained with the RATE algorithm used to compute transition rates.[3] The alternative to the single period-dependent model was three models, each confined to a single historical era at the end of which observations were censored. Censoring could have been avoided were it possible to assign each organizational unit to a unique historical era. But two problems arise in assigning to a single era units whose existence spans two or more eras. Figure 6-1 illustrates the nature of the problems. In Figure 6-1, organizational units are classified by cohort, that is, they are assigned to the eras in which they were born. One obvious problem is misspecification. Comparison of cohorts, vertical comparisons in Figure 6-1, and comparison of historical eras, horizontal comparisons in the figure, are not the same things. They would be the same things if no units spanned two or more eras, but this is very much not the case. A second problem, nearly obvious, is the correlation of cohort with death rates. Because the longest lived units are confined to the earliest cohort, death rates will increase, other things being equal, as one moves from earlier to later cohorts in Figure 6-1. If units were classified by era of death rather than birth cohort, the opposite result would obtain: Death rates would decrease over time. If units were assigned to the historical era in

---

[3] We do not know why maximum-likelihood estimates failed to converge. The problem may have been due to either a software error or the high correlation of age with historical era. We are grateful to Nancy Brandon Tuma for her advice in attempting to resolve this problem.

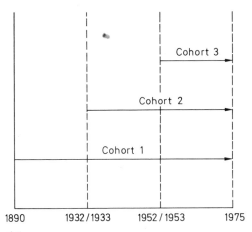

Figure 6.1
Cohort versus Period Comparisons of Organizational Mortality

which they spent the bulk of their existence, death rates would be lowest in the middle period, again other things being equal.

Some censoring beyond that in the original observations is therefore necessary to estimate the impact of historical eras on organizational death rates. Such censoring may bias estimates of age-dependence in mortality unless it can be accomplished without creating a correlation of censoring with age. In fact, this can be accomplished partially, but not fully.

Table 6.2 displays age-dependent estimates for death rates *within* three historical eras. The dependent variable, mortality, again, is computed *within* each era. The age of each unit, however, is not limited to its period of existence within each era. It is instead *either* its actual age at death if it died within an era *or* its age at the end of each era if it did not die in that era. Since only twelve of the 559 units covered in this research were formed before 1890 (and are treated as founded in 1890 since their birth dates are not known), most of the long-lived units are right-censored in the first era. There is a correlation of age with censoring. Relatively fewer long-lived units are censored in the second era than in the first, and there is even less right-censoring of long-lived units in the third era than in the second. In other words, the correlation of age with censoring drops over time and is about the same in the third era as in the relatively uncensored observations used in Table 6.1. Consider Figure 6.1 again. All units exceeding 42 years of existence are censored in the first era; units living more than 62 years are censored in the second era; while only units exceeding 85 years are necessarily censored in the third era.

Table 6.2
Effects of Age and Other Variables on Death Rates for 1890–1932, 1933–1952, and 1953–1975 Intervals

	exp[b]	c
1890–1932 (N = 124)		
Parameter	.061**	−.026
Department	.252**	
Log Size	.561**	
New Mayor	2.304#	
Chicago	3.638*	
Detroit	2.049	
1933–1952 (N = 179)		
Parameter	.188**	−.037**
Department	.080**	
Log Size	.534**	
New Mayor	1.612	
Chicago	.334**	
Detroit	.707	
1953–1975 (N = 382)		
Parameter	.129**	−.005
Department	.126**	
Log Size	.687**	
New Mayor	1.510#	
Chicago	.482**	
Detroit	.560**	

# $p < .1$
* $p < 0.05$
** $p < .01$

The estimates displayed in Table 6.2 can be read in several ways. To begin, net of other things, differences in organizational mortality across the three cities vary with historical era. Philadelphia has the lowest death rates in the 1890–1932 interval but has the highest rates thereafter. Organizational units in Chicago have higher mortality than in Detroit in the first historical era but lower rates thereafter.[4] The estimates in Table 6.2 also show departments to have much lower mortality than divisions and sections throughout, larger units to have lower death rates than smaller units, and changes in municipal administration to increase death rates, although not always significantly. These results are consistent with the estimates in Table 6.1. Finally, the estimates in Table 6.2 show age-dependence of mortality to be nonsignificant in two of the three historical periods. From 1890 to 1932, the estimated

[4] In the next chapter, where period-dependent models are estimated without censoring because age is not considered, differences in organizational mortality across the three cities vary over time in almost exactly the same pattern. See below, pp. 159-161.

effect of age on death rates is −.026, which while rather large in absolute terms does not approach statistical significance because its standard error is also large. From 1933 to 1952, age is estimated to have a somewhat greater effect, −.037, which is statistically significant. But from 1953 through 1975, age has no discernible impact on mortality. Its coefficient is −.005, which does not approach significance.

The interpretation of the coefficients of age, the estimated level of age-dependence of mortality, poses some uncertainties for reasons discussed above. On the one hand, the effect of age in the first historical period may be nonsignificant because its range is somewhat restricted compared to the other two periods. On the other hand, the effect of age in the second historical period may be large and significant because considerable heterogeneity remains within the 1933–1952 interval. The interpretation of the coefficient of age in the third period poses no difficulties, however. The range of age in the 1953–1975 interval is not restricted compared to its range from 1890 to 1975, hence censoring does not bias downward the estimated effect of age here compared to its effect in Table 6.1. And since heterogeneity baises age effects upward, it cannot account for the nonsignificant effect of age in the 1953–1975 period. Furthermore, the absence of age-dependence in organizational mortality in the third interval can be understood substantively: Some of the oldest units, comptrollers' offices in Detroit and Philadelphia that were formed before 1890, were displaced by finance departments between 1953 and 1975.[5] Only Chicago did not subordinate accounting and control functions to a more inclusive department of finance. Importantly, the experience of Detroit and Philadelphia was not anomalous. Many cities replaced comptrollers' offices with finance departments in the 1960's and 1970's (Meyer, 1979).

Compared to Table 6.1, then, the estimates in Table 6.2 differ in two respects. First, Table 6.2 shows the intersection of city with time to influence rates of organizational mortality. Most of the differences due to city and time can be understood at least partially as functions of municipal reform and bankruptcy. Second, Table 6.2 shows that net of city and time, significant effects of age on death rates are confined to one historical period, the Depression and World War II years. The procedure used to control for history could have yielded the nonsignificant age effect in the 1890–1932 interval (but could not have from 1953 on). And inadequate control for history could have yielded the significant age effect from 1933 to 1952. The

---

[5] Philadelphia retained a Comptroller's Office under the Home Rule charter, but it had only postauditing rather than accounting and financial control functions and its head became an elected rather than an appointed official. The post-1952 Comptrollers' office is treated as a new organization in this research.

absence of any "liability of newness" in the post-World War II era is not readily explained, however, save by the hypothesis that age does not advantage organizational units of the type studied. It is also important that the differences between Tables 6.1 and 6.2 not be overstated. The coefficient of age in the bottommost panel of Table 6.1, which is $-.015$, indicates that death rates will take forty-seven years to decline by half. While the coefficient is statistically significant, it hardly indicates an immunity to death after the first few years of existence.

6.3 Discussion

Two issues require discussion at this point. One, which applies to organizational research generally, is the appropriateness of Gompertz and Gompertz-like models for testing the hypothesis of "liability of newness" in organizational populations. The second, which is central to this research, is whether age contributes to the persistence of units of bureaucratic organization and thereby contributes to the accumulation of organizational units, hence bureaucratic growth, over time.

The first issue, the appropriateness of Gompertz models for testing "liability of newness," divides into two questions. One concerns their limitations; another concerns alternatives to them. As to the former, some key assumptions underlying models of age-dependence in death rates, of which the Gompertz is one, are rarely met in organizational populations. In particular, organizational populations are rarely homogeneous, nor are their environments. Heterogeneity in organizations or in environments that is not controlled can yield exaggerated estimates of age-dependence in death rates. It does so because variables causing mortality may also be associated inversely with age. As was shown in Table 6.1, estimated age-dependence of death rates decreases (in absolute value since its sign is negative) as causes of mortality are controlled. No test can demonstrate that all causes of mortality have been controlled. For this reason, it can always be argued that some omitted variable accounts for age-dependent deaths or "liability of newness." In general, then, the Gompertz model, then, can disprove but not prove "liability of newness" in organizations.

Heterogeneity arising due to variations in environments over time poses particularly vexing problems. Some censoring of observations may be necessary to separate intervals of expected high and low mortality should period-dependent models of age-dependence in mortality prove impossible to estimate. But censoring can suppress age-dependence in death rates by limiting the observed range of age. As was shown in Table 6.2, the impact of censoring on the observed range of age can be limited, but it cannot be removed completely. For this reason, where heterogeneity due to historical variations in environments is suspected and controlled, the Gompertz model cannot fully disprove "liability of newness" in organizations.

More data than have been heretofore available and simpler models than the Gompertz and Makeham's Law are required to test hypothesized "liability of newness." Stinchcombe's (1965) discussion of "liability of newness," it will be remembered, listed specific concomitants of age – consequences of age – that tend to reduce mortality in organizations. These include trust among strangers who must work together, familiarity with work roles, and the defeat of vested interests opposing the continued existence of an organization. Needless to say, this list could easily be extended. The theory of "liability of newness" does not assert, however, antecedents of age, such as historical period, to reduce mortality. Because any variable associated with mortality may be inversely associated with age, or, equivalently, because any variable associated with age may be inversely associated with mortality, some care must be taken to demonstrate that observed effects of age are due to its consequences for organizations and not to its antecedents. The easiest way to demonstrate this is to measure and introduce explicitly into models of mortality variables describing consequences of age. Whether or not a variable is antecedent or consequent to age can be determined partly on theoretical grounds and partly by its correlation with age. As a practical matter, of course, the concomitants of age specified in Stinchcombe's theory are not always available to researchers, especially when data are obtained from historical accounts of organizations rather than direct observation.

The second issue, whether or not there is "liability of newness" among the agencies studied, cannot be resolved definitively from the data available for this research, which do not include measures of the consequences of age. However, any age- dependence of death rates in these data is small, and no age dependence exists in the third historical interval where the impact of censoring is either negligible or nonexistent. Age, then, contributes only slightly or not at all to the persistence of the bureaucracies studied here. Age therefore appears not to contribute to the accumulation of organizational units, hence to bureaucratic growth, over time. Alternative models are required to explain long-term bureaucratic growth.

Chapter 7
Structure and Persistence in Organizational Hierarchies

This chapter addresses the third model of bureaucratic growth. The third model hypothesizes preferences for organization as a solution to problems to cause the amount of formal organization to increase over time and, ultimately, bureaucracies to grow. The preference model differs substantially from the two models of growth tested earlier. It differs from the task model of growth in that accommodation of change and uncertainties arising in the environment rather than quantitative variation in workload is claimed to propel long-term growth. It differs from the inertial model in that it specifies new organizational structures – the proliferation of subunits and sub-subunits within organizational hierarchies – rather than aging or inertia to be the principal cause of growth. The cornerstone of the preference model, the notion that proliferation of formal organization advantages existing units, will be explored in this chapter. The following chapter explores whether growth, in fact, follows increases in formal organization.

This chapter begins with a review of two kinds of ideas. The first asserts "spontaneous creation" of bureaucratic structures. The second alleges advantages of extended hierarchies – of new organization in the form of added subunits and sub-subunits – for existing organizations. Both kinds of ideas are familiar, and both are consistent with the problem-organization-problem-more organization cycle suggested by organizational theory. Here, the two kinds of ideas are linked in a way that allows the second, which is testable, to confirm or disconfirm the first, which is not testable as stated. The chapter then asks how one determines whether or not forming new organizations advantages existing units. The types of models estimated and their empirical results are then presented. The preference model of bureaucratic growth is then tested using data describing finance agencies in Chicago, Detroit, and Philadelphia.

7.1 The Problem

In a short book, *Are Government Organizations Immortal?* (1976), Herbert Kaufman observed a phenomenon that he labelled "spontaneous creation" of new federal agencies. He described the process as follows:

[Spontaneous creation] is governed by the internal dynamics of organizational life rather than by calculation and overall plan. The incessant, uncontrived division and subdivision of work gives many units their start ... Observers are prone to attribute these tendencies to the empire-building proclivities of bureaucrats, and there is little doubt that bureaucrats at all levels love to carve out their secure little niches. At the bottom, though, there seems to be a "built-in" thrust that encourages and assists the ever finer division of labor in organizations. Out of that come more organizations, products of a series of developments so small that they are hardly noticed individually as they occur. Collectively, if this hypothesis is valid, these insignificant changes could transform administrative structures without anyone ever having made a single, major, deliberate decision, to alter them (1976: 67–68).

Some of the details of the research on which this conclusion was based should be reviewed briefly. Kaufman's data describing agencies in ten of eleven executive departments were available for two points only, 1923 and 1973. Kaufman's definitions of organizational birth and death differed somewhat from those used here. Kaufman considered an organization to exist continuously, "as long as a boundary around a group of people included in the study was uninterruptedly maintained ... even if the composition, activities, outputs, and inputs of the group did not remain constant. When borders became indistinguishable, I ... declared the organization deceased" (1976: 28). Kaufman noted, of course, that the notion of "boundary" is not a simple and clear concept but was used as part of a "policy of leaning over backwards to find continuity rather than turnover" (1976: 32). Finally, Kaufman computed birth and death rates as probabilities of formation or dissolution during the fifty-year interval from 1923 to 1973, not as transition rates.

Kaufman was sensitive to the impact of external factors, especially changes in administration, on organizational births and deaths but found such factors insufficient to explain long-term trends. The one explanation proffered for "spontaneous creation" of government agencies is the tendency of individuals to specialize during the course of their careers and the corresponding tendency of bureaucracies to recognize expertise and seniority by forming new units. This argument is not unique. It is in fact, a more eloquent statement of "Parkinson's Law" (1957), which is not the accepted explanation for bureaucratic growth. While acknowledging the public's view that bureaucracies are self-perpetuating, most other scholars, especially economists, believe that growth is ultimately a function of external demand. Anthony

Downs, for example, writes that "... bureaus cannot expand without additional resources, which they must obtain either through voluntary contributions or from some government allocation agency. But, as we have seen, in a democratic society these external agents will not give a bureau such resources unless it produces outputs of commensurate value to them ..." (1967: 258).[1] The hypothesis of "spontaneous creation" also approaches nonfalsifiability. In asserting "built-in" growth of bureaucratic organization, concrete causes of growth are not specified hence conditions not favorable to growth are assumed exceptional and possibly nonexistent. A rigorous evaluation of the "spontaneous creation" hypothesis requires that it be transformed into one or more causal propositions that can, at least in principle, be falsified. Two such propositions are developed here. One is that creation of new organization advantages existing organizations. The second is that advantages of creating new organization accrue at all levels of organizational hierarchy. Together, these two propositions account for "spontaneous" or "built-in" growth of bureaucratic structures.

Advantages of New Organization

Perhaps the best way to begin recasting the idea of "spontaneous creation" is to search for underlying processes that could lead to this outcome. Normally, biases toward persistence and expansion of existing organizations are attributed to individuals, but control mechanisms within organizations and, in the case of business firms, market forces are expected to check expansionist tendencies (Williamson, 1975: 120–122). The failure of internal control mechanisms, thus, would be sufficient to explain "spontaneous creation" of bureaucratic structures. This explanation merely begs the question, however, since one must then ask why reasonable and rational organizations would permit their internal controls to lapse so that individuals can exercise, willy nilly, preferences for new organization. Two answers are possible. One is that the environment does not constrain bureaus to behave reasonably or rationally; officials proliferate offices as they please. Another answer, somewhat different, is that forming new organization is understood as reasonable and rational, and in fact enhances outcomes, especially for public bureaucracies whose outputs are not easily quantified. The bulk of the organizational literature, it will be argued, favors the second answer.

At least a half dozen advantages of extending organization, possibly more, are suggested in theory. The following benefits, among others, are noted:

---

[1] Others treating large size as a function of demand include Niskanen (1971), whose model shows, ceteris paribus, bureaus to have larger budgets than profit organizations, and Migue and Belanger (1974), who argue that bureaucrats behave like discriminating monopolists in extracting "rents" from offices.

- Organization allows rational division of labor (Weber, 1946).
- Organization economizes on bounded rationality and thereby contributes to decision making (Simon, 1947).
- Organization removes uncertainty from power relationships by transforming power into legitimate authority (Pfeffer, 1981).
- Organization allows substitutability of personnel thereby limiting failures (Simon, 1962).
- Organization induces requisite variety, allowing inconsistent and shifting environmental demands to be accommodated (Weick, 1976).
- Organization is myth used to represent symbolically that rational procedures exist for dealing with problems otherwise fraught with uncertainty (Meyer and Rowan, 1977).
- Organization maintains formal rationality, that is, the joining of purpose with consistency, by allowing new programs to be treated as subsets of established programs (Allison, 1971).

Interestingly, the first three of these properties – division of labor, economizing on bounded rationality, and legitimation of authority – suggest that fixity contributes to effectiveness and efficiency. The other four – substitutability, variety, symbolic representation, and maintenance of formal rationality under uncertainty – suggest that the function of formal organization is to absorb change and mask inconsistencies so that shifting environments can be accommodated. Below, whether organizations are advantaged due to fixity or flexibility will be explored. For the present, it suffices to note that theory asserts numerous if somewhat diverse advantages of organization.

Do Advantages of Organization Hold Across Levels of Hierarchy?

The hypothesis of "spontaneous creation" of organization requires not only that new organization should advantage existing units, but also that this advantage should obtain for units at all levels of hierarchy. Two issues are raised. One is whether the behavior of units at different levels is sufficiently similar so that they gain similar advantages from extended organizational structures. The second is whether large systems will seek to limit the extensiveness of organization at lower levels.

The first issue, whether existing units gain similarly from new organization at all levels of hierarchy cannot be decided from theory. For the most part, researchers have directed their attention toward deciding which level of organization yields the most appropriate units for analysis – for example, firms, departments within firms, or work groups – and not whether units at different levels behave similarly. In the few instances where theories have been tested at more than one level, results have been comparable across levels (Blau and Schoenherr, 1972; Kasarda, 1974), suggesting the possibility of isomorphism. Since no strong reason exists to reject the hypothesis that similar benefits from new organization accrue to units at different levels, this hypothesis will be tested against data.

The second issue, whether larger systems will seek to limit the extensiveness of organization at lower levels, requires that potential disadvantages of new organization be considered. Three kinds of problems arise when organizational structures are extended. One is cost. Staffing and maintaining complex structures incur substantial and permanent expenditures. A second problem is undue emphasis on procedures and insufficient attention to objectives in highly differentiated organizational systems. Suboptimization or "displacement of goals" (Merton, 1957) occurs. A third problem is communication distortion and associated control loss (Katz and Kahn, 1978). Other things being equal, one would expect the first two of these problems, cost and suboptimization, to regulate the extensiveness of organization so long as costs are salient, the value of outputs can be measured against costs, and objectives are well defined so that performance is more valued than compliance. But where these conditions do not obtain, which is often the case in bureaucratic settings, cost and suboptimization may be of little significance, and control loss alone may be insufficient to cause managers to limit the extensiveness of organization at lower levels.

In short, the advantages of new organization for existing units, which may be identical to the advantages of forming organizations in the first place, are often greater than its disadvantages. Where they are, one would expect extended organizational structures to offer advantages. The advantages of new organization additionally, may hold for units at all levels of administrative hierarchies. To the extent that these advantages hold, "continuous creation" of organization or "built-in" organizational growth is the expected outcome.

7.2 Ascertaining the Advantages of Organization

In principle, determining whether or not extended organizational structures advantage existing units of organization is not complicated. If one can assume, as was done in the previous chapter, that longevity is a valid measure of advantage, then one need only ask whether units having internal organization live longer or have lower mortality than units not so organized. The reader is referred to Figure 0-1 in the Introduction that displayed so-called "one-blob" and "three-blob" forms of organization, the former consisting of a single undifferentiated unit, the latter consisting of a unit containing two suborganizations or subunits. Presumably, advantages of organization obtain to the extent that "three-blobs" outlive or have lower mortality than "one-blobs."

In fact, several complications must be considered before any statistical test can be used to ascertain the advantages of organization for existing units. Two complications are of a practical nature. One arises from the nature of the data available for this research: For many of the units studied, it is impossible to determine whether or not they had suborganization or subunits. A second arises from the fact that while the dependent variable, mortality, describes the entire period of existence of a unit, the independent variables describing formal organization are static and can be measured only at discrete points in time. Two further complications reflect the possibility that organization may be an outcome and not a cause of advantages observed in existing units. One possibility is that the hypothesized cause of organizational persistence, formal organization, is in fact an artifact of historical time. In growing organizational systems, units living the longest will also have accumulated the most formal organization. Another possibility is that an invisible quantity, power, accounts for the apparent advantages offered by formal organization.

Units Used to Test the Preference Model

In the previous chapter, some 559 departments, divisions, and sections that had finance functions in Chicago, Detroit, and Philadelphia in the 1890–1975 interval were used to test the inertial model of bureaucratic growth. Not all of these units can be used to test the preference model because little information on the internal structure of sections, which are subunits of divisions, is given in municipal records. This does not mean that sections did not develop any formal organization, but it does mean that the extensiveness of organization within sections could not be determined in most instances. For this reason, tests of the preference model are confined to the 267 departments and divisions having finance functions in the three cities.

Even fewer units are available for models where we attempt to determine whether the advantages of organization are due to its fixity or flexibility. Measures of internal change could be constructed for only those departments and divisions ever having divisions and sections respectively. Some eighty-three departments and divisions of finance agencies in Chicago, Detroit, and Philadelphia had subunit organization at some time during their existence.

Measures of Organization

The key independent variables in the preference model are measures tapping the extensiveness of formal organization of both departments and divisions (but, again, not of sections). As noted two chapters above, the range of organizational variables that can be captured in research that relies on historical sources is limited compared to the range of variables that can be incorporated into observational studies. Basically, each department or division is described by its array of divisions or sections. Several measures of the extensiveness of and change in organization are yielded by these data. At any point in time, every department and division can be classified as either having or not having organizational structure, that is, having or not having subunits. At any point in time, every department and division can be described by its extensiveness of formal organization, that is, its number of subunits, if any. Organisational change within each unit having subunit structure can also be described.

Because static measures of organization are available for every year when each unit existed, some choices as to which measures would be included in the analysis and which would be excluded had to be made. Below, three measures indicating the extensiveness of organization are used. The first describes whether or not a unit ever had subunit structure at any point in its history. The second describes whether or not a unit had subunit structure in its last year of existence (or in 1975, if it did not go out of existence). The third measure of the extensiveness of organization is the number of subunits present in a unit in its last year of existence (or, again, in 1975 if it did not got out of existence). No claim is made that any of these measures of organization is superior to any other measure of organization that could have been constructed from our data. It should be noted, however, that considerable experimentation was undertaken with measures of organization that are not discussed here, and all produced essentially the same results.

The Impact of Historical Time

Possible effects of historical time must be considered when the preference model is tested. As shown in Chapter 5 above, there is a long-term trend toward growth in personnel and in formal organization among the finance agencies studied. This is characteristic of most government, indeed most administration in the U.S. Given this growth trend, the organizational units in existence toward the end of our series, which in many instances are the longest-lived units with the lowest mortality, will also be those units having subunit organization. Historical time, which is correlated with mortality, may thus be the cause of subunit organization, and the expected inverse association of subunit organization with mortality, if it materializes, may be spurious due to effects of time.

Historical time must therefore be controlled when estimating the effects of subunit structure on mortality of larger units. This is done in some instances below. Period-dependent models can be tested successfully here, unlike in the previous chapter, since age is no longer considered as a cause of mortality. Importantly, because the analysis in the previous chapter showed mortality rates within the three cities to vary substantially over time, the effects of city will also be treated as period-dependent in those models where historical time is controlled.

The Impact of Power

Possible effects of power must also be considered before the preference model is tested. The problem is not whether more powerful units of organization experience more or less mortality than less powerful units. We assume more powerful units to experience less mortality. The problem is, instead, whether power renders potentially spurious any observed relationship of subunit organization to mortality. No simple answer to this question is possible. On the one hand, to the extent that power has tangible consequences for organizational units, such as increased resources, these consequences must be controlled in models of mortality. In the estimates displayed below, the size of individual organizational units is explicitly controlled. On the other hand, to the extent that growth in formal organization is itself a manifestation of power, there may be no way to determine whether organization or power ultimately sustains individual units. But whether organization or power ultimately sustains units under these circumstances may also be immaterial to the theory we are testing since a preference for formal organization is indicated in either case.

The notion that power is manifested in the extensiveness of administrative organization is of some interest, for it suggests that individual bureaucrats seek continually to enlarge their responsibilities or domains, and that more powerful administrators succeed in doing so. One must ask, however, whether there are limits to this process. Management theory argues that preferences for large size and internal expansion will ultimately be checked by the inefficiencies they create. This may be the case where efficiency measures alone gauge organizational performance. But where other considerations operate – such as problem-solving capacity, the benefits of which cannot always be calculated – there may be no limits to internal expansion. Importantly, even if power explained the association of subunit organization with longevity and subunit organization contributed nothing directly to outputs or effectiveness, organization would remain the mechanism through which nonlegitimate power is transformed into legitimate authority. Again, there is a preference for formal organization.

7.3 Models and Results

Variation in organizational mortality is explored using age-independent models of two kinds. One model assumes variables $x_1 \ldots x_n$ to be causes of $r(t)$ such that:

$$r(t) = \exp[b_0 + b_1 x_1 + \ldots],$$

where $b_1 \ldots b_n$ are coefficients of variables $x_1 \ldots x_n$. In the second type of model, some, but not all, of the b_i's are estimated separately for each of three historical periods. In particular, the effects of city are assumed in these models to be period-dependent, consistent with the apparent effects of city shown in the previous chapter. Age-dependent models of death rates are not estimated here. As was shown in the previous chapter, mortality among the units studied exhibits little or no age dependence. As before, Tuma's (1980) RATE algorithm is used to generate maximum-likelihood estimates of parameters of the models.

Subunit Organization and Persistence

The hypothesis that the presence and extensiveness of subunits preserve larger organizational units will now be tested directly. Three measures of subunit organization are used. These include whether or not a unit ever had subunits, whether subunits were present in the last year of a "spell" of a unit's existence, and the number of subunits in the last year of a "spell." The three measures are highly correlated with one another and are for this reason entered into models one at a time. In the initial models, organizational mortality is estimated as a function of size, whether a unit is a department or division, and the three different measures of subunit organization. Estimates of mortality rates are then made separately for departments and divisions in order to test the hypothesis that the effects of organization hold across different levels. (Recall that sections, for which no data describing subunits are available, are excluded from this analysis.) Separate estimates are then made for the three cities to insure that elements at the city level do not confound results. Finally, change in municipal administration and historical time are introduced as additional controls. The anticipated effects of subunit organization on the persistence of departments and divisions hold throughout.

The models estimated in the uppermost panel of Table 7.1 confirm that, net of other things, subunit organization increases the survival chances of organizations. This result holds for all three measures. In the leftmost column, the extensiveness of organization is measured by whether or not a unit – a department or division – ever had subunits. Net of other things, having had subunits reduces mortality to a multiple of .401. In the center column, the extensiveness of organization is indicated by whether or not subunits were

Table 7.1
Effects of Substructure on Rate of Dissolution (N = 267)

	(1) exp[b]	(2) exp[b]	(3) exp[b]
Parameter	.091**	.087**	.090**
Log Size	.971	.927	.876
Department	.234**	.224**	.232**
Ever had Subunits	.401**		
Had Subunits in *Last* Year		.453**	
Number of Subunits in Last Year			.861*
Departments (N = 27)			
Parameter	.035**	.028**	.021**
Log Size	1.281	.938	1.119
Ever had Subunits	.095**		
Had Subunits in *Last* Year		.249**	
Number of Subunits in Last Year			.736#
Divisions (N = 240)			
Parameter	.888**	.084**	.089**
Log Size	.992	.996	.873
Ever had Subunits	.436**		
Had Subunits in *Last* Year		.479**	
Number of Subunits in Last Year			.880*
Chicago (N = 90)			
Parameter	.047**	.044**	.043**
Log Size	1.358	1.235	1.253
Department	.285**	.326**	.431*
Ever had Subunits	.400**		
Had Subunits *Last* Year		.458**	
Number of Subunits in Last Year			.790*
Detroit (N = 61)			
Parameter	.086**	.082**	.083**
Log Size	.826	.874	.823
Department	.745	.854	.731
Ever had Subunits	.311**		
Had Subunits in *Last* Year		.245**	
Number of Subunits in Last Year			.790*
Philadelphia (N = 116)			
Parameter	.146**	.147**	.160**
Log Size	.895	.814	.726
Department	.037**	.032**	.032**
Ever had Subunits	.424**		
Had Subunits in *Last* Year		.518**	
Number of Subunits in Last Year			.914

\# $p < .10$
* $p < .05$
** $p < .01$

present in the last year a unit existed (or in 1975). Having or having had subunits in the last year decreases mortality by a multiple of .453. The third measure or subunit organization is the number of subunits attached to a unit in its final year. Its effects are indicated in the rightmost column. Each subunit reduces mortality by a multiple of .861, indicating again that extensive formal organization preserves larger units.

Two additional results in the uppermost panel of Table 7.1 should be noted. First, the coefficients of the dummy variable for departments, which range from .224 to .234 depending upon which model is estimated, indicate that net of other things the mortality of departments is less than one quarter that of divisions. Second, the models estimated in the uppermost panel of the table show size to have no significant effect on mortality net of subunit structure. The coefficients of the logarithm of size are .971 in the leftmost column, .927 in the center, and .876 at the right. None of these coefficients approaches statistical significance.

Effects of Organization within Departments and Divisions

In order to determine whether the effects of subunit organization hold within departments and divisions hence, by implication, throughout administrative hierarchies, rates of dissolution are estimated separately for departments and divisions in the second and third panels of Table 7.1. The dummy variable for departments is, needless to say, omitted from these models. The results of these estimates can be summarized succinctly: Extensive organization preserves both departments and divisions. All three measures of subunit organization reduce significantly or nearly so mortality among both departments and divisions. This holds even though only twenty-seven departments with finance functions existed in Chicago, Detroit, and Philadelphia from 1980 through 1975 and even though death rates for departments were much lower than for divisions. Having had subunits at any time reduces mortality by a multiple of .095 for departments and .436 for divisions; having subunits in the last year reduces death rates for departments and divisions by .453 and .249 respectively; for each subunit in the last year, mortality is reduced by a factor of .736 for departments (which is significant at the .10 level) and .880 for divisions. Furthermore, no significant effect of size on death rates appears for either departments or divisions. To the extent that it is possible to test whether subunit organization preserves larger units throughout administrative hierarchies, the data confirm that it does.

Effects of Organization Net of Exogenous Change

Sources of exogenous change must be controlled to remove the possibility that the observed effects of subunit organization are due to shifts occurring

Table 7.2
Effects of Substructure on Rate of Dissolution Controlling for City, and Changes in Administration (N = 267)

	(1) exp[b]	(2) exp[b]	(3) exp[b]
Parameter	.089**	.089**	.091**
Log Size	1.044	.974	.932
Department	.240**	.226**	.238**
Chicago	.709**	.654**	.642**
Detroit	.734	.783	.790
New Mayor	1.774*	1.667*	1.683*
Ever had Subunits	.386**		
Had Subunits in *Last* Year		.448**	
Number of Subunits in Last Year			.853**

* p < .05
** p < .01

in the environment. Not all exogenous change can be controlled, but some key external elements such as city differences, changes in municipal administration, and historical time can be introduced into estimates of mortality.

– Controlling for city. The effects of subunit organization on mortality are estimated separately for Chicago, Philadelphia, and Detroit in the fourth, fifth, and sixth panels of Table 7.1. These estimates confirm the earlier findings. Ever having had subunits reduces mortality by multiples of .400 in Chicago, .311 in Detroit, and .424 in Philadelphia. Having subunits in the last year of existence reduces death rates by multiples of .458, .245, and .518 in the three cities respectively; for each extant subunit in the last year, mortality declines by multiples of .790 in both Chicago and Detroit, and by .914 (which is not significant) in Philadelphia.

Comparison of the fourth, fifth, and sixth panels of Table 7.1 also shows Chicago to have had, overall, the lowest rate of organizational mortality among the three cities net of other variables and Philadelphia to have had the highest rates. A similar overall pattern was noted in the previous chapter where sections as well as departments and divisions were included in the analysis. This pattern can be attributed, in part, to events affecting the cities individually, such as municipal reform and bankruptcy. Chicago experienced neither municipal reform nor municipal bankruptcy during the 1890–1975 interval, while Detroit and Philadelphia experienced both. Reform in Detroit occurred early and did not cause the same extensive reorganization triggered by the reform process in Philadelphia, which began just after World War II and culminated in a 1952 Home Rule charter.

Table 7.3
Effects of Substructure on Rate of Dissolution Controlling for City, Changes in Administration, and Era (N = 267)

	(1) exp[b]	(2) exp[b]	(3) exp[b]
1890–1932			
Parameter	.025**	.022**	.022**
Chicago	3.535	4.052	4.122
Detroit	2.698	3.199	3.303
1933–1952			
Parameter	.077**	.075**	.077**
Chicago	.566#	.448**	.434**
Detroit	.462*	.489*	.490*
1953–1975			
Parameter	.119**	.118**	.120**
Chicago	.534**	.516**	.503**
Detroit	.704#	.731	.727
Period-Independent Effects			
Log Size	.965	.932	.892
Department	.236**	.232**	.237**
New Mayor	2.271**	2.268**	2.276**
Ever had Subunits	.477**		
Had Subunits in *Last* Year		.507**	
Number of Subunits in Last Year			.880*

# $p < .1$
* $p < .05$
** $p < .01$

Chicago escaped bankruptcy in the Depression through short-term borrowing; Detroit was bankrupt by 1937 and Philadelphia was virtually so at that time.

– Controlling for changes in municipal administration. In Table 7.2 mortality rates among the 267 departments and divisions are estimated as functions of their size, whether or not a unit is a department, city (for which two dummy variables, one for Chicago and one for Detroit are used), change in municipal administration, and the three measures of subunit organization. Changes in administration are indicated by a dummy variable coded one for inaguration of a new mayor during the last year of a unit's existence. Table 7.2 shows changes in administration to increase significantly mortality rates among organizational units, but it also shows the measures of substructure to decrease mortality significantly as in the previous estimates. Death rates increase by a factor of approximately 1.7 following mayoral succession but decrease by a multiple of .386 if subunits existence of a department or division, .448 if subunits were present during the last year of existence, and .853 for every subunit present in the last year.

– Controlling for historical time. Historical time or period is controlled in estimates of death rates displayed in Tabel 7.3. Time or period is controlled in order to remove the possibility that subunit organization decreases mortality because the longest live units are those existing in the later historical eras when organizational structures were most extensive. Here, unlike in the previous chapter, no censoring of series is needed to estimate the impact of historical time or period. Consistent with the previous chapter where the effects of city differences on mortality varied across historical eras, the effects of city are treated here as time- or period-dependent.

Coefficients of the constant parameters and the dummy variables for Chicago and Detroit are estimated within three historical eras, 1890–1932, 1933–1952, and 1953–1975. These coefficients reproduce almost exactly the pattern of city differences over time that were shown in the previous chapter. Philadelphia, for example, has the lowest mortality for organizational units in the 1890–1932 interval and the highest mortality thereafter. Chicago has higher organizational mortality than Detroit in the first period and lower mortality than Detroit in the third. Table 7.3, however, suggest few differences between Chicago and Detroit in the second period, the era of the Depression and World War II, whereas the previous chapter indicated Detroit to have higher mortality during this period. The similarity of the present period-dependent estimates based on 267 departments and divisions with the earlier results that were based on 559 departments, divisions, *and* sections is of note both because the units involved differ and also because the impact of censoring in the previous chapter appears to have been slight.

The lower portion of Table 7.3 displays time- or period-independent estimates of the impact of size, whether a unit is a department or division, change in municipal administration, and the three measures of subunit organization. The effects of these variables shown earlier are reproduced here. Size has no significant impact on mortality, departments have substantially lower death rates than divisions, and changes in municipal administration increase mortality substantially. Importantly, subunit organization continues to attenuate rates of dissolution. Having had subunits at any time reduces death rates by a multiple of .477, having subunits in the last year of existence (or in 1975) attenuates death rates by .507, and each subunit present in the last year reduces mortality by a multiple of .880. All of these coefficients are statistically significant. All of these coefficients are, however, somewhat larger than in Table 7.2 where historical period was not controlled. To some small extent, then, the effects of subunit organization on mortality estimated earlier are artifacts of history, whereby units existing later in time, which on balance are somewhat older than units existing at earlier points, also are more likely to have grown hence to have accumulated subunits.

Is Persistence Due to Fixity or Flexibility?

A further question to be explored is whether the advantages of subunit organization are due to fixity or flexibility. The fixity argument is essentially that of classical and neo-classical organizational theory: Determinate organizational patterns yield efficiencies in administration and augmented decision capacity. The flexibility argument, which is contemporary, claims that variety within organizations allows accommodation of changes and inconsistencies arising externally. The findings developed above favor neither the fixity nor the flexibility argument since they show subunit organization to advantage departments and divisions similarly. If the principal benefit of extensive formal organization were more efficient administration and augmented decision capacity, then one would expect to find forces tending toward elaboration of organization operating mainly at higher levels of administration since decision making and efficiency considerations are most salient at this point. If the principal benefit of organization were absorption of changes and inconsistencies, then the opposite outcome would be expected since greater adaptive capacity is demanded at lower than at higher levels of organization. A direct test of the impact of flexibility, or change within organizational subunits, on the persistence of larger units is suggested.

Data describing eighty-three departments and divisions having subunits are available to evaluate the impact of change in subunit organization on mortality. Only this small number of units can be used because change measures cannot be computed where no subunit organization exists. To assign change measures scores of zero during intervals when there were no subunits is to confound effects of existence and variation in organization. Table 7.4 displays estimates of dissolution rates for these eighty-three "spells" of existence when organizational units had subunits. Organizational mortality is treated as a function of size, a dummy variable for departments, change in municipal administration, and four measures of variation in substructure, including whether or not any births of subunits occurred, the birth rate or the average annual rate of formation of new units, whether or not any deaths occurred among subunits, and the average annual rate of dissolution of subunits. Dummy variables for Chicago and Detroit are not included in Table 7.4 since dissolution rates are unaffected by city in the subsample of 83. One change measure is entered into each of four models reported in Table 7.4. The estimates displayed in Table 7.4 show three of the four

Table 7.4
Effects of Change in Substructure and Other Variables on Rate of Dissolution (N = 83)

	(1) exp[b]	(2) exp[b]	(3) exp[b]	(4) exp[b]
Parameter	.041**	.040**	.062**	.056**
Log Size	1.488	1.485	1.428	1.142
Department	.151**	.132**	.167**	.144**
New Mayor	2.474#	2.575#	1.905	2.684#
Ever had Births	.650#			
Annual Birth Rate		.012**		
Ever had Deaths			.153**	
Annual Death Rate				1.059

\# p < .10
** p < .01

measures of variation in substructure to reduce significantly or nearly so the dissolution rate for larger units. Having had any births of subunits during intervals when subunits were always present reduces by a multiple of .650 the likelihood of dying (which is significant at the .10 level). An average annual rate of formation of new subunits of 100 per cent, which is many times higher than actual birth rates, is estimated to reduce death rates by a multiple of .012. Having had any deaths of subunits reduces by a multiple of .153 the likelihood of dissolution, but the average annual death rate of subunits, whose coefficient is 1.059, does not affect organizational unit mortality at all.

The results in Table 7.4 can be read in one of two ways. On the one hand, they can be understood as supporting the flexibility hypothesis: The greater the rate of change in subunit structure, the greater the persistence of larger units. On the other hand, they can be understood as confirming the findings developed earlier: Given that substructure is present, the greater the birth rate of new subunits, that is, the faster organizational structure is extended, the greater the persistence of larger units. No choice between these two interpretations is possible given that the coefficient of the death rate for subunits is almost exactly one. Were this coefficient significantly smaller, the flexibility hypothesis would be supported; were it significantly larger, Table 7.4 could be viewed as extending the earlier findings showing structure to preserve organizations.

Summary of Findings

The presence and extensiveness of subunits preserves organizations. This result holds across two levels of organization, departments and divisions, in municipal agencies having finance functions. The result holds within each of

the three cities for which time series were assembled; it holds when historical time, changes in municipal administration, size, and other conditions are
controlled. Why extensive formal organization is associated with lower mortality among the agencies studied cannot be determined definitively from
the data at hand. The argument that the advantage of organization lies in
fixity, hence administrative efficiency and improved decision making, is
plausible but appears not to be consistent with the results showing some
measures of variability to decrease mortality. The argument that the advantage of organization lies in its flexibility is more consistent with the effects of
variability shown above, but alternative interpretations of these results are
possible.

7.4 Implications

The present results do not prove "spontaneous creation" or "built-in"
growth of bureaucratic structures. But the results are not inconsistent with
these ideas, which heretofore have had their basis in description rather than
in tests of propositions that are falsifiable. If extensive formal organization
sustains individual units of public bureaucracy – that is, if other things being
equal there is a preference for organization – and if this preference operates
unrestrained throughout administrative hierarchies, then organizational
growth will result. That organizational growth has occurred in the agencies
that are the subject of this research is indisputable. As noted earlier, Chicago, Detroit, and Philadelphia each had four organizational units responsible for finance functions in 1890. By 1975, Chicago had sixty-three,
Detroit fifty, and Philadelphia sixty-three such units.

Confirmation that bureaucratic structures tend toward growth because of
preferences for formal organization requires much more extensive investi-
gation and analysis than is possible in one research study. It is the case,
however, that alternative explanations for growth have been considered and
have been shown either not to be operate or not to affect the processes
described here. In particular, bureaucratic growth has been shown not to be
a function of immediate task requirements throughout much of the interval
studied, and growth has been shown for the most part not to be a function of
inertia whereby once formed individual units of organization are not easily
displaced. Kaufman (1976), it should be recalled, considered both of these
explanations and found both task demands and inertia not to account for the
increased numbers of government agencies he observed.

No wholesale revision of thinking about organizational structures is indicated by the present results, but a shift in emphasis may be. This chapter

began with a review of some of the alleged advantages of extensive administrative organization. The propositions listed are as fundamental as any in
organizational theory, and many appeared early in the history of theory. All
seek to explain organizational structures in terms of their consequences for
organizations, and all indicate positive consequences of structure. These
propositions are very different from ideas pursued in recent research that
have sought to explain structures in terms of antecedent conditions, such as
size, technology, intentions of participants, and the welter of environmental
elements that can impinge on organizations (see Scott, 1975). The results
presented in this chapter tend to give credence to the earlier ideas suggesting
advantages of extensive formal organization. But the results also suggest
lacunae in these ideas in that none anticipates limits to the organizing process. It may be that this gap in theory is also a problem for organizations, at
least public bureaucracies, to the extent that increase in formal organization, hence bureaucratic growth, are not easily limited.

The ultimate cause of the pattern observed here – extensive administrative
structure preserves organizations – is not indicated by the data at hand, and
it may be that no quantitative data can alone provide a satisfactory explanation. A preference for organization is nonetheless indicated. The one
explanation consistent with theory and with the results observed above is
that extensive organization allows change and, perhaps, uncertainty to be
managed better better than would be the case absent organization. Myriad
further explanations for our results could be proffered, but few could be
tested within the confines of this research. Suffice it to note that any explanation that relies upon managers' preferences for structure as a means of
protecting themselves or aggrandizing their offices must ask the further
question of why managers' preferences are not checked. It may be simply
that the facts of bureaucratic growth take years to surface hence the causes
of growth are not corrected quickly. But, more disconcertingly, it may also
be that one of the key presuppositions of bureaucracy – that diverse and
sometimes conflicting interests can be managed within the framework of
rational administration – can be maintained only under conditions of bureaucratic growth.

Chapter 8
The Bureaucratic Structure Hypothesis

The purpose of this chapter is to complete the test of the preference model of bureaucratic growth. In the previous chapter, extensive formal organization was shown to reduce mortality for organizational units with finance functions in the three cities studied. This result held for both departments and divisions, suggesting that preferences for organization are present at all levels of administrative hierarchies and suggesting, further, that such preferences yield long-term bureaucratic growth. Here, we will ask whether increased formal organization is followed by growth in staff or whether, contrariwise, increased numbers of personnel accounts better for growth in organization. This chapter will, therefore, develop a complete theory of the relationship of the size of organizations, as measured by numbers of personnel, to the structure of organizations, as measured by numbers of subunits. One component of this theory has been developed extensively in the literature and treats administrative organization mainly as a function of size: The larger a unit's staff, the greater its differentiation into subunits and sub-subunits. This is the size hypothesis. The second component of the theory treats size as a function of formal organization: The more categories of organization and the more elaborate formal organizational structure, the greater the claim to resources and the larger the staff. This is the bureaucratic structure hypothesis. Wholly different implications would be drawn depending on which of the hypotheses is most correct. The size hypothesis suggests organization to be epiphenomenal, mainly an accommodation to span-of-control constraints and the requirement that reporting relationships be represented hierarchically. The implication is that once certain classical principles of administration – division of labor, unity of command, span of control – have been satisfied, administrative organization makes little difference. The bureaucratic structure hypothesis suggests, by contrast, that organizational patterns are consequential for size and possibly other things, and are therefore central to organizations.

A further purpose of this chapter is to make explicit and to compare two fundamentally different conceptions of organizations. One, which is conventional, views organizations as permanent with well-defined boundaries separating organization from environment. The existence of organizations is assumed, and attention is directed toward interrelations of variables describing environments and organizations such as demand for services, size, measures of organizational structure, and the like. This conception of organization strongly favors the size hypothesis because it does not consider the kinds of fundamental changes, such as births and deaths of units, that are most likely to affect size. An alternative conception developed in the third chapter understands bureaucratic systems as units within units within still larger units, all of which are in some sense organizations. The existence of individual units is considered to be variable as are boundaries between organizations and environments. Attention is therefore directed to both causes and consequences of births and deaths of individual units. This alternative conception of organizations favors neither the size nor the bureaucratic structure hypothesis. The size of an organization may affect its array of units, the latter determined by the balance of births and deaths, or births and deaths of individual units may affect the size of a larger, more inclusive organizational system. The alternative conception of organizations also suggests an inconsistency in the conventional view since the latter assumes impermanence in organizational subunits, whose configuration constitutes administrative structure, yet permanence in larger units treated as organizations. When one treats all units as organizations that are at least potentially impermanent, this inconsistency is relieved.

Finally, and most importantly, this chapter completes a theory of bureaucratic growth. As noted earlier, bureaucratic growth has not heretofore been explained satisfactorily except as an outcome of fundamental social change (Weber, 1946; Stinchcombe, 1965). Economists have developed several models of bureaucratic *size* (Niskanen, 1971; Migue and Belanger, 1974) but not of bureaucratic *growth* despite its pervasiveness and obvious consequences. In the previous chapter, the existence and extensiveness of organizational subunits was shown to preserve larger units. This result proved robust when size, level of organization, age, time, and place were controlled. At issue here is whether, following the size hypothesis, organizational structure is principally an outcome of size, or, following the bureaucratic structure hypothesis, size is a function of administrative organization. To the extent that structure arises from size, a causal path from size to structure to organizational persistence can be traced. But to the extent that size follows elaboration of formal organization, organization must be understood as a source of both persistence and growth and must be explained in terms of other elements, especially the intersection of larger environmental forces generating preferences for new organizations and strategic choices made within existing organizations.

To date, most empirical evidence favors the size hypothesis (Blau, 1970; Meyer, 1972; Kimberly, 1976). Nonetheless, the size hypothesis remains unsatisfying as a theory of the relationship of formal organization to size for several reasons. First, the size hypothesis is partly truism. There cannot be more positions, job titles, or units than there are persons in an organization, at least not for long. Second, the size hypothesis is inconsistent with the premise that administrative structure is central to organizations, which is embodied in both classical sociological theory as well as in the contemporary literature on industrial organization.[1] Third, the size hypothesis runs contrary to the common sense observation that organizations grow as the result of new programs and activities, not the reverse. Precisely for this reason, some researchers have interpreted correlations of size with measures of administrative organization as supporting the bureaucratic structure hypothesis (Niskanen, 1975), while others have turned to retrospective accounts of organizational change for evidence that size follows formal organization (Daft and Bradshaw, 1980).

The limitations of the size hypothesis compel a rigorous evaluation of its obverse, the bureaucratic structure hypothesis. But because the size hypothesis holds by definition or nearly so under some circumstances, the bureaucratic structure hypothesis cannot be tested in isolation. Instead, the size and bureaucratic structure hypotheses must be evaluated simultaneously. This poses substantial difficulties, however, since there is no simple or elegant way to test the hypothesis that size is at once consequence and cause of organizational patterns. Why this is so will be explored in some detail in the next section. Absent an optimal model for estimating structure and size as simultaneous functions of one another, some alternative approaches, all deficient in some respects, are pursued. These models are developed and tested with time series in the following section. The concluding section outlines the implications of the empirical results, some of which go substantially beyond the structure-size question.

8.1 Structure and Size: Problems of Estimation and Inference

The Problem of Simultaneity

Let us begin with a simple simultaneous model of the relationship of administrative structure with size. Denoting size as s and measures of structure – it does not matter for the moment which – as d, the following model is indicated:

$$d = b_0 + b_1 s + e, \text{ and}$$
$$s = b_0' + b_1'd + e,$$

where b_0 is a constant term and e represents a residual or error term in each equation.

---

[1] This body of theory is reviewed in the previous chapter, pp. 149–151 above.

The first equation reflects the size hypothesis and the second the bureaucratic structure hypothesis. Unfortunately, the coefficients in this model cannot be estimated because the model is underidentified. Since each variable is solely a function of the other, it is not possible to separate the causal influence of one on the other.

Normally, exogenous variables determined outside of the system are introduced to relieve underidentification. The identification rule called the order condition states that the number of exogenous variables excluded from each equation must equal at least the number of endogenous variables included as explanatory variables. In the example most often used in econometrics texts, the supply of agricultural products increases with price and rainfall, the second exogenous, while demand decreases with price but increases with consumers' income, the second also exogenous. By excluding one of the two exogenous variables from each equation, the identification rule is satisfied, and coefficients of price, or, more accurately, supply and demand elasticities of price, can be estimated.

The issue to be pursued here is whether there are analogs to rainfall and income that would permit identification of the two-equation system above, or, at a minimum, one of the equations. Three questions arise. One is whether *any* variables are exogenous to the model. The answer is affirmative so long as environmental elements not constructed or enacted by organizations themselves can be found. The second question is whether any exogenous variables included in the equation predicting size can be excluded from the equation predicting structure. The answer is clearly affirmative as many external elements affecting size, such as demand, will influence structure only through their effects on size. The third question is whether any exogenous variables included in the equation predicting structure can be excluded from the equation predicting size. In principle, no difficulty is posed as decisions to pursue new policies or objectives may occur independently of size yet influence organizational patterns. In practice, however, there are substantial difficulties as many decisions and choices made by organizations are unobservable at the time the occur, and very few can be reconstructed fifty or more years after the fact. And even when past decisions can be reconstructed there remain problems in imputing causality: How can the fact of a decision or choice be ascertained except by its consequences?

In short, there exists no satisfactory way to identify models treating organizational structure and size as simultaneous functions of one another. Exogenous variables assumed not to affect structure net of size can normally be found, but elements not affecting size net of structure are often intangible decisions or choices that when found cannot be distinguished from their effects.

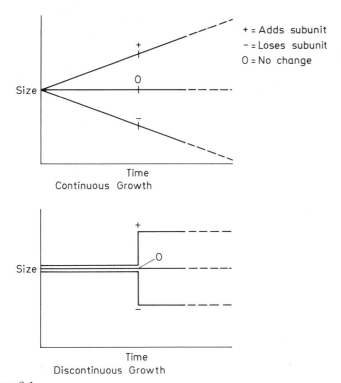

Figure 8.1
Continuous versus Discontinuous Growth in Organizations

The Problem of Falsifiability

In the absence of a solution to the identification problem, the two equations above or equations like them will have to be estimated separately. This, however, raises the question of what evidence, if any, could falsify the size hypothesis, the hypothesis that formal organization is a function of size. Measures of structure and size are expected to be correlated in both cross-sections and time series, hence models estimating structure as a function of size or size as a function of structure will almost always be confirmed when both size and structure are measured continuously. The possibility of disconfirmation exists, however, should change measures be utilized, but the bureaucratic structure hypothesis is most easily disconfirmed.

Figure 8-1 illustrates why the bureaucratic structure hypothesis is more vulnerable to disconfirmation than the size hypothesis. In the upper portion Figure 8-1, continuous changes in logarithmic size are accompanied by discrete changes in structure for two of three hypothetical organizations. For a third organization, size and structure remain unchanged over time. For these three cases, size would predict structural change. While structural change would predict subsequent growth or decline, it would not affect rates of growth or decline or account for large increments or decrements in size. The pattern represented in this portion of Figure 8-1, then, is more consistent with the size than the bureaucratic structure hypothesis, and for this reason the latter is disconfirmed.

The lower portion of Figure 8-1 depicts a somewhat different situation where structural change and discontinuous changes in size occur simultaneously for two of three hypothetical organizations. As before, size and structure remain unchanged for a third organization. Size would predict structural change in this instance, but structural change would also predict incremental or decremental changes in size. The bureaucratic structure hypothesis is supported, but the size hypothesis is not disconfirmed since changes in size and structure occur at the same time. The case for disconfirmation of the size hypothesis would be stronger had changes in structure preceded changes in size, but it would not be conclusive because one could argue that structure is often changed in anticipation of growth. The choice between the size and bureaucratic structure hypothesis will therefore rely as much on theory as empirical results, but results consistent with the bureaucratic structure hypothesis may be weighted somewhat more than results consistent with the size hypothesis because the latter is not easily disconfirmed.

8.2 Models of Size and Organizational Structure

Three models of the relationship of organizational structure to size are developed here. The first is conventional. It assumes size and formal organization to change in pattern similar to Figure 8-1a. The size hypothesis is tested by estimating numbers of subunits as functions of size and other characteristics of larger units. The second and third models assume change patterns similar to Figure 8-1b. In the second model, organizational changes are treated as transitions from one qualitative state to another. Rates of transition, that is, rates of adding or of losing subunits, are then estimated as functions of size and other variables in this second test of the size hypothesis. The third model also treats organizational change as a qualitative transition, but change becomes the independent variable and growth the dependent variable in a test of the bureaucratic structure hypothesis. The first and the third models are then reestimated using lagged and leading values of the independent variables. No one of these procedures is entirely defensible, but a consistent pattern of results from these models should permit evaluation of the relative merits of the size and bureaucratic structure hypotheses.

The units used in evaluating the size and bureaucratic structure hypotheses vary, depending upon which model is tested. Tests of the first model, where numbers of subunits are estimated as functions of logarithmic size, are undertaken, first, for the three cities over sixty-nine year series, second, for thirteen departments within these cities over twenty-two year series, and, third, for ten divisions in these departments over eleven year series. Tests of the second model, where rates of gaining or losing subunits are estimated as functions of logarithmic size, are undertaken for 329 "spells" of existence of departments and divisions. Tests of the third model, where logarithmic size is estimated as a function of organizational change and a linear growth trend, are undertaken, first, for thirteen departments over sixteen year series and, second, for ten divisions over sixteen year series. These units were selected somewhat opportunistically, based on available data and other considerations. Tests of the first model, for example, were conducted for the three cities for all years when the total size of their finance functions could be determined[2] but were restricted to those departments and divisions having one or more subunits for eight or more years. Tests of the third model were restricted to units experiencing a single organizational change between the eighth and ninth years of sixteen year series. As the reader is now aware, there is some mortality among individual departments and divisions in the finance agencies studied. The longer the series required to test models of size and organizational structure, the fewer departments and, especially, divisions available for study. The units used in the present tests of the size and bureaucratic structure hypotheses represent, we believe, the best compromise between numbers of units and length of series. Experiments with different numbers of units and lengths of series produced results essentially similar to those reported below.

Model I: *Structure as a Function of Size*

The first model estimates organizational structure as a logarithmic function of size, as is conventional in the literature, and of some other variables. Estimates of this model are made using a form of generalized least squares regression that assumes error terms to be correlated cross-sectionally and first-order autoregressive by time.[3] Formally:

$$d = b_0 + b_1 \log s + b_2 \log s' + b_3 d' + e,$$

where d is the measure of structure, s is size, s' is the size of the next higher or more inclusive level of organization, and d' is the same measure of structure for the next higher or more inclusive level and e represents a residual or

---

[2] While data on the organizational structure of departments are available for the 1890–1975 interval, some data on size are missing prior to 1907.

[3] No significant second- or higher-order autocorrelation appears in our series.

Table 8.1
Effects of Size and Other Variables on Numbers of Subunits

	b
(a) Effects of City Size on Number of Departments (N = 69 observations × 3 series)	
Constant	.339
Log_{10} City Size	1.637**
(b) Effects of Department Size on Number of Divisions (N = 22 observations × 13 series)	
Constant	.125
Log_{10} Department Size	2.922**
Log_{10} City Size	.166
Number of Departments in City	—.162**
(c) Effects of Division Size on Number of Sections (N = 11 observations × 10 series)	
Constant	2.014
Log_{10} Division Size	1.083**
Log_{10} Department Size	.159
Number of Divisions in Department	—.191**

** $p < .01$

error term. Separate estimates of Model I were made for cities (from which the s' and d' terms are omitted since there is no higher level), departments (for which cities are the next highest level), and divisions (for which departments are the next highest level). These estimates are displayed in Table 8.1.

The estimates in Table 8.1 are consistent with the size hypothesis in several respects. The size of a unit, whether, a city (i.e., all departments with finance functions), department, or division has the expected positive effect upon numbers of subunits, which are departments (for cities), divisions (for departments), and sections (for divisions). The coefficients of the logarithms of size range from 1.083 for divisions to 2.922 for departments, all of which are highly significant. This result is familiar: structural differentiation increases with size. Two other results in Table 8.1 are less familiar, however. One is that the size of more inclusive organizational units, which are cities in the second panel and departments in the third panel of Table 8.1, has no impact on numbers of subunits. The extensiveness of structure within a unit is a function of its size but not of the size of other units. The second less familiar result is that the structure of more inclusive units does affect subunit structure. Numbers of divisions increase with departmental size but decrease with the number of departments in a city. Similarly, numbers of sections in a division increase with divisional size but decrease with the number of divisions in a department. In both instances, the number of units at a given level is an inverse function of the number of units at the next higher level. These results indicate that choices as to where to locate functions may be made somewhat independently of size and suggest that the size hypothesis may be incomplete.

Model I: *Structural Change as a Function of Size*

The second model treats rates of structural change, of transition between one state of organization and another, as functions of size and other variables. The transitions of interest are those between not having and having and, alternatively, between having and not having subunits. For departments, in other words, rates of transition from not having to having divisions as well as from having to not having divisions are estimated. For divisions, the two transitions are from not having to having sections and, similarly, from having to not having sections. Model I, it should be noted, treated measures of organizational structure as continuously variable and, by implication, organizational change as a continuous process. Here, organizational change is considered to be a transition from one qualitative state to another.

There are several advantages to treating change in formal organization as a qualitative event. One is that dynamic models can be estimated using the same techniques that were introduced in earlier chapters to estimate organizational mortality. Model I, even though it makes use of time series, remains a static model. A second advantage is that two types of change, gaining and losing subunit organization, can be estimated separately as functions of size. The size hypothesis suggests the effects of size to be symmetrical and therefore approximately equal for the two types of transitions. Formal organization should increase and decrease with size similarly. Should, however, formal organization be constrained by size but not otherwise caused by size, an asymmetry can be anticipated: While large size may or may not cause increases in formal organization, small size, past a point, will necessarily cause contraction of formal organization since the number of organizational units cannot exceed total personnel. Should size merely constrain formal organization but not cause its growth, then, one would expect small size to predict loss of subunit organization better than large size to predict gain of subunit organization.

Formally, Model II is as follows:

$$\log r = b_0 + b_1 \log s + b_2 k,$$

or equivalently,

$$r = \exp[b_0] * \exp[b_1 \log s] * \exp[b_2 k]$$

Table 8.2
Effects of Size on Rates of Gaining and Losing Substructure (N = 329 "spells")

	exp[B]
(a) Gaining Substucture	
Parameter	.005
Log_{10} Size	2.202
Department Dummy	1.776
(b) Losing Substructure	
Parameter	.407
Log_{10} Size	.247**
Department Dummy	.561#

# p < .10
** p < .01

where r is the instantaneous rate of transition from one qualitative state to another, s size whose logarithm is taken to the base ten, and k a dummy variable coded one for departments and zero for divisions. The second form of the model is the one actually estimated in Table 8.2 as its results are more easily interpreted.

The estimates in Table 8.2 show size to have the expected impact upon rates of organizational change, although the effect is significant for only one of two transitions. The reader should remember that exponential rather than linear coefficients are displayed in Tabel 8.2. Thus, for example, the exponential coefficient for log size in the upper panel of the table, 2.202, indicates that the likelihood of adding subunit organization when none had existed previously is approximately doubled with each order of magnitude increase in size. The exponential coefficient for log size in the lower panel of Table 8.2 is .247 and indicates that the likelihood of losing subunit organization decreases by a factor of approximately four with each order of magnitude increase in size. The coefficient of size is not statistically significant in the model estimating rates of gaining substructure, but it is statistically significant in the model where rates of losing subunit organization are estimated.[4] Table 8.2 also shows that departments are about twice as likely to gain and half as likely to lose subunit organization compared to divisions. The first result is somewhat anomolous and reflects the early history of agencies studied during which relatively small departments added numerous divi-

[4] The coefficients in Table 8.2 are of the form exp[b]. Should b equal zero, exp[b] is unity. For this reason, the null hypothesis, save for the constant, is exp[b] = 1.

sions, but divisions tended not to add sections as they grew. In neither model is the coefficient of the dummy variable for departments significant, however. Model II, then, shows size to be a somewhat better predictor of losing than of gaining organizational substructure. It provides, at best, weak support for the size hypothesis.

Model III: *Size as a Function of Structural Change*

A direct test of the bureaucratic structure hypothesis is now undertaken. Size is treated as a function of organizational change and of time over sixteen-year intervals as follows:

$$s = b_0 + b_1 k + b_2 t + e, \qquad \text{(eq. 4)}$$

where s is the logarithm to the base ten of size, k has values of zero for the first eight years of a series and is otherwise a constant indicating the magnitude of structural change occuring between the eighth and ninth years, and t is time, running from year one to year sixteen. The model assumes a constant rate of organizational growth or decline, which is interrupted only by structural change. Sixteen year intervals, as noted earlier, were chosen somewhat arbitrarily to balance the need for extended series with the need for multiple series. The longer the series, the fewer series available in which units existed continuously.

The coefficient b_1 is crucial to the bureaucratic structure hypothesis. In the equation predicting the size of organizational systems responsible for finance functions in the three cities, k is the number of departments gained when it is positive and the number of departments lost when it is negative. In the equation predicting departmental size, k indicates whether the divisional

Table 8.3
Effects of Organizational Change on Log_{10} Size

	b	Antilog [b]
(a) Effects of Departmental Change on Size of finance Function (N = 16 observations × 13 series)		
Parameter	2.643	
Departments added/lost	.044**	.106
Year	.014**	.034
(b) Effects of Divisional Change on Department Size (N = 16 observations ×10 series)		
Parameter	1.612	
Divisional structure formed/dissolved	.043**	.103
Year	.012**	.028

** $p < .01$

level of organization was added, in which case k equals 1, or lost, in which case k equals −1. All changes in departmental or divisional organization occur at the midpoint of series between years 8 and 9. Should the coefficient of k prove nonsignificant, that is, should no significant increments or decrements in size be associated with organizational change as in Figure 1a, then the bureaucratic structure hypothesis would be rejected. Should k prove significant and size change with formal organization as in Figure 8-1b, then the evidence would favor the bureaucratic structure hypothesis, although not conclusively. A similar method is used by Niskanen (1975) to test the bureaucratic structure hypothesis.

The impact of departmental change on the overall size of the city finance functions is shown in the upper panel of Tabel 8.3, and the impact of adding or removing the divisional level of organizations from departments in shown in the lower panel of the table. As in Table 8.1, a form of generalized least squares regression that assumes the error term to be first-order autoregressive and correlated in cross-sections is used. The results displayed in Table 8.3 are straightforward, consistent across the two levels of organization for which estimation is possible, and consistent with the bureaucratic structure hypothesis. The estimated coefficients of both year and organizational change are highly significant, the latter substantially greater than the former. Antilogs of the estimated coefficients, which are also displayed in Table 8.3, show the annual rates of growth for all city finance functions and

Table 8.4
Lagged and Leading Effects

	Lagged	Contemporaneous	Leading
(a) Effects of Size on Number of Subunits[a]			
For Cities	.756*	1.637**	1.227**
For Departments	.506	3.080**	1.664**
For Divisions	1.298**	1.376**	1.326**
(b) Effects of Size on Rates of Gaining and Losing Substructure[b]			
For Gaining Substructure	2.202		4.753*
For losing Substructure	.247**		.200**
(c) Effects of Organizational Change on Size			
For Cities	.025**	.044**	.025**
For Departments	.031**	.43**	.011**

[a] Model is $d = b_0 + b_1 \log s + e$.
[b] There are no contemporaneous effects in Model II since dependent variable is *transition* between observations.
* $p < .05$
** $p < 01$

departments to be about three per cent – 3.4 per cent for the former and 2.8 per cent for the latter – net of other things in the sixteen-year series. Structural change accelerates or retards growth by an additional ten to eleven percentage points. For each new department added (or lost), the size of the city finance function increases (or decreases) 10.6 per cent beyond the normal rate of growth. Each department that adds (or removes) the divisional level of organization gains (or loses) an additional 10.3 per cent of its employees. The size of organizational units, then, changes discontinuously and substantially at points of structural change. While this result is not inconsistent with the size hypothesis, it is certainly consistent with its obverse, the bureaucratic structure hypothesis.

Lagged and Leading Effects

We now turn to the question of temporal ordering – does size precede organization, are the two contemporaneous, or does formal organization precede size? Normally, size is assumed to precede organization (Blau, 1970), but our time series data suggest otherwise. The three models developed above are now reestimated using lagged and leading values of the independent variables. This procedure permits us to experiment, in effect, with different temporal orderings of size and formal organization to determine which best fits the data.

Table 8.4 displays lagged, contemporaneous, and leading coefficients of size for Models I and II and of organizational change for Model III. The results for Model I are displayed in the uppermost panel, Model II in the center panel, and Model III in the lower panel of the table. Model I, it should be noted, is altered somewhat in this table. Numbers of subunits are treated as a function of size but of neither the size nor the extensiveness of organization in more inclusive units, d' and s' respectively in the second equation above, in order to avoid complexities arising from lagging and leading these variables. Two results emerge from the upper panel of Table 8.4. First, the effects of size on numbers of subunits are greatest when both are measured contemporaneously. Second, the leading coefficients of size are consistently larger than lagged coefficients. In other words, the estimated effects of size on organization are greater when size is measured a year *later* than organizational patterns rather than a year before, but the greatest effects occur when both are measured in the same year. In the center panel of Table 8.4, the estimated effects of size on gaining and losing substructure are reproduced from Table 8.2 under the "lagged" heading since size was measured in the year immediately preceding the transitions that are dependent variables in this model. Under the "leading" heading, transition rates are estimated as a function of size measured in the year *following* gain or loss of substructure. Again, the leading coefficients of size are of greater magnitude than the two lagged coefficients: The likelihood of gaining substructure increases and the likelihood of losing substructure decreases more rapidly with size when the latter is measured after transitions rather than before. Finally, the results in the lower panel of Table 8.4 are much like those in the upper panel. The contemporaneous effects of structural change on size, which are reproduced from Table 8.3, are larger than either lagged or leading effects. For cities, lagged and leading effects of organizational change are identical, but at the departmental level, the lagged effect of structural change is much larger than its leading effect. Structural change predicts growth or decline for departments somewhat better when it is measured before rather than after departmental size.

Overall, the estimates in Table 8.4 show organizational patterns and size to be for the most part contemporaneous events. However, to the extent that organization and size can be ordered temporally, the extensiveness of organization tends to precede size rather than the reverse. When numbers of subunits were estimated as a function of size, leading values of size had larger coefficients than lagged values in all instances. When size was treated as a function of organizational change, the lagged coefficient of organizational change was greater than its leading coefficient in one instance and identical to it in another. The bureaucratic structure hypothesis finds somewhat more support in these data than the size hypothesis.

8.3 Implications

Elaboration of organization and growth are largely contemporaneous events in bureaucracies. When the evidence does permit choice between the size hypothesis – size causes organization – and the bureaucratic structure hypothesis – formation and dissolution of organizational units cause size – it favors the latter. This is of some significance since the bureaucratic structure hypothesis is more easily falsified than the size hypothesis. How this result extends earlier findings, whether the traditional conception of organizations as fixed units separable from their environments yet subject to internal change can be maintained, and whether long-term bureaucratic growth can be attributed entirely to causes wholly external to organizations should now be explored.

Extension of Earlier Results

At this point, some results presented in earlier chapters should be reviewed. Three models of bureaucratic growth, it will be recalled, were proposed above. One model tied long-term growth to growth in quantifiable task demands. This model held to some extent for the interval beginning in 1907 and ending in 1932 – personnel counts were not available for all three cities prior to 1907 – but from 1933 onward task measures did not predict growth well. A second model tied bureaucratic growth to inertia or aging whereby over time individual organizational units become more closely linked to their environments hence less vulnerable to displacement requiring that new units be formed to accommodate change. No wholly satisfactory test of the inertial model was possible because of the difficulty of separating effects of historical period or time from effects of age on organizational mortality. To the extent that the inertial model could be tested, the effects of age on survival rates for individual units were either small or nonsignificant. Age or inertia, apparently, does not account for the excess of organizational unit births over deaths. A third model hypothesized bureaucratic growth to be the outcome of preferences for organization or a problem-organization-problem-more organization cycle whereby the capacity of existing units to accommodate environmental change is augmented by extending formal organizational structure. The evidence presented in the previous chapter showed that, controlling for other causes of mortality, units having subunit organization had significantly lower mortality than units not having subunits. This result, importantly, held for both departments and divisions, suggesting preferences for organization throughout administrative hierarchies. The previous chapter also showed size not to influence mortality net of measures of subunit organization. This chapter has shown size and the extensiveness of organization to be largely contemporaneous events but, on balance, changes in organization to be better predictors of size than size to predict changes in organization. Formal organization, not size, appears to drive bureaucratic growth.

None of the empirical results presented here or in previous chapters can demonstrate why preferences for organization driving long-term growth are ubiquitous. Historical and theoretical explanations are required. These explanations, outlined in the first three chapters, are tied to conceptions of rational administration that emerged in the first decade of this century and have persisted since. Precisely because the data cannot explain why preferences for organization have operated in the past, they cannot predict when these preferences will shift, or if they ever will. This is a matter for speculation. Clearly, however, bureaucratic growth cannot continue indefinitely.

The Concept of Organization Reconsidered

The present results add credence to the argument made in the third chapter, namely that the conception of organizations as fixed units with variable properties is insufficient to account for bureaucratic growth. Under conventional conceptions of organization, bureaucratic growth is understood only as increase in size, not also as increase in formal organization. Under the conception of organization developed above, where organizations consist of units within units within still larger units, the quantity of organization is variable hence growth can be understood as both increase in size and increase in formal organization. The results developed here and in the previous chapter show that bureaucratic growth cannot be understood easily so long as the conventional conception of organization is maintained. Large size appears not to advantage organizational units net of other things. Preferences for increased size, therefore, do not explain bureaucratic growth. Extensive formal organization does appear to offer advantages – there are preferences for organization – and extensive formal organization also appears to give rise to large size in organizations. The conception of the quantity of organization as variable, thus, is more useful than the conception of organizations as fixed units whose properties are variable.

There is another way to approach this problem of defining organization. Assuming the conventional conception of organizations and assuming the empirical result demonstrated above that, on balance, the configuration of organizational subunits predicts size better than size predicts subunit organization, one must ask how this finding would be articulated using the conventional conception of organization. Roughly, one would say that organizational structure causes size. But since structure connotes fixity, or, at least, predictability, one must ask how that which is fixed or predictable can account for size, which is variable. Using the variable conception of organization developed here, the term structure is largely replaced by phrases such as extensiveness of formal organization, subunit organization, and the like. To state that the extensiveness of organization causes size does not encounter the same difficulty as saying that structure causes size because the extensiveness of formal organization, just like the existence and variability in subunit organization, is a variable property that can reasonably be considered as a cause of other variable properties of organizations, including their size.

The Role of the Environment in Bureaucratic Growth

In a chapter such as this one, it is easy to overlook the centrality of the environment to bureaucratic growth. The environment enters into bureaucratic growth in two ways. First, the larger environment, what some have called the institutional environment of organizations, has legitimated bureaucratically structured organizations as appropriate solutions to problems where market mechanisms do not provide solutions. Concepts of rational administration have become so deeply embedded in modern societies that it is difficult to imagine solutions to many problems that do not involve building organizations. Second, perturbations in the environment trigger the process of building new organizations and organizational units. In this book, no theory of the environment has been developed, that is, we have attempted no theory explaining why environmental perturbations occurred as they did at the time they did. Each shift in the environment of municipal finance can, of course, can be explained in terms of events immediately preceding it. But overall shifts in the larger environment of the agencies studied cannot be explained and, indeed, probably do not require explanation. Whatever changes have occurred objectively, the environments in which public bureaucracies believe themselves to be operating contain much of their history, all of the perturbations of the past, plus the present. Over time, then, these environments increase in complexity, like the organizations to which they give rise.

Both our theoretical argument and research findings suggest that environments do not enter into bureaucratic growth in one key respect. Quantitative increases in task demands, to the extent that tasks can be quantified, appear not to be the principal cause of bureaucratic growth. This is not to say that tasks performed by bureaucracies have not increased. This is to say, however, that the tasks demanded externally of bureaucracies have shown little consistent relationship to growth. Those tasks performed that are not demanded externally consist mainly, of course, of tasks demanded of bureaucracies by bureaucracies themselves. The logic of rational administration gives rise to this internal demand. The environment poses uncertainties; bureaucracies accommodate these uncertainties within the framework of formal administrative rationality that requires consistency of present and past action; the array of elements bureaucracies confront, hence their formal organization and size, increase over time. Importantly, as was shown in the previous chapter, organizational units failing to incorporate new elements tend to survive less well than others. And, as shown in this chapter, new elements of organization tend, on balance, to precede rather than to follow increased numbers of personnel.

Even though task elements appear not to determine bureaucratic growth or to do so only partially, the theory of the relationship of organization to size developed here incorporates environmental elements to a much greater extent than earlier theories of size and organizational structure. The size hypothesis posits changes in administrative organization to be calculated responses to growth or decline in numbers of personnel. The bureaucratic structure hypothesis, which is favored here, posits new units to be created and later staffed. The size hypothesis says nothing whatever about the role of environments in growth of either staff or of formal organization. The bureaucratic structure hypothesis is embedded in a larger theory explaining why new organizational units are constructed by environments. Thus, even though this chapter has not focused directly on environmental causes of bureaucratic growth, its results are consistent with a theory of bureaucratic growth where the conjunction of uncertainty with the constraint of administrative rationality cause organizational elements to accumulate over time hence long-term growth to occur.

Chapter 9
Alternatives to Bureaucratic Growth

This concluding chapter has three purposes. Its first purpose is to review the theoretical arguments and empirical research results developed above and to determine whether the theory is sustained by the research results. Its second purpose is to add to the earlier theoretical development by addressing the issue – which is the title of this book – of limits to bureaucratic growth. If theory predicts bureaucratic growth, as we believe it does, then theory should also consider limits to growth. One might expect that limits to growth are approached when the complexity of organization itself meets or exceeds the complexity of environments it purportedly addresses. Yet the absence of failure mechanisms in public bureaucracies renders uncertain any prediction about limits to growth so long as current concepts of rational administration are retained. A final purpose of this chapter is to suggest how alternatives to bureaucratic growth may emerge. Many of the same elements that were present in traditional systems of administration – complexity, uncertainty, and politicization of action – are now present in bureaucratic administration to an unacceptable degree. These elements alone are probably insufficient to cause any fundamental rethinking of the premises of organization. Nonetheless, just as the advantage of bureaucracy over traditional forms of organization seventy-five years ago was its simplicity and certainty, any form that challenges prevailing concepts of rational administration will also have to offer these advantages.

It is fitting that this book ends roughly where it began, with a further reconsideration of prevailing ideas about organizing. The last section of this chapter assumes what was established earlier, that much of organizational theory can be understood as prescribing bureaucratic growth. It asks whether the growth and increasing complexity of bureaucratic systems do not account for the inconsistent evaluations of large-scale organization that have permeated theory. It suggests that classical theory evaluated bureaucracy positively because it compared simple and therefore efficient bureaucracies with complicated and inefficient traditional patterns. It suggests, further, that while bureaucracy has evolved toward complexity and inefficiency in recent years, bureaucracy persists because the legitimacy of concepts of rational administration has not been challenged. The last section suggests also that while contemporary theory offers alternatives to the bureaucratic models, these alternatives may not be satisfactory in some settings, such as in municipal finance administration, where control of behavior and consistent outcomes are demanded without exception. This last section suggests finally that research should focus attention on bureaucratic growth, evaluate the consequences of alternative organizational forms, and examine whether alternative types of social institutions can rationalize human conduct as effectively as large-scale organizations have in the past. Importantly, asserting that the private sector should displace government offers no alternative to bureaucratic growth. Unless one assumes that organizational hierarchies in firms operate differently from organizational hierarchies in the public sector – and the evidence presented in the second chapter suggests that this is very much not the case – long-run economies may not be achieved by substituting private for public administration.

9.1 Toward a Theory of Bureaucratic Growth

A theory of bureaucratic growth emerges from the joining of organizational theory with historical analysis and quantitative research results that are consistent with theory and that explain bureaucratic growth. Existing organizational theory, to be sure, has been extended und reinterpreted in some instances in order to address the phenomenon of bureaucratic growth. And both the historical and quantitative research undertaken here suffers some limitations that again must be acknowledged. Nonetheless, the result of these efforts is a set of ideas, in fact a fairly simple set of ideas, potentially explaining why bureaucratic growth has been ubiquitous in modern societies and why it has occurred at explosive rates.

The Theoretical Analysis

The theoretical premises of this book are straightforward. It was argued that ideas of rational administration, which emerged at the turn of the century, were attempts to impose a business or machine model of organization on public bureaucracies. The reform movement, in particular, sought to substitute "businesslike" methods for the spoils system that had sustained urban political machines throughout the 1800's. The ideas of rational administration, however, contained some important inconsistencies that its proponents ignored or attempted to mask. One of these appears in Woodrow Wilson's work: Public administration was to be efficient and, again, businesslike, yet at the same time democratic. Another appears in Max Weber's writings on bureaucracy: Bureaucracy is consistent with democratic governance only if democracy is understood as equal treatment of citizens by the bureaucratic apparatus of the state but not their participation in governance. For both Wilson and Weber, then, the vagaries of democratic governance were incompatible with the demand for predictability and control in organizations. Wilson obfuscated with appeals to Americanism; Weber redefined democracy to escape the dilemma.

Classical organizational theory elaborated a number of formalisms for structuring organizations and did not consider the possibility that the machine model did not apply in all settings. Neoclassical theories of administration substituted a set of cognitive assumptions for the formalisms of classical organizational theory and thereby provided a theoretical footing for thinking about organizations. Much to its credit, the neoclassical framework attempted to resolve the problem of organizing in truly uncertain environments, but the problem could not be resolved fully. Organization was asserted to overcome bounded rationality limits of individual persons by dividing complicated problems into successively less complicated ones thus extending ends-means chains. A number of specific propositions deriving the structure of organizations from their environments flowed from this core hypothesis. But no propositions linking uncertainty in the environment to organizational design could be adduced, either theoretically or in research. The small number of research studies addressing the consequences of uncertainty for organizations did arrive at one consistent result: Regardless of the actual level of variability or volatility in the environment, perceived uncertainty was in inverse proportion to the extensiveness of formal organization. These findings, in a way, confirmed the basic premise of neoclassical theory: Organization does help reduce complicated environments to manageable proportions. But they also suggested that there may be no stable equilibrium or match between organizations and their environments. Assuming irreducible uncertainty, there are no permanent organizational solutions, only more formal organization. A spiral of growth results.

Interestingly, nonrational theories of organizations anticipated this outcome. There is no need to review here the models of bureaucratic dysfunctions and of increasing bureaucratization outlined in the second chapter. Suffice it to note that nonrational theories have not for the most part been tested in research. This has occurred partly because these theories involve feedback loops and predict disequilibrium.

A theory of bureaucratic growth is thus at least implicit in existing organizational theory. Organizations, as indicated in classical and neoclassical theories, offer satisfactory if not optimal solutions to problems. They satisfice, to use Simon's language. Because organizations satisfice, they are retained. But problems change unpredictably, requiring new organizations. A problem-organization-problem-more organization cycle of the sort anticipated in nonrational theories is thus set in motion.

The History of Municipal Finance Administration

The history of municipal finance agencies is one of the progressive extension of administrative, control. Various control mechanisms were developed from the 1910's onward. Some were innovations in accounting and budgeting, while others were innovations in organization. Two arguments were made concerning these innovations. The first is that, in one way or another, all of these mechanisms of control contributed to the construction of formal organization, to the elaboration of bureaucratic process. Generally, the accounting and budgeting innovations contributed to development of additional units of organization at lower levels of administrative hierarchy, while the organizational innovations, which were entirely in the direction of centralization of functions, contributed to development of the larger and more inclusive units of organization. In both cases, however, a "lack of definite and accountable organization," to use J. O. McKinsey's phrase, was perceived and corrected with more organization. The second argument is that while these control mechanisms may have succeeded partially or temporarily in ordering the financial administration of cities, they did not succeed permanently. If the measure of success of control mechanisms is the fiscal condition of municipalities in periods of recession or depression, then the experience of the three cities studied suggests that they were little better prepared for the recession of the mid-1970's than they were for the Great Depression.

These arguments aside, the historical analysis suggests strong parallels between the ideas about bureaucratic growth adduced from organizational theory and the ways organizational forms and practices deemed appropriate for the municipal finance function evolved over time. Organizational theory, as noted, contains an implicit problem-organization-problem-more organization cycle. The history of municipal accounting is one of the displacement of simpler with more complicated accounting standards in an effort to control and account properly for revenues, expenditures, and indebtedness. Budgets, which were intended as cost-controlling mechanisms, the fund structures of municipal accounts, whose purpose was to insure that monies allocated for different purposes were not commingled, and attempts to find a satisfactory compromise between the full cash and full accrual bases of accounting added substantially to this complexity. The history of municipal finance organization is one of continuous extension of hierarchy in an effort to centralize control of and thereby maintain uniformity and predictability in administrative functions. Comptrollers' offices grew initially as final responsibility for accounts was centralized in them, and as the payroll, purchasing, and postauditing functions were later centralized. Purchasing was later placed in a separate department in many cities, as were budgeting and, as computer technology developed, data processing. All of these functions, in turn, were placed within single centralized departments of finance in many cities.

The demand for control, which was persistent and could never be satisfied, led to almost continuous construction of organization in the interval covered by our research. The history of the finance agencies studied thus confirms the problem-organization-problem-more organization cycle suggested in theory.

The Quantitative Analysis

The analysis of quantitative data describing the organization of finance functions in Chicago, Detroit, and Philadelphia from 1890 through 1975 has yielded results anticipated in theory and implicit in the history of the agencies studied. The analysis proceeded in several steps. To begin, the unit of analysis was defined as individual organizational units – departments, divisions within departments, and sections within divisions, and sometimes the set of all departments with finance functions – consistent with the manner in which organization was understood by those constructing it, and consistent with the use of the term "organizational unit" in the municipal accounting literature. Bureaucratic growth was defined next. Bureaucratic growth is conventionally understood as increase in administrative or supervisory personnel or in bureaucratic process, and one measure of bureaucratic growth used here was increase in total employment in municipal finance functions. Another measure of bureaucratic growth was increase in numbers of organizational units with finance functions. Increased numbers of units, it was noted, could also be understood as a rate of formation of organizational units in excess of the death rate of such units.

Three models of bureaucratic growth were then developed. The first treated growth as increased staff or numbers of units. Growth was hypothesized to be a function of quantitative task measures in this model. These task measures included city size, expenditures, and indebtedness, as well as the length of budget documents and, for the period beginning in 1953, the amount of state and Federal aid to the cities studied. This task environmental model succeeded in accounting for growth of finance functions only in the interval preceding 1933. From 1933 on, the task measures exhibited almost no significant effects on the size of finance functions in Chicago, Detroit, and Philadelphia. Furthermore, qualitative task measures, with one exception, also exhibited no significant effects on growth. The exception was the impact of the Great Depression in Detroit. Detroit, it will be recalled, exhausted its treasury in 1937 and defaulted on all obligations. In the 1930–40 interval, no growth took place in Detroit's finance functions. This occurred even though bankruptcy required refunding – conversion of short- into long-term notes – of the city's outstanding debt that demanded lengthy negotiations with creditors and substantial paperwork.

The second model treated growth as an excess of organizational unit births over deaths. This excess was hypothesized to occur because, first, existing units of organization are characterized by inertia in that they are insulated somewhat from dissolution once they have been in existence for a short period, and, second, new units of organization are formed at a more or less constant rate. The second model, in other words, hypothesized bureaucratic growth to be a function of what others have called "liability of newness" or declining death rates with age. This inertial model did not succeed well. While age appeared initially to insulate units against dissolution, its effect diminished once other variables were controlled. These variables included certain organizational characteristics as well as change in municipal administration and the intersection of city with historical time, the last a surrogate for events such as reform and bankruptcy. Indeed, once all relevant control variables were entered into the equation testing this second model, the effect of age was rendered nearly nonsignificant. The inertial model does not fully explain bureaucratic growth.

The third model also treated growth as an excess of organizational unit births over deaths, but it hypothesized a different cause of this excess than the second model. The third model hypothesized the excess of births over deaths to be a result of preferences for new units of organization as a means of solving problems arising in existing units. As a test of this hypothesis, dissolution rates for organizational units were estimated as a function of the extensiveness of subunit structure. The existence and extensiveness of substructure was found to be strongly related to the longevity of units, whether departments or divisions of departments administering municipal finances. This result held when other variables were controlled. As a further test of the third model, it was asked whether increased staff tends to precede or follow the development of substructure. While no conclusive answer was possible because organizations tend to be formed and their staffs hired at the same time, results from lagged models of structure and size suggest creation of new organizational structures more often to precede than to follow increases in staff. Of the three models of bureaucratic growth tested, then, the model of growth as a function of preferences for organization succeeded best. Of the three models of growth, this one is also the most consistent with the theory of bureaucratic growth developed earlier and with the history of the agencies studied.

Unresolved Questions

The quantitative evidence on bureaucratic growth lends further credence to a theory of bureaucratic growth based in the premise that organizations are constructed to solve problems, that they do solve problems and are therefore retained, but that new problems arise continually requiring new organizations to be formed. As stated, this theory is most appropriate to organizations operating under uncertainty or in environments posing patently inconsistent constraints. It may not apply in settings where uncertainties are few, where outcomes are predictable, where there is reliable cause-and-effect knowledge. And it may not apply in organizations, or in segments of organizations, where objectives are few and highly specific.

The set of organizations to which the theory does apply is not known and cannot be ascertained within the bounds of this research. Clearly, it would be useful to know whether other municipal organizations that have experienced growth have also experienced the same continual redefinition of their tasks that has occurred in municipal finance. It would perhaps be even more useful to know whether growth of administration that has occurred in the private sector can also be attributed to increased uncertainty and complexity *in administration itself*. Heretofore, growth in administration in production organizations has been attributed principally to the need for coordination and control of their production activities. While this may be the case in some instances, the theory developed here together with the data on bureaucratic growth in industry developed in the second chapter suggests that a set of administrative tasks posing uncertainties or inconsistent demands have been imposed on firms that had and still have relatively certain production tasks. Government regulation and other legal constraints are among the possible sources of these uncertainties and inconsistencies triggering administrative growth.

Also unknown is whether the theory developed here applies with equal force in all societies. Ultimately, it was argued in the first chapter, the idea of rational administration, the notion that rationalized bureaucratic structures offer solutions to problems posed in environments, accounts for the fact of bureaucratic growth. The research results reported here are consistent with this argument, but they do not demonstrate it conclusively. The idea of rational administration is more deeply embedded in some societies than in others, and societal differences in the extensiveness of formal organization also exist. Whether or not a connection exists between organizing ideas and bureaucratic growth across societies could not be explored here but does deserve close examination. The present research was deliberately limited to a small set of organizations so that specific mechanisms linking ideas about administration and bureaucratic growth could be identified and their effects explored. This approach to bureaucratic growth needs to be complemented by a more macroscopic research strategy that compares prevailing ideas about organizing with past rates of growth and the present extensiveness of administration. Such research is not easily undertaken. Not only have ideas about organizing converged dramatically in recent years, but comparable measures of bureaucratization may not be obtainable. Furthermore, historical differences and differences across national economies would have to be controlled carefully.

The theory of bureaucratic growth developed here, then, emerges from small strands of evidence that should be augmented in further empirical studies. One would not want to allow sweeping generalizations about bureaucratic growth to rest permanently on the limited observations that were possible in this research. But theorizing must begin somewhere, and it must be connected early in its development with systematic data whose consistency or inconsistency with theory can be ascertained. This is the essence of social science. Whatever the limitations of the current research, then, its most important result is that it has yielded some results consistent with a theory of bureaucratic growth, which, in turn, can be explored and modified in subsequent research.

9.2 Limits to Bureaucratic Growth

A theory of bureaucratic growth must also consider limits to growth. The theory developed above does not specify limits to growth, and we are not sanguine that limits to growth exist. It is argued here that the complexity of organizations may meet or exceed the complexity of environments that organizations were intended to address in the first place and that such complexity in organizations then challenges bounded rationality limits just as complexity in environments does. Past a point, organizations cannot be fully understood – by their members or anyone else. Nonetheless, it is argued, the kinds of failures that may be induced in firms by the bounded rationality problem, displacement of individual firms or of organizational forms, do not occur in bureaucracies. Discontent and loss of public confidence in government caused by the bounded rationality problem also does not cause failures in bureaucratic systems because the systemic nature of the problem is not understood. Finally, attempts to induce failure through fiscal restraints are for the most part unsuccessful because outputs are cut while the administrative structures of governmental bureaucracies remains intact.

Bounded Rationality Reconsidered

Neoclassical organizational theory posits organizations to overcome the cognitive limitations of individual persons by dividing complicated problems into simpler ones. No exposition of the theory is required here. What needs emphasis at this point is the theory's assumption that the bounded rationality problem is posed only in the environment, that only problems external to organizations exceed the ability of individual persons to grasp much less to solve them. To be sure, recent revisions of neoclassical theory have suggested that conditions within organizations can also pose bounded rationality difficulties. But these revisions to neoclassical theory, which constitute the "new industrial organization," suggest solutions to these difficulties only for firms whose outputs are separable. No alternatives to bureaucratic organization hence no alternatives to bureaucratic growth are suggested.

The theory of bureaucratic growth developed here suggests that these revisions of neoclassical theory are too limited, that concepts of rational administration themselves generate complexity beyond that imposed by task demands. Concepts of administration are, of course, products of external forces just as task demands are. But they derive from beliefs about how organizations ought to be constructed, not from the necessity of accomplishing specific tasks. At the core of the theory of bureaucratic growth is the idea that organizations solve problems and are therefore retained, but that problems shift unpredictably requiring new organization. Organizations suitable for past problems remain in place for the simple reason that these problems were solved, or at least solved satisfactorily. Organizations suitable for present problems are invented as a matter of necessity. Importantly, the mechanism that simultaneously retains old and elaborates new organization is organizational structure itself, or organizational hierarchy. As new problems arise, new organizational units or categories emerge to address these problems. These new units or categories do not displace existing units but are treated as subunits or subsets of existing organizational units or categories. Over time, then, environments change unpredictably, but change within organizations is for the most part in the direction of greater complexity. Eventually, complexity within organizations approaches the complexity of the environment and in some instances exceeds it. At this point, organization begins to pose the same challenge to bounded rationality that the environment does. Organization becomes as much of a problem as a solution to problems. We arrive at the paradoxical situation where organizations charged with managing problems are unable to implement solutions because they cannot master their internal processes.

There is no way to prove that the agencies responsible for administering the finances of Chicago, Detroit, and Philadelphia increased in complexity to the point where bounded rationality limits were exceeded, where their internal processes could not be understood. Some impressionistic evidence tends toward this conclusion, however. The financial performance of Chicago, Detroit, and Philadelphia during the Depression and in the mid-1970's suggests, for example, that officials did not fully understand the condition of their cities. This may be a generous interpretation of official malfeasance, but we think it not. Anyone who has attempted to master the details of recent budgets and financial statements of U.S. municipalities will be overwhelmed by the myriad categories of revenues, expenditures and indebtedness and the numerous transactions taking place between categories. Clearly, the public and the financial community did not fully understand the fiscal condition of cities in the early 1970's. Precisely this level of complexity led to the demands for simplification of accounting. Furthermore, accounting and financial reporting standards themselves began to pose challenges to understanding by the early 1970's. There is no need to repeat here the history of municipal accounting. It suffices to note again Allan Drebin's 1979 comment, which closed the first chapter, that "there has been no general agreement as to what the objectives of governmental accounting and financial reporting are."

Organizational Failure in Public Bureaucracies

It is argued by some theorists, especially Oliver Williamson and his students, that the solution to the bounded rationality problem is organizational failure. Organizational failure, in Williamson's (1975) framework, occurs when either inefficient firms are displaced by more efficient producers or less efficient organizational structures or *forms* are displaced by more efficient forms. The classic case of displacement of organizational form is the shift from unitary or functional organizational structures to the decentralized multiunit pattern that occurred in many U.S. industries beginning in the 1920's. Almost all observers agree that this shift was necessary to preserve the economic viability of these enterprises. Failure of firms was averted by changing organizational structures or forms.

Neither of the two kinds of organizational failure outlined by Williamson – failure of firms and failure of forms – offers a viable solution to the bounded rationality problem in public bureaucracies. With rare exception, public bureaucracies do not liquidate their assets and got out of business. No matter how dismal their performance, bureaucracies are not subject to displacement by competitors. Budgets may be cut and responsibilities realigned, but the essential functions performed by a bureau persist in most instances because there is no apparent alternative to continuation. Furthermore, reorganization of public bureaucracies does not yield changes in organizational form as in industry. The history of the bureaus studied, indeed the history of almost all public bureaucracy, is the history of centralization of administrative functions. There have, of course, been experiments in bureaucratic decentralization, but the essential features of the decentralized firm – the division of a single organization into quasi-autonomous profit centers and the allocation of capital to these profit centers on the basis of expected return – have never been present. No single metric can gauge the performance of public bureaucracies, or, for that matter, the performance of various administrative departments of business firms. And no return-on-investment calculus, save perhaps for a political calculus that eludes quantification, can guide the investment of administrative effort.

Another kind of organizational failure has been suggested by Hirschman (1970). Hirschman argues that the expression of voice or of discontent is the principal mechanism signaling failure of public bureaucracies. This same mechanism, voice or discontent, also allows recuperation of failed organizations because, following Hirschman's reasoning, dissatisfaction with existing policies contains at least the implicit suggestion of alternatives that might quell discontent. Cast in the language of traditional political analysis, the process of articulation of interests yields failures hence corrections in the conduct of public business. Hirschman's theory is apt for the formation and reconsideration of public policy. It is inapplicable, we believe, to the problem of bureaucratic growth. Its inaplicability stems from two sources. First, while bureaucratic growth may generate discontent, it is an unfocused discontent, a discontent that finds its expression in loss of confidence in institutions rather than in opposition to what governmental organizations are doing. The bounded rationality problem arises with bureaucratic growth not because government agencies are doing the wrong things but because they are attempting to do too many things whose relationship to one another cannot be understood. That confidence in government and in business have eroded in recent years cannot be disputed. To be sure, opinion polls show distrust of government to stem from perceptions of inadequate or inept leadership (Lipset and Schneider, 1983: 351–52), not from bureaucratic growth. But no leadership can manage organizations, public or private, that do not understand what they are doing and therefore can neither articulate clear policies nor correct policies that are in error. Second, the kind of discontent generated by bureaucratic growth, loss of confidence or malaise, does not aid recuperation because it suggests no alternatives to an unsatisfactory state of affairs. Alternatives to bureaucratic growth and the bounded rationality problem are not stimulated, in part, due to the unfocused nature of discontent. Absent a known cause, no remedy is possible. Perhaps more importantly, alternatives do not emerge because the rationality of bureaucratic systems remains unchallenged. Organizations that have been constructed to accomplish public purposes, whatever their inefficiences, conform to concepts of rational administration and are therefore believed rational. The inadequacies of these organizations are thus failures of people, the corrective for which is replacing people. This fundamental misunderstanding leads almost inevitably to erosion of confidence in institutions of governance, one-term officeholders, and a sense that the political system is unresponsive like the administrative structures it is intended to direct.

Citizens have from time to time attempted to induce failures in public bureaucracies through means other than ordinary political channels. In the

U.S. this has occurred principally through grass-roots efforts to limit government revenues, indebtedness, and expenditures, mainly at the local level. All of the three cities studied here were at one time or another subject to revenue, debt, and expenditure restrictions, but these restrictions ultimately had little effect. Revenue limitations fell when statutory limitations on property tax rates were amended; debt limitations became meaningless as special districts were empowered to incur new debt and forms of indebtedness not secured by the full faith and credit of cities; expenditure limitations, embodied in the idea of budgeting, were never truly operative. Fiscal limitations such as these proved ineffective not because they did not reduce, at least temporarily, the cost of government, but rather because they could not cause replacement or fundamental reorganization of outmoded and inefficient structures. Some of the economists' models of bureaucratic behavior are instructive on this point. Migue and Belanger's (1974) portrait of bureaucrats as price-discriminating monopolists who are maximizing emoluments of office rather than profit is particularly useful. While not explaining bureaucratic growth, Migue and Belanger anticipate what bureaucrats do under scarcity: They limit output and raise prices, or raise prices effectively by screening requests for service more carefully, allowing queues to lengthen, and otherwise increasing the inconveniences experienced in dealing with government. The logic of the argument developed in this book suggests a similar outcome: Formal organization will be preserved at the expense of outputs should a choice between the two be forced. Bureaucratic structures are maintained and services suffer.

The Problem of Growth Redefined

The upshot of the present discussion is this: The problem of bureaucratic growth, if there is a problem of growth, is one of our inability to induce failures – our inability either to replace existing organizations or to reorganize and simplify them – in bureaucratic systems. Persistence and growth of public bureaucracies may be taken as evidence of the brute power of bureaucratic systems, which Weber attributed to their expertise and quasi-military command hierarchies. But it may also be taken as evidence of the force of the idea of rational administration, which has attributed to modern organizational structures the capacity not only to accomplish tasks beyond the abilities of unorganized persons, but also the capacity to accomplish tasks of limitless complexity. Clearly this image of organizations is inaccurate. When organizations increase in complexity and exceed the same cognitive limitations of individual persons that impede understanding of tasks and environments, the capacity of organizations to accomplish their purposes, indeed any purpose, diminishes. But the theoretical arguments and evidence developed above indicate that complexity has, at least in the past, increased rather than decreased the persistence and permanence of bureaucratic structures, and that this mechanism of persistence has led to long-term bureaucratic growth rather than to failure. The pattern cannot continue without limit, however. Indeed, it is likely that we are now approaching limits to bureaucratic growth beyond which new organization, new bureaucracy, creates more problems than it solves. This is not a satisfactory state of affairs, however, because the inability to form new organization also leaves many problems without solutions and blocks needed change.

The problem of bureaucratic growth, then, becomes the problem of finding concepts of administration that permit failure – replacement or fundamental reorganization of existing units – in complex systems that otherwise tend toward persistence and growth. These concepts, needless to say, cannot be found in routine administrative procedures that only add to rather than reduce organizational complexity and growth.[1] They must instead originate outside of existing organizations and convey unambiguously the facts of bureaucratic complexity and growth as well as the idea that organization, especially new organization, is not the solution to every problem.

9.3 Alternatives to Growth

What, then, are the alternatives to continuous bureaucratic growth? Within the framework of rational administration, as the term rational is now understood, there may be no alternatives to growth. Rational solutions to problems are almost always administered solutions requiring augmented regulations, administrative hierarchies, and staff. Until now, increases in complexity and size, themselves products of successive administered solutions, have not been considered to be problems, much less problems requiring unconventional solutions. Indeed, it is not clear that one can develop solutions to organizational problems outside of the framework of rational administration. The needed language does not exist. The only

---

[1] The U.S. government's Paperwork Reduction Act has succeeded mainly in adding to the administrative burden of agencies publishing forms and regulations; California's Office of Administrative Law, whose purpose is to reduce the complexity of regulation, has similarly added enormously to the burdens placed on agencies attempting to change existing statutes, even in instances where simplification is proposed. We are also reminded of President Nixon's edict that the number of governmental committees should be reduced. Its main effect was reclassification of existing committees as subcommittees, such that formation of new committees charged with supervising these subcommittees was required.

known alternatives to rational administration, what Max Weber called rational-legal authority, are two other types identified by Weber. One of these, traditional authority, existed mainly in the past, although some vestiges of traditional administration still exist. The other, charismatic authority, is inherently unstable and is the antithesis of administration in that it rejects all precedent. There will be no reversion to traditional authority. Nor can the force of a single charismatic personality transcend administration permanently. Perhaps, however, the past can suggest conditions under which one system of administration succeeds another. Perhaps also, the present state of thinking about organizations can be understood as anticipating what organizations will actually be like in the future. Perhaps finally, the role of research in overcoming the limits of bureaucracy can be sketched briefly.

The Failure of Earlier Administrative Forms

One asks with some trepidation why traditional systems of administration failed. The problem is not a paucity of explanation but a surfeit of them. On the one hand, it is not at all clear that either traditional or rational-legal authority, as Weber used these terms, consisted of single types.[2] There were, thus, many kinds of failures of traditional authority. On the other hand, traditional systems of administration, when they did give way to rational-legal authority, failed at identifiable points in history. Almost any of the forces operating at or near these points could be cited as causes for failure in traditional administration, and no one of them could be identified as the principal cause.

With these limitations in mind, two conditions facilitating the transformation from traditional to rational bases of administration can be noted. The first of these is the weakness or absence of central control under traditional authority. Vernon Dibble's (1965) description of the administration of justice in sixteenth century England remains perhaps the most vivid account of prebureaucratic patterns in the literature. Figure 9-1 reproduces from Dibble's article his chart showing relations among traditional offices – justices of the peace, sheriffs, the privy, council, so forth – in the Elizabethan era. Of particular interest in Figure 9-1 is the lack of any clear ordering among offices as would be expected in modern organizations. There was no hierarchy of authority, jurisdictions were unclear, and concerted action was possible only with the consent of the notables in each community. Conflict was endemic in traditional organizations and was limited mainly by restricting access to office to the upper classes.

---

[2] Bendix (1974) argues forcefully that there are multiple types of both traditional and rational-legal authority.

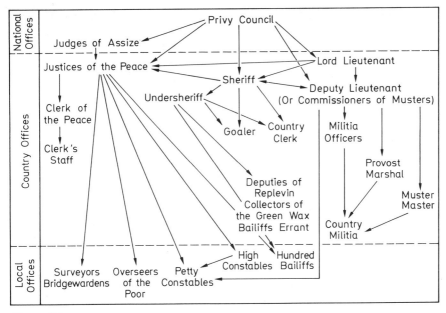

Figure 9.1
Organization of Country Government in Sixteenth Century England
Source: Dibble (1965: 881).

Traditional patterns of administration were also inordinately cumbersome and inefficient compared to the bureaucratic structures that succeeded them. Weber observed, among other limitations of traditional authority, ambiguities as to whether decisions were to be governed by precedent or by the discretion of a chief (1947: 344), and arbitrary regulation of the substance of economic activity that made rational calculation of results difficult (1947: 356–57). The virtues of bureaucracy compared to traditional administration were, at the time Weber wrote, bureaucracy's efficiency and exactitude:

... the fully developed bureaucratic mechanism compares with other organizations exactly as does the machine with the non-mechanical modes of production.

Precision, speed, unambiguity, knowledge of the files, continuity, discretion, unity, strict subordination, reduction of friction and of material and personal costs – these are raised to the optimum point in the strictly bureaucratic administration, and especially in its monocratic form. As compared with all collegiate, honorific, and avocational forms of administration, trained bureaucracy is superior on all these points. And as far as complicated tasks are concerned, paid bureaucratic work is not only more precise but, in the last analysis, it is often cheaper than formally unremunerated honorific service (1946: 214).

Whether or not contemporary bureaucracy retains the efficiency and exactitude of its original form is an open question. We believe it does not. But we also believe that Weber's positive assessment of bureaucracy was based on a comparison of fully developed and complicated traditional forms with primitive and therefore simple bureaucratic structures.

The second condition facilitating the transformation from traditional to rational bases of administration was legitimation of the latter. Complexity and cumbrousness alone did not defeat traditional organizations. To be sure, where traditionally and bureaucratically organized firms have been in competition, traditional organizations have usually been disadvantaged. But as Weber, Bendix, and many others have pointed out, the belief that rational-legal authority is an appropriate basis for organizing action has been much more powerful than any economic advantages of rational-legal authority. In the U.S., for example, concepts of rational administration were tied closely to political reform. The movement for reformed government that initially sought merit personnel administration, then budgeting, and later the application of scientific principles to a range of management issues always claimed that reform innovations would aid economy and efficiency in government. The reformers, of course, had no proof for their claims, but they implemented their innovations nonetheless. The application of rational concepts of administration in industry was also due in part to social and political agitation. Taylorism was spread by a vocal and contentious cult. Taylor's ideas eventually had palpable effects at the production level, for example in time-and-motion studies, but they were put into place in almost all instances well before their effectiveness had been demonstrated. Traditional administration failed, then, not only because of its inadequacies but also because an alternative model, rational administration, was available.

One of the two conditions that marked the change from the traditional to the rational-legal basis of authority is again present. Just as traditional prerogatives accumulated and thereby limited the power of central authority, bureaucratic structures and procedures have moved from simplicity to complexity over time, also weakening central control. There may be little difference between the complexity of the most developed traditional systems of administration and fully developed bureaucracies, assuming that modern bureaucracy has approached its limits. There are substantial differences, however, in the way complexity developed. Under traditional authority, rights and privileges accumulated in a haphazard way. Under rational-legal authority, bureaucratic growth is highly rationalized in that each new element requires justification as a logical extension of one of the elements already in existence. Precisely because bureaucratic growth is the outcome of a rationalized process, demands for new administration can be pressed by any of a number of constituencies, not just traditional leaders.

For this reason, complexity in bureaucratic systems has emerged much more rapidly than under traditional administration. Thus, while the Elizabethan system of justice changed slowly or not all over a period of three centuries, the current rate of bureaucratic growth, if it continues, augers fundamental change in the near future.

The second condition marking the shift from traditional to rational-legal authority, beliefs legitimating alternative forms of organization, is not yet present. To be sure, sensitivity to government expenditures and to costs in the private sector has increased enormously in the past decade, and some economies have been achieved. But other than in the realm of political rhetoric where attacks on bureaucracy are ritual, existing organizational patterns remain unchallenged. Those who were the most articulate critics of bureaucracy in the past have retreated from predicting its imminent demise. Warren Bennis, in particular, has moved from proclaiming "The Coming Death of Bureaucracy" (1967) to ambivalence. Bennis now maintains that while some organizations attempt to move beyond bureaucracy, there remains a "strong undertow toward greater bureaucratization" (1979: 24). Ambivalence also characterizes the assessment of bureaucratic patterns in organizational theory. Early in its development there was widespread acceptance of Weber's assertions as to the superior efficiency and responsiveness of bureaucracy. Bureaucratic dysfunctions were later recognized, and debate focused on whether they were aberrational or endemic. At this point, there remains almost no debate. The issue is considered to be either uninteresting or insoluble. Perhaps the historical approach taken in this book will again sensitize organizational theory to the problem of bureaucratization. The long-term patterns of bureaucratic growth revealed above suggest that bureaucracy was once an efficient and dependable mechanism for accomplishing collective tasks but has evolved toward such complexity that it may now be inefficient and undependable.

The Contribution of Contemporary Theory

Even though contemporary organizational theory has offered no explicit alternative to the rational model, it has contributed substantially to thinking by departing from the earlier rationalistic bias. Three streams of thought that have developed somewhat independently of one another together suggest a possible new basis for organizing. One set of ideas treats organizations as social institutions, as units whose principal purpose is legitimating activity rather than accomplishing specific objectives. John W. Meyer and his associates have contributed most to the institutional perspective in recent years. (See, for example, J. Meyer (1977); Meyer and Rowan (1977; 1978); Meyer et al. (1978)). A second set of ideas acknowledges that uncertainty is inevitable in organizations and that uncertain processes may offer some advantages over determinate ones. An essay by Simon (1962) introduced the notion that error detection and correction were facilitated by organizational complexity; Weick (1976) outlined advantages (and disadvantages) of "loose coupling" within organizations; the idea of evolution, which is now prominent in theory (see especially Weick (1969) and McKelvey (1982)), introduced chance events to explain diversity among organizations; and theories of "garbage-can" processes in organizations and "organized anarchies" (March and Olsen, 1976) suggested choice processes to be essentially random. A third set of ideas introduces culture as an important element in organizations. The study of organizational cultures is not fully developed. At present, this field asserts that attention to values can contribute to productivity (Pascale and Athos, 1981; Peters and Waterman, 1982). But what values make what contributions under what conditions are not specified. The reader is also alerted to a collection of articles on organizational cultures in the September, 1983, issue of *Administrative Science Quarterly*.

These insights may or may not contribute to a new basis for constituting organizations. One could view them as contributing little to ideas about organizing because they ignore the purposive character of organizations in emphasizing legitimacy rather than efficiency, uncertainty rather than planning, and diffuse cultural prescriptions rather than specific objectives. At another level, these insights can be understood as amending the rational model by identifying the limits of organized action but not altering it fundamentally. Formal rationality must have legitimacy for formal organization to function; the rational model describes administration but not decision processes; beliefs held by people in organizations must be supportive of stated objectives. These insights, perhaps in conjunction with the results from this research, could also be understood as the kernel of a new theory of organizing that departs in substantial ways from received beliefs about how organizations ought to be constructed. Such a theory might rest on the following premises:

1. Innovation and experimentation need greater legitimacy, formal organization less. As contemporary organizational theory has suggested, many formal structures persist because of their legitimacy rather than demonstrated efficiency or effectiveness. Indeed, the idea of rational administration as synonymous with creation of rules and formal structures is so deeply embedded in modern cultures that few people can imagine alternatives. Academic theorizing and bureaucratic practice, furthermore, have emphasized that managerial intentions are best made concrete and communicated to individuals through formal procedures and structures. To formalize an activity is to make it visible, external, and apparently stable. Formalization thus contributes to the belief that organized activity is buffered from uncertainties arising in the environment. The results from this research both confirm and challenge the belief that formalization induces stability in organizations. As noted above, roughly ten per cent of the organizational units in

the finance agencies studied underwent change in any given year. Change was not randomly distributed, however. The existence of and change in lower-level units preserved larger and more inclusive units suggesting preferences for formal organization. In this sense, formalization induced stability. But the resulting proliferation of organizational units cannot but have added complexity and uncertainty within bureaucratic hierarchies. In this sense, formalization ultimately contributed to instability. For the same reasons that formalization contributes, in the long run, to complexity and instability within organizations, innovation and experimentation may, in the long run, lead to more stable systems of administration. By regarding organizing as a continuous process and individual organizational units as temporary solutions to problems that are transient in nature, the capacity of larger systems to manage internal processes and accommodate external change may be enhanced.

2. Many errors should be corrected, not prevented. Contemporary theories of organizations suggest that experimentation, chance events, and error may contribute positively to organizational outcomes because uncertainty is endemic. This view is very much in contrast to prevailing practice, which treats as rational any extension of formal organization that promises to remove uncertainty and thereby minimize future errors. The aversion to error is so extreme under the rational model that costs of error prevention are rarely compared to costs of errors themselves. This is particularly the case where expenditures incurred in error prevention are easily externalized – passed on to an administrative budget or to taxpayers – whereas the costs to individual persons of making mistakes cannot be. A legal system that punishes errors severely but is insensitive to the costs of error prevention compounds this tendency. While theory now indicates that greater tolerance for error would serve some organizations well, there is not yet indication of what kinds of error are tolerable and what kinds are not in different settings. Accidents in nuclear plants or nuclear war are clearly not acceptable, but tolerance of ambiguities and inconsistencies in ordinary administrative bureaucracies may limit pressures toward long-term growth.

3. Complexity should be discouraged, purposiveness encouraged. Little in the literature on organizational culture and values describes more than the content of culture. Here, we wish to suggest several functions of explicit attention to culture and values. Attention to the distinctive aspects of an organization's culture or its "superordinate values" simplifies and focuses procedures and otherwise complex patterns of structure and regulation. Attention to culture and values, therefore, is a partial corrective to bureaucratic growth. However, cultures and value systems having distinctiveness are also exclusive. Some ends are encouraged, others discouraged. This is in marked contrast to the ethical neutrality of modern bureaucracy, which, following Weber's analysis, pursues all ends with equal vigor.

Some differences between the kinds of organizations suggested in contemporary organizational theory and classical bureaucracy can be sketched briefly. The logic of bureaucracy utilizes formal organization – organizational structure – to map complicated environments. The construction of organization is a response to uncertainty or change, as shown in theoretical argument and in empirical research results, leading to almost unending organizational growth. The organizing patterns suggested by contemporary theory operates somewhat differently. Individuals are assembled for well understood purposes and dispersed when these purposes are accomplished, organization evolves from trial-and-error, and unspoken culture as well as explicit values limit the tendency toward evolving complexity. For these reasons, growth is not built into the contemporary model. Classical bureaucracy and contemporary theories also place different demands on the individual person. For the individual, classical bureaucracy overcomes bounded rationality limits by constructing micro-environments presenting fixed decision premises and limited choices. Contemporary theory, by contrast, is less attentive to the bounded rationality problem because it believes the problem ultimately insoluble. Much more is therefore demanded of the individual under the contemporary model than in classical bureaucracy, for the costs of uncertainty and chance are imposed directly on him or her rather than absorbed by a larger organization. The model of organization presented by contemporary theory, finally, is even further removed from traditional organization than is bureaucracy. Traditional organization preserves the past relentlessly. Bureaucratic organization attempts both to preserve the past and to accommodate change. The contemporary model of organization is distrustful of the past as a model for the present since workable solutions are more highly valued than consistent conduct.

Whether the model suggested by contemporary theory could function for organizations where the bureaucratic model has been used in the past is unknown. The bureaucratic model aims for complete control of behavior leading to outcomes, and it aims for consistent outcomes. It also aims to shield individuals from change by providing a stable set of alternatives and rules for deciding among alternatives. Complete control of individual behavior is not achieved in the contemporary model. Weakened control is combined with a reliance on trial and error guided by overarching values to achieve adaptability and, ultimately, effectiveness. Consistency in administration is not achieved in the contemporary model. It is instead rejected as unrealistic given endemic uncertainty in environments. And the contemporary model says little or nothing about how individuals are to cope with a world of infinite choices that may or may not lead to desired outcomes. If one moves from the realm of the abstract to concrete cases, such as municipal finance administration, the limitations of contemporary theory become even more evident. Financial accounts become meaningless if transactions are not in fact controlled closely. Accounts become impenetrable if not maintained consistently on a year-to-year basis. And since the application of accounting rules is the substance of work, limitless choices cannot be made available to individuals. The rules are ends in themselves and, as such, cannot be dispensed with.

Viewed in this perspective, the bureaucratic model becomes somewhat more palatable than alternative models of administration, at least for some tasks. Neither the traditional nor the contemporary model of administration can maintain control and consistency in the application of a set of principles or rules. Control and consistency are costly, however, because neither can be maintained in other than wholly benign environments without augmenting complexity and staff over time. A choice between the bureaucratic and contemporary models of organizing then, must be made in some settings. Organizational theory, or perhaps we should say theories, is thus cast into an unfamiliar and perhaps uncomfortable role. The theories themselves, just like organizations constructed consistent with theories, have limits beyond which their contradictions overwhelm their contributions to the functioning of organizations. The traditional model engenders conflict in large-scale administration, the bureaucratic model engenders complexity and growth, while the contemporary model forgoes control of actions and lessens predictability of outcomes.

Whether or not it is possible to construct a simple model of organizations that achieves the aims of bureaucratic administration without incurring its costs is unknown. We think it is not. Indeed, we rather hope that such a model cannot be developed. The danger posed by bureaucratic administration, acknowledged fully by Weber, is its power. Limits to bureaucratic growth are ultimately also limits to bureaucratic power. The contemporary model of organization that subordinates control and consistency to adaptation offers, therefore, not only an alternative to bureaucratic growth but also an alternative to bureaucratic domination. But the contemporary model cannot be applied everywhere. It certainly cannot be implemented where mistakes are intolerable. A theory of organizations to be genuinely useful, then, will present not only alternative models of organizing but also some suggestions as to where each model best applies and, importantly, at what points the contradictions of each model require a search for alternatives. To be sure, such a theory would be much more complicated than the prescriptive statements that now pass for organizational theory, for it would reflect the messiness of the world much more vividly than present theories do. But it would sensitize people to the ineluctable fact of organizational life, namely that the inconsistency of the world is such that no consistent set of principles from any one model of organizing can produce positive outcomes indefinitely.

The Contribution of Research

This book is a research study, one concerned simultaneously with explaining long-term patterns of growth of a set of municipal agencies and constructing a theory that both explains bureaucratic growth and identifies limits to growth. As the reader is now aware, theory entered into discussion in two ways. As is conventional in social science research, theory was used to predict the behavior of organizations. As is exceptional in research, one of the principal independent variables or causal forces driving the systems studied was a theory of organizing embodied in concepts of rational administration. The research showed theory, as prediction, to anticipate actual behavior somewhat. The research also showed theory, as a causal force, to produce contradictory effects. Concepts of rational administration appeared, in the short run, to contribute positively to organizations. The presence and extensiveness of formal organization increased the survival prospects of individual units. But in the long run, concepts of rational administration caused continuous increase in organization, possibly to the point of unmanageability. At this juncture, limits to bureaucratic growth are encountered and set boundary conditions on theories predicting growth. Theory is thus rendered an uncertain guide to future patterns of organizing.

The limits to bureaucratic growth, which are also the limits of theories of bureaucratic growth, demonstrate vividly why theoretical analysis alone will not suffice for the social science enterprise. Theory cannot alone reveal its own inconsistencies or limitations. Only research can identify these limits. Moreover, since there are competing theories of organizing, only research can identify which is operating in any particular setting. Thus, as mundane as it may sound, theory and research are inextricably tied. Neither is of much utility without the other. With this is mind, we would like to suggest that research can contribute to solutions to some of the dilemmas indicated above.

Research can, first, focus attention on the phenomenon of bureaucratic growth. The data on growth of government and of administration in the private sector presented in Chapter 2 indicate long-term patterns of change that have not been widely understood. Data like these, in our judgment, should be available for individual organizations whenever their performance is appraised, whether by directors and shareholders or by public authorities. If attention to bureaucratic growth is built into thinking about organizations, then one partial corrective to growth, continual scrutiny of it, is in place. Importantly, the measurement tools needed to gauge bureaucratization are readily available. They need only be applied to extant organizations for purposes of evaluation rather than for purposes of research having no consequences for the units studied. Quantitative performance measures have been used in both the public and private sectors for years. Assessment of organization, however, has either been haphazard or restricted to qualitative criteria. We believe that quantitative measures of bureaucratization should be applied to all large organizations and should be an ongoing responsibility of management. Research can, second, draw attention to the consequences of alternative organizing models for different kinds of organizations. To date, academic studies of organizations, whether public or private, have tested single theories or models of organizational process. Each empirical study has been designed, as it were, to demonstrate whether or not a particular model holds for the units studied. Extant organizations, however, do not need to know whether their behavior fits a given model. They do need to know whether an alternative model of organizing would serve them better, if only for a short period. The popularity of books on Japanese management demonstrates that there is demand for alternatives to present organizing principles. Research must, then, treat organizing principles or models of organization as independent variables and organizational outcomes, such as bureaucratic growth, as dependent. The research reported in this book is flawed in this respect. The ultimate causal force, the concept of rational administration, is invariant here. The present research has shown behavior consistent with rational concepts to yield long-term growth. It has suggested that these concepts yield bureaucratic growth in both government and private firms. But it was not able to show that fundamentally different organizing principles would yield different outcomes. Greater variation over time and across societies will have to be captured so that the effects of different organizing principles can be known. Introducing such variation into research is fraught with difficulties since it sacrifices some precision almost inevitably.

There is a further role for research, one that transcends organizations and organizational theory yet is linked to the problem of bureaucratic growth. It goes without saying, but has not yet been stated, that people occupy organizations and use organizations to order and organize their lives. As Herbert Simon noted, "The rational individual is, and must be, an organized and institutionalized individual" (1947: 102). One question that must be considered eventually is whether permanent organizations, which in many instances will mean growing organizations, are the only institutions capable of rationalizing conduct. In the past, before there were large formal organizations, families, communities, and societies were the principal agencies rationalizing conduct. Large-scale organizations grew rapidly during this century because they were able to generate definitive solutions to problems that had proved intractable in other settings. But the limits of organizing are apparent. Research now has the task of addressing whether new kinds of institutions are equally capable of rationalizing conduct without incurring the permanent costs of organizations. The emerging emphasis on informal social networks, which in some instances appear to overcome bounded rationality limits better than structured organizations (see Granovetter, 1973; 1983), suggests that research should pursue the consequences of innovations in social institutions that have appeared in recent years, not just innovation in formal organizations. Like research spanning lengthy intervals and multiple societies, research comparing institutions poses challenges for which there are no routine solutions. But such research must be undertaken if we are not to be trapped by obsolete theories of human action.

9.4 Conclusion

This purpose of this book was to construct a theory of bureaucratic growth that was based in research. Such a theory was constructed – the reader knows the arguments too well at this point – and suggested that the limits to bureaucratic growth occur when organizations are no longer able to manage their internal processes. The alternatives to bureaucratic growth are much less clear than its limits, however. This occurs in part because there has been little experience with alternatives. This occurs also because whatever the limits of bureaucratic organization, the limits of alternatives may be greater. This book, then, offers a problem but not a panacea.

Precisely because there is and will remain a problem of bureaucratic growth and its limits, and precisely because alternative organizing models that may be appropriate in some settings, such as business firms, may not be appropriate in other settings, such as the finance agencies studied here, the social sciences will not be able to abandon the study of bureaucracy. It is unlikely that any definitive resolution of the issues raised in this book will be found. But social science can at least define these issues and delineate the choices that can be made. Even if the alternatives are limited, it is better knowing than not knowing what they are.

An earlier book by the senior author of this work (Meyer, 1979) was described as an interim report and promised to extend over time the studies of organizational structure that it reported. What was planned has been accomplished in large measure. But it has changed and complicated somewhat the way organizations, organizational structures, and environments are understood. Changes over time render the boundaries of organizations variable. Organizational structures appears to be mechanisms through which organizations order environments. And environments appear to contain two components, prescriptions about how rationally to manage complexity and uncertainty, and complexity and uncertainty themselves. Importantly, the mechanism of administrative structure allows organizations to manage rationally complicated and uncertain environments, but at the cost of increasing complexity within organizations.

Other social institutions have increased in complexity in recent years, like public bureaucracies, and other institutions may also be approaching unmanageability. One wonders, for example, whether changes in law, accounting doctrine, and administrative regulation generally have not reflected some of the same processes we have observed in bureaucratic structures. One wonders also whether the current efforts directed toward deregulation and delegalization do not reflect some of the same limits to growth and complexity that we believe to operate in bureaucracies. Our research agenda, then, does not call for more studies of bureaucratic structures. It calls, instead, for comparative studies of growth in both the complexity and size of several institutional domains. Such research, like this, will be historical, but it will perhaps be more attentive to qualitative detail and less attentive to quantification than has been the case here. It will be directed toward general laws of social organization, not of bureaucracies or of formal organizations. Comparisons across institutions are, of course, even riskier than comparisons of relatively simple organizations over time. But we are convinced that studies of this sort must be undertaken to test the notion that there are laws of social process that transcend laws of individual behavior.

References

Ahlbrandt, R. (1973): "An empirical analysis of public and private ownership and the supply of municipal fire services." *Public Choice* 16: 273–309.

Aldrich, Howard E. (1979): *Organizations and Environments*. Englewood Cliffs, N. J.: Prentice-Hall.

Aldrich, Howard E., and Albert J. Riess, Jr. (1976): "Continuities in the study of ecological succession: Changes in the race composition of neighborhoods and their businesses." *American Journal of Sociology* 81: 846–66.

Allen, William H. (1908): "Wanted – one thousand efficient accountants for municipal research." *Journal of Accountancy* 6: 187–193.

Allison, Graham T. (1971): *Essence of Decision*. Boston: Little-Brown.

American Accounting Association, Comittee on Nonprofit Organizations (1971): "Report of the committee on not-for-profit organizations." *American Accounting Review* 46: Supplement. (1975): "Report of the committee on not-for-profit organizations." *American Accounting Review* 46: Supplement.

American Institute of Certified Public Accountants, Committee on Governmental Accounting and Auditing (1974): *Audits of State and Local Governmental Units*. New York.

Armour, Henry O. and David J. Teece (1978): "Organizational structure and economic performance: A test of the multidivisional hypotheses." *Bell Journal of Economics* 9: 106–122.

Arrow, Kenneth (1970): *Limits of Organization*, New York, Norton.

Balderston, C. Canby (1957): "Present problems and possible plight of local finance." *Municipal Finance* 30: 10–14.

Barnard, L. M. (1935): "The Kansas cash basis law." *Municipal Finance* 7: 18–19.

Bendix, Reinhard (1956): *Work and Authority in Industry*. Berkeley: Univ. of California Press. (1974): "Introduction." *Work and Authority in Industry*. 2nd ed. Berkeley: Univ. of California Press.

Benjamin, B. (1965): *Social and Economic Factors Affecting Mortality*. The Hague: Mouton.

Bennis, Warren (1967): "The coming death of bureaucracy." *Management Review* 56: 19–24. (1979): "Beyond bureaucratic baiting." *Social Science Quarterly* 60: 20–24.

Bernhardt, Elmer F. (1937): "Baltimore's payroll bureau." *Municipal Finance* 10: 11–21.

Binford, Chalres W. (1975): "The best approach to governmental budgeting: The large unit." *Municipal Finance* 47: 20–29.

Bird, Frederick L. (1935): "The five-year trend in tax delinquency." *Municipal Finance* 7: 25–29.

Blau, Peter M. (1955): *The Dynamics of Bureaucracy*. Chicago: Univ. of Chicago Press. (1970): "A formal theory of differentiation in organizations. *American Sociological Review* 35: 201–218.

Blau, Peter M. and Richard A. Schoenherr (1971): *The Structure of Organizations*. New York: Basic Books.

Borcherding, Thomas S. (1977): *Budgets and Bureaucrats: The Sources of Government Growth*. Durham: Duke Univ. Press.

Boughey, Arthur S. (1968): *Ecology of Populations*. New York: Macmillan.

Buck, A. E. (1930): *Municipal Finance*. New York: Macmillan. (1941): "Whither the budget?" *Municipal Finance* 13: 3–6. (1949): "Next steps in local budgeting." *Municipal Finance* 21: 2–6.

Byers, Paul E. (1948): "Economy through budget control." *Municipal Finance* 20: 15–19.

Carroll, Glenn R. (1982): *Dynamic analysis of discrete dependent variables: a didactic essay*. Dept. of Sociology, Brown Univ.

Carroll, Glenn R. (1983): *A stochastic model of organizational mortality: review and reanalysis*. School of Business Administration, Univ. fo California, Berkeley.

Carroll, Glenn R. and Jacques Delacroix (1982): "Organizational mortality in the newspaper industries of Argentina and Ireland: an ecological approach." *Administrative Science Quarterly* 27: 169–198.

Casstevens, Thomas W. (1980): "Birth and death processes of government bureaus in the United States." *Behavioral Science* 25: 161–165.

Chandler, Alfred, D., Jr. (1977): *The Visible Hand: The Managerial Revolution in American Business*. Cambridge, Mass.: Harvard Univ. Press.

Chapman, Richard M. (1910): "Municipal accounts." *Journal of Accountancy* 1910: 17–26.

Chatters, Carl H. (1957): "Municipal financial needs v. credit restraints." *Municipal Finance* 30: 15–22.

Coleman, James S. (1981): *Longitudinal Data Analysis*. New York: Basic Books.

Coopers & Lybrand and the Univ. of Michigan (1976): *Financial Disclosure Practices of American Cities: A Public Report*. New York: Coopers & Lybrand.

Cotton, John F. (1968): "Planning-programming-budgeting systems for local government." *Municipal Finance* 41: 26–33.

Crozier, Michel (1964): *The Bureaucratic Phenomenon*. Chicago: Univ. of Chicago Press.

Cyert Richard and James G. March (1963): *A Behavioral Theory of the Firm*. Englewood Cliffs, N. J.: Prentice-Hall.

Daft, Richard L. and Patricia J. Bradshaw (1980): "The process of horizontal differentiation: Two models." *Administrative Science Quarterly* 25: 441–446.

Daft, Richard L., and Norman B. Macintosh (1981): "A tentative exploration into the amount and equivocality of information processing in organizational work units." *Administrative Science Quarterly* 26: 207–224.

Davidson, Sidney, D. Green, W. Hellerstein, A. Mandansky, and R. Weil (1977): *Financial Reporting by State and Local Governmental Units*. Chicago: Univ. of Chicago Center for Management of Public and Nonprofit Enterprise.

Davies, David (1971): "The efficiency of public versus private firms: The case of Australia's two airlines." *Journal of Law and Economics* 14: 149–165.

Dibble, Vernon (1965): "The organization of traditional authority." Ch. 19 in J. G. March (Ed.): *Handbook of Organizations*. Chicago: Rand-McNally.

Dill, William R. (1958): "Environment as an influence on managerial autonomy." *Administrative Science Quarterly* 2: 409–443.

DiMaggio, Paul J., and Wlater, Walter W. Powell (1983): "The iron cage revisited: Institutional isomorphism and collective rationality in organizational fields." *American Sociological Review* 48: 147–160.

Donaho, John A. (1950): "The performance budget." *Municipal Finance* 22: 103–107.

Downs, Anthony (1967): *Inside Bureaucracy.* Boston: Little-Brown.

Drebin, Anthony (1979): "Government versus commercial accounting: The issues." *Governmental Finance* 8: 3–8.

Duncan, Robert B. (1972): "Characteristics of organizational environments and perceived environmental uncertainty." *Administrative Science Quarterly* 17: 313–327.

Durham, J. Edgar (1961): "Desirable features of line-item budgeting." *Municipal Finance* 34: 93–95.

Edwards, Richard (1979): *Contested Terrain.* New York: Harper and Row.

Emery, F. E., and E. L. Trist (1965): "The causal texture of organizational environments." *Human Relations* 18: 21–32.

Fayol, Henri (1923): "The administrative theory in the state." Ch. 4 in L. Gulick and L. Urwick (Eds.): *Papers on the Science of Administration.* New York: Columbia Univ. Institute of Public Administration.

Fennell, Mary L. (1980): "The effects of environmental characteristics on the structure of hospital clusters." *Administrative Science Quarterly* 25: 485–511.

Force, Harold D. (1909a): "New York City's revision of accounts and methods. I. Historical and descriptive." *Journal of Accountancy* 8: 1–7. (1909b): "New York City's revision of accounts and methods. II. Leading factors and installation." *Journal of Accountancy* 8: 106–123. (1909c): "New York City's revision of accounts and methods. II. Leading factors and installation (continued)." *Journal of Accountancy* 8: 182–189. (1909d): "New York City's revision of accounts and methods. II. Leading factors and installation (concluded)." *Journal of Accountancy* 8: 270–286.

Freeman John H., and Michael T. Hannan (1975): "Growth and decline processes in organizations." *American Sociological Review* 40: 215–228. (1978): "Internal politics of growth and decline." Ch. 7 in M. W. Meyer et al.: *Environments and Organizations.* San Francisco: Jossey-Bass.

Freeman, John, Glenn R. Carroll, and Michael T. Hannan (1983): *The liability of newness: age dependence in organizational death rates.* School of Business, Univ. of California, Berkeley.

Glick, Edward J. (1937): "New Rochelle attains cash basis." *Municipal Finance* 9: 20–23.

Goddard, J. Percy (1924): "Municipal budgets." *Journal of Accountance* 38: 430–434.

Gompertz, Benjamin (1825): "On the nature of the function expressive of the law of human mortality and on a new mode of determining the value of life contingents." *Philosophical Transactions of the Royal Society* 115: 513–580.

Gouldner, Alvin W. (1954): *Patterns of Industrial Bureaucracy.* Glencoe: Free Press.

Granovetter, Mark (1973): "The strength of weak ties." *American Journal of Sociology* 78: 1360–1380. (1983): *Labor mobility, internal markets, and job matching: A comparison of the sociological and economic approaches.* Dept. of Sociology, State University of New York at Stony Brook.

Gulick, Luther (1933): "Science, values, and public administration." Ch. 11 in L.

Gulick and L. Urwick (Eds.): *Papers on the Science of Administration*. New York: Columbia Univ. Institute of Public Administration. (1937): "Notes on the theory of organization." Ch. 1 in L. Gulick and L. Urwick (Eds.): *Papers on the Science of Administration*. New York: Columbia Univ. Institute of Public Administration.

Hannan, Michael T. and John H. Freeman (1977): "The population ecology of organizations." *American Journal of Sociology* 82: 929–964. (1981): *Dynamics of niche width in organizational populations*. Institute for Mathematical Studies in the Social Scienes, Stanford Univ.

Hatton, A. R. (1915): "Forward." *The Annals* 62: vi-xiv.

Hendershot, Gerry E., and Thomas James (1972): "Size and growth as determinants of administrative-production ratios in organizations." *American Sociological Review* 37: 149–153.

Hickson, D. J., C. R. Hinings, C. A. Lee, R. H. Schneck, and J. M. Pennings (1971): "A strategic contingencies theory of intraorganizational power." *Administrative Science Quarterly* 16: 216–229.

Hirsch, Werner (1965): "Cost functions of government service: Refuse collection." *Review of Economics and Statistics*.

Hirschman, Albert O. (1970): *Exit, Voice, and Loyalty*. Cambridge, Mass.: Harvard Univ. Press.

Hofstadter, Richard (1955): *The Age of Reform*. New York: Vintage.

Holdaway, Edward A., and Thomas A. Blowers (1971): "Administrative ratios and organizational size: A longitudinal examination." *American Sociological Review* 36: 278–286.

Huber, George P., Michael J. O'Connell, and Larry L. Cummings (1957): "Perceived environmental uncertainty: effects of information and structure." *Academy of Management Journal* 18: 725–740.

Inkson, J. H., D. S. Pugh, and D. J. Hickson (1970): "Organizational context and structure: an abbreviated replication." *Administrative Science Quarterly* 15: 318–329.

James, Robert M. (1950): "Three major concepts in governmental accounting theory." *Accounting Review* 25: 307–314. (1951): "Some aspects of a governmental audit." *Accounting Review* 26: 347–351.

Kasarda, Jack D. (1974): "The structural implications of social system size: A three level analysis." *American Sociological Review* 39: 19–28.

Katz, Daniel, and Robert L. Kahn (1978): *The Social Psychology of Organizations*. 2nd ed. New York: Wiley.

Kaufman, Herbert (1976): *Are Government Organizations Immortal?* Washington, D. C.: Brookings Institution.

Kimberly, John R. (1976): "Organizational size and the structuralist perspective: A review, critique, and proposal." *Administrative Science Quarterly* 21: 571–597.

King, Clyde L. (1924): "Forward." *The Annals* 113: vi-xi.

Kohler, E. L. (1941): "Accounting as management control." *Municipal Finance* 21: 3–8.

Lancaster, Lane W. (1924): "The trend in city expenditures." *The Annals* 113: 15–22.

Lawrence, Paul R., and Jay W. Lorsch (1967): *Organization and Environment*. Boston: Graduate School of Business Administration, Harvard University.

Lawton, W. H. (1921): Review of F. Oakey: "Principles of Government Accounting and Auditing." *Journal of Accountancy* 32: 472.

Leblebici, Huseyin, and Gerald R. Salancik (1981): "Effects of environmental uncertainty on information and decision processes in banks." *Administrative Science Quarterly* 26: 578–596.

Leifer, Richard, and George P. Huber (1977): "Relations among perceived environmental uncertainty, organizational structure, and boundary-spanning behavior." *Administrative Science Quarterly* 22: 235–247.

Liebert, Roland (1976): *Disintegration and Political Action*. New York: Academic Press.

Lipset, Seymour Martin, Martin Trow, and James S. Coleman (1956): *Union Democracy*. Glencoe: Free Press.

Lipset, Seymour Martin and William Schneider (1983): *The Confidence Gap*. New York: Free Press.

Luther, Robert A. (1968): "PPBS in Fairfax County: A practical experience." *Municipal Finance* 41: 34–42.

Lybrand, William M. (1906): "Municipal accounting in the City of Philadelphia." *Journal of Accountancy* 1906: 275–279.

Lyon, Oswald (1919): "Municipal accounts." *Journal of Accountancy* 27: 125–133.

MacDonald, Austin F. (1924): "The trend in recent state expenditures." *The Annals* 113: 8–15.

Makeham, W. M. (1959): "On the law of mortality and the construction of annuity tables." *The ASSU Magazine* 8: 301–310.

March, James G. and Johan P. Olsen (1976): *Ambiguity and Choice in Organizations*. Bergen: Universitetsforlaget.

March, James G., and Herbert A. Simon (1958): *Organizations*. New York: Wiley.

Marris, Robin (1964): *The Economics of Managerial Capitalism*. New York: Free Press.

McKelvey, Bill (1982): *Organizational Systematics: Taxonomy, Evolution, Classification*. Berkeley and Los Angeles: Univ. of California Press.

McKelvey, Bill, and Howard Aldrich (1983): "Populations, natural selection, and applied organizational science." *Administrative Science Quarterly* 28: 101–128.

McKinsey, J. O. (1923): "Municipal accounting." *Journal of Accountancy* 35: 81–94.

Merton, Robert K. (1936): "The unanticipated consequences of purposive social action." *American Sociological Review* 1: 809–904. (1940): "Bureaucratic structure and personality." *Social Forces* 18: 560–568.

Meyer, John W. (1977): "The effects of education as an institution." *American Journal of Sociology* 83: 55–77.

Meyer, John W., and Brian Rowan (1977): "Institutionalized organizations: Formal structure as myth and ceremony." *American Journal of Sociology* 83: 440–63. (1978): "The structure of educational organizations." Ch. 4 in M. W. Meyer et al.: *Environments and Organizations*. San Francisco: Jossey-Bass.

Meyer, John W., W. Richard Scott, Sally Cole, and Jo-Ann K. Intili (1978): "Instructional Dissensus and Institutional Consensus in Schools." Ch. 9 in M. W. Meyer et al.: *Environments and Organizations*. San Francisco: Jossey-Bass.

Meyer, Marshall W. (1972): "Size and the structure of organizations: A causal analysis." *American Sociological Review* 37: 434–440. (1979): *Change in Public Bureaucracies*. New York: Cambridge Univ. Press.

Migue, Jean-Luc, and Gerard Belanger (1974): "Toward a general theory of managerial discretion." *Public Choice* 17: 27–43.

Miller, Gary and Terry Moe (1983): *"The positive theory of hierarchies."* Paper presented to the American Political Science Association, Chicago.

Moak, Lennox L. and Albert M. Hillhouse (1975): *Concepts and Practics in Local Government Finance*. Chicago: Municipal Finance Officers Association of the United States and Canada.

Morey, Lloyd (1928): "Fund and proprietary accounts in governmental accounting." *Accounting Review* 1: 76–84. (1933a): "Fundamentals of municipal accounting." *Municipal Finance* 7: 31–34. (1933b): "Municipal and governmental accounting." *Journal of Accountancy* 56: 350–364. (1934): "Principles of municipal accounting." *Accounting Review* 9: 319–325.

National Committee on Governmental Accounting (1979): *Government Accounting, Auditing, and Financial Reporting*.

National Committee on Municipal Accounting (1936): *Municipal Accounting Statements*. Chicago: Municipal Finance Officers Association. (1941): *Municipal Accounting Statements*. Rev. ed. Chicago: Municipal Finance Officers Association.

Nelson, Daniel (1975): *Managers and Workers*. Univ. of Wisconsin Press, 1975.

Niskanen, William A., Jr. (1971): *Bureaucracy and Representative Government*. Chicago: Aldine. (1975): "Bureaucrats and politicians." *Journal of Law and Economics* 18: 617–643.

O'Leary, James J. (1970): "Prospects for long-term municipal borrowing." *Municipal Finance* 43: 13–21.

Olson, Mancur, Jr. (1968): *The Logic of Collective Action*. New York: Schocken.

O'Reilly, Charles A., III (1980): "Individuals and information overload in organizations." *Academy of Management Journal* 23: 684–696.

Padgett, John F. (1981): "Hierarchy and ecological control in Federal budget making." *American Journal of Sociology* 87: 75–129.

Parkinson, C. Northcote (1957): *Parkinson's Law*. Boston: Houghton, Mifflin.

Pascale, Richard T. and Anthony G. Athos (1981): *The Art of Japanese Management*. New York: Simon & Schuster.

Pennings, Johannes M. (1975): "The relevance of the structural-contingency model for organizational effectiveness." *Administrative Science Quarterly* 20: 393–410.

Penrose, Edith (1959): *A Theory of the Growth of the Firm*. New York: Wiley.

Perrow, Charles (1979): *Complex Organizations: A Critical Essay*. 2nd ed. Glenview, Ill.: Scott-Foresman.

Peters, Thomas J. and Robert H. Waterman, Jr. (1982): *In Search of Excellence*. New York: Harper & Row.

Pfeffer, Jeffrey (1981): *Power in Organizations*. Marshfield, Mass.: Pittman. (1983): *Organizations and Organizational Theory*. Marshfield, Mass.: Pittman.

Pfeffer, Jeffrey, Jerry Ross, and Marshall W. Meyer (1983): *Organizational demography and the size of the administrative component.* School of Business, Stanford Univ.

Pfeffer Jeffrey, and Gerald R. Salancik (1978): *The External Control of Organizations.* New York: Harper & Row.

Pianka, Eric R. (1983): *Evolutionary Ecology.* 3rd ed. New York: Harper and Row.

Pielou, E. C. (1969): *An Introduction to Mathematical Ecology.* New York: Wiley.

Poole, Robert H. (1974): *An Introduction to Quantitative Ecology.* New York: McGraw-Hill.

Rusk, Stephen G. (1928): Review of L. Morey: "Introduction to Governmental Accounting." *Journal of Accountancy* 45: 73–74.

Savas, E. E. (1977): "As empirical study of competition in municipal service delivery." *Public Administration Review* 37: 717–724.

Scott, W. Richard (1975): "Organizational structure." *Annual Review of Sociology* 1: 1–20.

Seidemann, Henry P. (1924): "The preparation of the national budget." *The Annals* 113: 40–50.

Selznick, Philip (1949): *TVA and the Grass Roots.* Berkeley: Univ. of California Press.

Simon, Herbert A. (1947): *Administrative Behavior.* New York: MacMillan. (1962): "The architecture of complexity." *Proceedings of the American Philosophical Society* 106: 467–82.

Singleton, David W., Bruce A. Smith, and James R. Cleaveland (1976): "Zero-based budgeting in Wilmington, Delaware." *Governmental Finance* 5: 20–29.

Spann, R. (1977): "Rates of productivity change and the growth of local expenditure." Ch. 4 in T. Borcherding (ed.): *Budgets and Bureaucrats: The Sources of Government Growth.* Durham: Duke Univ. Press.

Starbuck, William (1965): "Organizational Growth and Development." Ch. 10 in James G. March (ed.): *Handbook of Organizations.* Chicago: Rand McNally.

Stinchcombe, Arthur L. (1965): "Social structure and organizations." Ch. 4 in James G. March (ed.): *Handbook of Organizations.* Chicago: Rand McNally.

Suffern, Edward L. (1922): "Municipal accounting in New Jersey." *Journal of Accountancy* 33: 321–330.

Taussig, Russell (1963): "Internal control: The new look." *Municipal Finance* 35: 148–152.

Taylor, Frederick Winslow (1911): *The Principles of Scientific Management.* New York: Harper.

Tenner, Irving (1951): "Recent developments in municipal accounting." *Municipal Finance* 24: 70–77.

Terreberry, Shirley (1968): "The evolution of organizational environments." *Administrative Science Quarterly* 12: 590–613.

Thompson, James D. (1967): *Organizations in Action.* New York: McGraw-Hill.

Tosi, Henry, Ramon Aldag, and Ronald Storey (1973): "On the measurement of the environment: An assessment of the Lawrence and Lorsch environmental uncertainty scale." *Administrative Science Quarterly* 17: 28–36.

Tullock, Gordon (1965): *The Politics of Bureaucracy*. Washington, D. C.: Public Affairs Press.

Tuma, Nancy Brandon (1980): *Invoking Rate*. Menlo Park, CA: Stanford Research Institute.

United States Bureau of Labor Statistics (1979): *Employment and Earnings, United States, 1909–78*. Washington, D.C.: U.S. Government Printing Office. (1980): *Employment and Earnings*, 27, No. 6. Washington, D.C.: U.S. Government Printing Office. (1983): *Employment and Earnings*, 30, No. 6. Washington, D.C.: U.S. Government Printing Office.

United States Department of Commerce (1975): *Historical Statistics of the United States*. Washington, D.C.: U.S. Government Printing Office. (1980): *Subject and Special Statistics*. Vol. 1. 1977 Census of Manufactures. Washington, D.C.: U.S. Government Printing Office.

Upson, Lent D. (1924): "Half-time budget methods." *The Annals* 113: 69–74.

von Mises, Ludwig (1944): *Bureaucracy*. New Haven: Yale Univ. Press.

Weber, Max (1946): "Bureaucracy." Pp. 196–244 in H. Gerth and C. W. Mills (Eds.): *From Max Weber: Essays in Sociology*. New York: Oxford Univ. Press. (1947): "Three types of legitimate authority." Pp. 324–423 in *The Theory of Social and Economic Organization*. Glencoe: The Free Press.

Weick, Karl E. (1969): *The Social Psychology of Organizing*. Reading, Mass.: Addison-Wesley. (1976): "Educational organizations as loosely compled systems." *Administrative Science Quarterly* 21: 1–19.

Weston J. Fred, and S. K. Mansinghka (1971): "Tests of the efficiency performance of conglomerate firms." *Journal of Finance* 26: 919–936.

White, Charles P. (1924): "The trend in Federal expenditures." *The Annals* 113: 1–8.

White, Harrison (1981): "Where do markets come from?" *American Journal of Sociology* 87: 517–547.

Wildavsky, Aaron (1964): *The Politics of the Budgetary Process*. Boston: Little-Brown.

Williamson, Oliver (1975): *Markets and Hierarchies*. New York: Free Press.

Wilson, Woodrow (1941): "The study of administration." *Political Science Quarterly* 56: [1887] 481–506.

Zucker, Lynne G. (1983): "Organizations as institutions." *Research in the Sociology of Organizations* 2: 1–47.

Author Index

Subject Index

de Gruyter Studies in Organization

An international series by internationally known authors presenting current research in organization.

Editorial Board: *Michael Aiken*, USA (University of Wisconsin) · *Franco Ferraresi*, Italy (University Torino) · *David J. Hickson*, Great Britain (University Bradford) · *Alfred Kieser*, Federal Republic of Germany (University Mannheim) · *Cornelis J. Lammers*, The Netherlands (University Leiden) · *Johan Olson*, Norway (University Bergen) · *Jean-Claude Thoenig*, France (INSEAD, Fontainebleau)

The Japanese Industrial System
By *Charles J. McMillan*
2nd revised edition
1985. 15,5 × 23 cm. XII, 356 pages. Cloth DM 88,–.
ISBN 3 11 010410 5

Political Management
By *Hall Thomas Wilson*
1984. 15,5 × 23 cm. 230 pages. Cloth DM 76,–.
ISBN 3 11 009902 0

Guidance, Control and Evaluation in the Public Sector
Edited by *F. X. Kaufmann, G. Majone, V. Ostrom*
1985. 15,5 × 23 cm. Approx. 650 pages. Cloth approx. DM 150,–.
ISBN 3 11 009707 9

International Business in the Middle East
Edited by *Erdener Kaynak*
1985. 15,5 × 23 cm. Approx. 250 pages. Cloth approx. DM 90,–.
ISBN 3 11 010321 4

Forthcoming Title:
Management in China
By *Oiva Laaksonen*
1985. 15,5 × 23 cm. Approx. 290 pages. Cloth approx. DM 88,–.
ISBN 3 11 009958 6

Prices are subject to change without notice

WALTER DE GRUYTER · BERLIN · NEW YORK

ORGANIZATION STUDIES

An international multidisciplinary journal devoted to the study of organizations, organizing and the organized in, and between societies

Editor-in-chief: David J. Hickson, University of Bradford

Co-Editor: Alfred Kieser, Mannheim

Managing Editor: Susan van der Werff

Editorial board: F. Agersnap, Copenhagen; K. Azumi, Newark; G. Benguigui, Paris; S. Clegg, Queensland; P. Coetsier, Gent; F. Ferraresi, Turin; J. Hage, Maryland; B. Hedberg, Stockholm; F. Hegner, Berlin; B. Hinings, Alberta; G. Hofstede, Arnhem; J. de Kervasdoué, Paris; C. Lammers, Leiden; B. Mannheim, Haifa; R. Mayntz, Cologne; G. Morgan, Toronto; I. Nonaka, Tokyo; J. Olson, Bergen; J. Padioleau, Paris; J. Pennings, Pennsylvania; G. Salaman, Milton Keynes; B. Stymne, Stockholm; A. Teulings, Amsterdam; H. Thierry, Amsterdam; J.-C. Thoenig, Fontainebleau.

Organization Studies is a supranational journal, based neither on any one nation nor on collaboration between any particular nations. Its aim is to present diverse theoretical and empirical research from all nations, spanning a broad view of organizations and organizing. Its current Editorial Board is drawn from thirteen nations, and its contributors are worldwide.

O.S. is published in English because that language is the most widely read in this field of research. But manuscripts in other languages can be reviewed in those languages prior to translation. O.S. reviews books published in languages other than English to bring them before its international readership, and News and Notes cover conferences and research in many countries.

O.S. has published papers by authors from sociology, political science, management and public administration, psychology and economics. Some among the range of titles are listed overleaf. O.S. is not only about the study of "the organization", though that is central. It is also about the processes of organizing people, whether in business, public services, or public administration and government; and it is about the response of "the organized". It is not only about the contemporary scene, especially differences around the world, but also about the historical developments which have led to that scene.

Subscription rates 1985

Per volume of four issues. Libraries and institutions **DM 108,–**/approx. US $ 38.75. Individuals (except FRG and Switzerland) **DM 54,–**/approx. US $ 19.25 (DM-prices are definitive, $-prices are approximate and subject to fluctuations in the exchange rate).

Published in collaboration with the European Group for Organizational Studies (EGOS) and the Maison des Sciences de l'Homme, Paris by

WALTER DE GRUYTER · BERLIN · NEW YORK

Verlag Walter de Gruyter & Co., Genthiner Straße 13, D-1000 Berlin 30, Tel.: (0 30) 2 60 05-0
Walter de Gruyter, Inc., 200 Saw Mill River Road, Hawthorne, N. Y. 10532, Tel.: (914) 747-0110